PROMOTING ACTIVE READING COMPREHENSION STRATEGIES
A Resource Book for Teachers

JUDITH W. IRWIN
University of Connecticut

ISABEL BAKER
Trenton State College

PRENTICE HALL, *Englewood Cliffs, New Jersey 07632*

LIBRARY OF CONGRESS
Library of Congress Cataloging-in-Publication Data

Irwin, Judith Westphal.
  Promoting active reading comprehension strategies: a resource
book for teachers/Judith W. Irwin, Isabel Baker.
    p.   cm.
  Bibliography: p.
  Includes index.
  ISBN 0-13-731241-5
  1. Reading.   2. Reading comprehension.   I. Baker, Isabel
  II. Title
LB1050.I78 1989
428.4'3—dc19   88-22466
                                                    CIP

Editorial/production supervision and interior design: **Susan E. Rowan**
Cover design: **Lundgren Graphics, Ltd.**
Manufacturing buyer: **Peter Havens**

 © 1989 by Prentice-Hall, Inc.
A Division of Simon & Schuster
Englewood Cliffs, New Jersey 07632

Printed in the United States of America
10 9 8 7 6 5 4

ISBN 0-13-731241-5

PRENTICE-HALL INTERNATIONAL (UK) LIMITED, *London*
PRENTICE-HALL OF AUSTRALIA PTY. LIMITED, *Sydney*
PRENTICE-HALL CANADA INC., *Toronto*
PRENTICE-HALL HISPANOAMERICANA, S.A., *Mexico*
PRENTICE-HALL OF INDIA PRIVATE LIMITED, *New Delhi*
PRENTICE-HALL OF JAPAN, INC., *Tokyo*
SIMON & SCHUSTER ASIA PTE. LTD., *Singapore*
EDITORA PRENTICE-HALL DO BRASIL, LTDA., *Rio de Janeiro*

**Dedicated to Alice and Ian MacDonald
and all those who encourage others to share
in the joy of reading**

CONTENTS

PREFACE

This is a book of practical ideas for busy teachers. It can be used as a supplemental text in any reading methods course. It would be especially useful in courses accompanied by teaching experiences. It could also be used by classroom teachers, reading specialists, and reading clinicians who are looking for new and useful ideas for promoting active reading comprehension strategies.

The theory on which this book is based is explained in the first five chapters and in the chapter introductions throughout the book. The specialist perusing these chapters will note that this theory is a blend of cognitive-processing theory, whole-language theory, and direct-instruction approaches. From cognitive-processing theory we get analytical tools that enable the teacher to gain insights into the students' specific comprehension strategies. Whole-language theory reminds us to always teach reading comprehension in the context of real, meaningful language activities. Finally, direct-instruction researchers have taught us the importance of explaining and modeling strategies that would be useful to the students. Thus, we have resisted the pressure to be put in any one of these camps, trying instead to use the best advice from each.

This was not an easy task. Throughout the book we have added warnings to activities that focus on isolated strategies so that the teacher will remember to use them sparingly and to tie the strategies into more meaningful reading situations. Many activities begin with very specific instructions about how to explain and model a strategy to students. They end with reminders to reinforce the strategy in other meaningful situations.

Of course, it is possible that this book will be misused. It is possible that teachers will use the activities as isolated skill activities. It is possible that they will not use meaningful, relevant, exciting materials. Possible, but not probable. Teachers are looking for activities that actively involve learners in meaning-making. They are looking for activities that are meaningful to their students. This book is addressed to those teachers. We hope that they and their students will find that the activities stimulate exciting literacy events.

Judith W. Irwin
Isabel Baker

INTRODUCTION: HOW TO USE THIS BOOK

This is a book of ideas for teaching reading comprehension. It is intended for both remedial reading teachers and classroom teachers. It contains activities for all ages and ability levels. Though it contains the most current and exciting new approaches, it requires no extra training beyond that given to teachers who already teach reading in some way.

Observations of classrooms and basal readers conducted in the past few years have shown that comprehension is rarely taught directly. Instead, students are asked to read and answer questions or to complete work sheets and workbook pages but receive little instruction about how to do this. Moreover, these work sheets and skill activities have been isolated from the real reading tasks for which the skills could be used. Many students, therefore, have failed to learn to comprehend in practical situations. This is evidenced by the recent National Assessment of Educational Progress data, which show that many students are unable to complete tasks requiring anything beyond simple, literal understanding.

The approach and activities provided in this book were not available even a decade ago. Innovative research methods have led to an understanding of comprehension and how to teach it that is clearly new to the field of education. Now we can begin to show students how to comprehend better. We can directly teach the processes that good readers use to comprehend and recall their reading materials, and we can teach these processing strategies within the context of meaningful reading tasks.

The best way to use this book is to begin by reading the first five chapters. All of the basic concepts you need are explained there in simplified form. If you need more information about a specific strategy, you may refer directly to the corresponding chapter in this book, or you may do some background reading. Several useful books on comprehension are listed at the end of this chapter.

After you have familiarized yourself with the material in the first five chapters, you are free to use the rest of the book in any order you choose. It is designed to be used as a handy reference when you want activities and teaching ideas. Simply choose the active comprehension strategy you are targeting and turn to the corresponding chapter. Read over the general suggestions. Then, choose the appropriate objective from the list provided and turn to the activity set for that objective. Select the appropriate activity for your students by using the key provided in Figure A.

We have tried to include activities that are both effective and enjoyable. We have tried to use a variety of formats and materials. We have provided activities that can be used in content-area lessons as well as in reading lessons. Remedial reading teachers can use these content lessons to help students with homework and reading at the same time.

Teachers who have used the approach in this book have told us that their classrooms have become more rewarding places to be. They feel that they are finally teaching comprehension. Their students are more interested in the lessons than ever before. We hope you will have the same success.

Possible Age Level:

> P = primary, grades 1–3 (sometimes kindergarten)
> I = intermediate, grades 4–6
> J = junior high, grades 7–8

H = high school, grades 9–12
A = college, adult

Special characteristics:

FIGURE A: Symbol Key

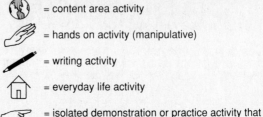

= content area activity

= hands on activity (manipulative)

= writing activity

= everyday life activity

= isolated demonstration or practice activity that must be followed by application to a meaningful reading task

Numbering system:

> roman numeral = chapter number
> letter = objective
> arabic numeral = activity number
> Example: Activity II.B.3 = the third activity for objective B in Chapter 2.

BIBLIOGRAPHY

ANDERSON, R., E. HEIBERT, J. SCOTT, AND I. WILKINSON. *Becoming a Nation of Readers*. Washington D.C.: National Institute of Education, 1984.

DEVINE, T. G. *Teaching Reading Comprehension: From Theory to Practice*. Newton, Mass.: Allyn & Bacon, 1986.

DUFFY, G., L. ROEHLER, AND J. MASON. *Comprehension Instruction: Perspectives and Suggestions*. New York: Longman, 1984.

FLOOD, J. *Understanding Reading Comprehension*. Newark, Del.: International Reading Association, 1984.

IRWIN, J. W. *Teaching Reading Comprehension Processes*. Englewood Cliffs, N.J.: Prentice-Hall, 1986.

McNEIL, J. *Reading Comprehension: New Directions for Classroom Practice*. Glenview, Ill.: Scott, Foresman, 1984.

PEARSON, P. D. AND D. D. JOHNSON. *Teaching Reading Comprehension*. New York: Holt, Rinehart & Winston, 1978.

chapter 1

BASIC COMPREHENSION PROCESSES: WHAT ARE WE TEACHING?

In order to teach students what to do when they want to comprehend, you have to understand what comprehension involves. So, this book must begin with a brief description of the comprehension process.

Of course, in order to even begin to comprehend, students must be able to decode the words they are reading and understand what those words mean. They must also have some prior knowledge of the subject and be somewhat motivated. These and other prerequisites for the comprehension process will be discussed in more depth in Chapter 2.

For the purposes of the following discussion, we will assume that the students can read and understand the individual words, that they have adequate background knowledge, and that they are motivated. Most of this description of comprehension involves skills you have heard of before, but the synthesis of all these skills into one process may be new to you.

Let's take a trip through the comprehension process. Let's pretend that good readers are reading the following passage:

Many people think that New York City is a very exciting place to visit. It has many museums. The exhibits

come from around the world. It has a national center for stage plays and musicals. Many famous actors and actresses live near there. New York also has one of the most famous neighborhoods for seeing art, called SoHo. It has the Statue of Liberty. It is truly a horn of plenty for American sightseers.

The first thing our good readers would have to understand is the meaning of each sentence. To do this, they would divide the sentences into their meaningful phrases. For instance, the first sentence would be divided into at least four phrases, as follows:

Many people think/ that New York City is/ a very exciting place/ to visit.

Students who cannot see which words go with which, or who read sentences as lists of unconnected words, cannot make sense of them. (To help your students with this, see Chapter 9.)

Another thing our good readers would do is select the most important idea or word from each sentence and keep it in mind for interpreting upcoming sentences. For instance, New York City is definitely the most important concept in the first sentence. Readers must keep this in mind while reading the rest of the paragraph in order to make sense of it. If instead they selected "exciting," choosing to remember only that something was exciting, the rest of the paragraph would express exciting things, rather than characteristics of New York City. Selecting important details is a critical comprehension skill. (To help your students with this, see Chapter 10.)

The final thing our readers need to do to understand the individual sentences is to understand any ambiguous or figurative language they contain. The last sentence of our sample passage contains an idiom that requires specialized knowledge and an understanding of metaphor as comparison. Our good readers know that "horn of plenty" is a biblical reference to an abundance of food, and that New York is being compared to this because it has an abundance of things for sightseers to do. (To help your students with this, see Chapter 11.)

So our good readers understand each sentence. But they have been doing something else while reading these sentences—tying them together into a unified whole. This requires an understanding of pronouns, in this case the constant repetition of "it" in reference to New York City. Also, "there" is used to refer to New York's "national center for stage plays and musicals." (To help your students with this, see Chapter 12.)

Our readers also connect the sentences by inferring conjunctive concepts such as "because." In our passage, readers can connect the first sentence to the next by inferring this word. Sentences 4 and 5 can be connected with "so," and so on. (To help your students with this, see Chapter 13.)

Finally, in order to connect sentences good readers will infer information that the author has implied. For instance, to connect sentences 2 and 3 of our passage, readers need to infer that the exhibits are in the museums. This may seem obvious to us, but young readers who are not familiar with museums may not realize this and not know how to link these two sentences. Authors must assume many of these inferences, or their writing would be too explicit for the normal reader. (To help your students with this, see Chapter 14.)

Let's stop a minute and summarize. What have our readers done so far? First, they have understood individual sentences by using the syntax to create meaningful phrases and by selecting the important parts to remember. They have linked sentences together whenever possible, in one of three ways—pronouns, connective concepts, and inferences of assumed information.

Our good readers are not only linking up sentences, however. They are trying to tie them all into one neat package—a summary. Good readers do not try to remember every detail. Instead, they summarize as they go. (To help your students with this, see Chapter 15.) Since our passage consists of one paragraph, summarizing it involves simply finding the main idea, which is stated in the first sentence (to help your students with this, see Chapter 16), and combining the remaining statements into one—something like "it has museums, plays, a famous art neighborhood, and the Statue of Liberty." (See Chapter 15.)

Our readers would be aided in this summarizing process by an understanding of the basic organization of the paragraph. Our passage consists of a generalization followed by details that support it. (To help your students with this, see Chapter 17.) Thus, the summary would be a restatement of the generalization and a synthesis of the details.

Now stop and think about what you know about comprehension. Are readers limited to understanding the individual sentences, linking them together, and summarizing? What else do good readers often do?

They go beyond the intended meaning of the author and add meaning of their own. (To help your students with this, see Chapters 18–20.) They may form mental images of the content being explained. (Did you get any pictures in your mind while you were reading the sample paragraph? Read it again to see.) They may make predictions about what is coming next. After reading the first sentence, could you have predicted that the rest of the paragraph would list some of the sights of New York City? Many of our good readers probably did this. They also integrated the new information with what they already knew. For instance, one reader may have thought about the restoration of the Statue of Liberty and pictures he or she saw of this. Another may have wondered whether his or her favorite actress lived in New York and vowed to find out. These kinds of personal elaborations actually help readers to remember the literal content. The readers who made the aforementioned elaborations would be more likely to remember the part of the passage about actors and actresses or the part about the statue.

Good readers also read critically and creatively. They analyze, evaluate, apply, and synthesize. For instance, one of our good readers may be questioning whether museums are really exciting places to visit. Another may be wondering if the New York City Tourist Bureau wrote the paragraph. Another may wonder if the addition of museums to his or her own city would increase tourism. Another may be thinking of other things in big cities that might attract attention. (To help your students with this, see Chapters 21 and 22.)

Finally, good readers monitor the success of

their comprehension processes and use appropriate remedies when they are having trouble. If our good readers did not know what the horn of plenty was, they might have asked someone or looked it up in an encyclopedia. If midway through they forgot which city the paragraph was about, they would have gone back to the beginning to check. There are many such remedies for comprehension problems. Readers must learn to actively look for meaning in what they are reading and to use these fix-up strategies when something fails to make sense. (To help your students with this, see Chapter 23.)

Related to this is the use of flexible strategies. If our fictional good readers expected to be tested, they would have used study strategies such as rehearsal and review. If they weren't sure about the purpose of the task, they would have asked. Good readers know that their approach to the material is affected by the type of material, their background in the subject, and the purpose of the reading task. (To help your students with this, see Chapters 24 and 25.) Indeed, this entire book is about helping students actively choose comprehension strategies that work for them.

That is all you need to know about comprehension processes! Let's review so you can see how simple it is. Figure 1-1 diagrams the processes for you. Good readers understand individual sentences by dividing them into phrases and selecting what is important. They may also need to interpret figurative language. They tie sentences together with pronouns, conjunctive concepts, and inferences of assumed information. They understand the whole by finding the main ideas and summarizing. They use the author's organizational pattern to do this. They elaborate on the material through predictions, mental images, integration with their previous knowledge, and critical and creative thinking. They expect the text to make sense, and when it doesn't they do something about it. Finally, they adjust their strategies to the type of text, their own background, and the purpose of the task.

All of these processes interact with each other. A breakdown in one affects all the others. For instance, a student who does not understand the individual sentences can hardly be asked to find the main idea. A student who does no elaboration is unlikely to remember any details. A student who makes no connective inferences is unlikely to see the organization pattern (and vice versa!). Moreover, students can choose to use one process to help themselves in another.

Of course, as an experienced teacher, you know that all this is not as simple as it sounds. Different students comprehend differently. Sometimes students know how to use all the processes but lack the decoding skill, prior knowledge, or motivation to understand the passage. Different texts pose different problems. Different situations result in different kinds of performance. Many factors influence these basic processes. You must be aware of these factors to effectively teach

FIGURE 1-1   Basic Comprehension Processes

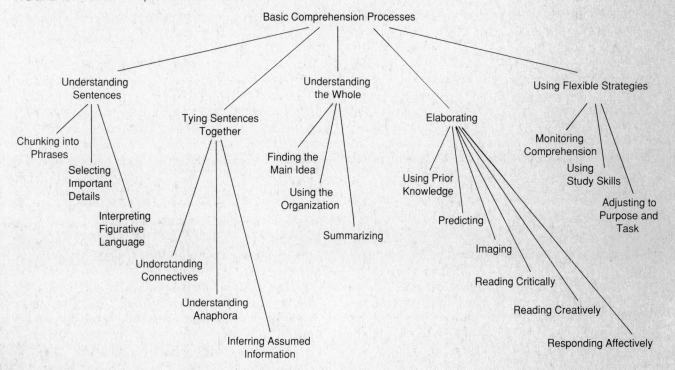

real people in real situations. Thus, you will probably want to read the next chapter, which discusses these factors, before getting started.

Finally, and most important, all of the processes in this chapter can be subsumed under the word *active*. Readers must take an active approach to these processes. Readers must *actively* chunk, select, organize, summarize, infer, elaborate, and so on. In other words, all of the activities in this book encourage readers to take active control of their own comprehension processes. To stress that the reader is actively in control, we classify comprehension processes as *strategies*. Strategies are active comprehension processes that a reader chooses in order to comprehend better. Thus, this is a book about promoting active reading comprehension strategies.

BIBLIOGRAPHY

BAUMANN, J. F. *Teaching Main Idea Comprehension*. Newark, Del.: International Reading Association, 1986.

FLOOD, J. F. (ed.) *Understanding Reading Comprehension*. Newark, Del.: International Reading Association, 1984.

IRWIN, J. W. *Teaching Reading Comprehension Processes*. Englewood Cliffs, N.J.: Prentice-Hall, 1986.

IRWIN, J. W. (ed.) *Understanding and Teaching Cohesion Comprehension*. Newark, Del.: International Reading Association, 1986.

PEARSON, P. D. AND D. D. JOHNSON. *Teaching Reading Comprehension*. New York: Holt, Rinehart & Winston, 1978.

SPIRO, R. J., B. C. BRUCE, AND W. F. BREWER (eds.) *Theoretical Issues in Reading Comprehension*. Hillsdale, N.J.: Erlbaum, 1980.

VAN DIJK, T. A. AND W. KINTSCH. *Strategies of Discourse Comprehension*. New York: Academic Press, 1983.

chapter 2

FACTORS THAT INFLUENCE COMPREHENSION PROCESSES: WHO, WHAT, WHY, WHEN, AND WHERE?

Every act of comprehension is affected by the who, what, why, when, and where of the situation. That is why you must be aware of these things whenever you are teaching. You will need to adjust all of the activities in this book to these factors. The *who* is the reader and his or her individual characteristics. The *what* is the reading material and its specific qualities. The *why*, *when*, and *where* are the other aspects of the situation, such as the purpose, the task, and the environment. Let's look at each of these factors separately.

THE READER

Each reader is unique. Each reader brings a unique set of background experiences to each reading act, and therefore each comprehends a little differently. This is as it should be.

The reader-related characteristics that affect comprehension most directly are the reader's background knowledge and experiences (including diverse cultural and linguistic experiences), motivation and interest, and ability to read the words easily.

To effectively comprehend, students need various kinds of prior knowledge. They need knowledge of the vocabulary in order to understand the individual sentences. They need knowledge of the content in order to make the inferences required to tie sentences together. They need knowledge beyond the content to make elaborations that go beyond the content.

Let's go back to our good readers in Chapter 1. Here again is the paragraph they were reading:

Many people think that New York City is a very exciting place to visit. It has many museums. The exhibits come from around the world. It has a national center for stage plays and musicals. Many famous actors and actresses live near there. New York also has one of the most famous neighborhoods for seeing art, called SoHo. It has the Statue of Liberty. It is truly a horn of plenty for American sightseers.

In order to connect the second and third sentences, our readers needed to know that museums house exhibits. To understand the figurative language in the last sentence, they needed to know that "horn of plenty" is a biblical reference to an abundance of food.

You will also remember that at least one of our readers formed a mental image of the Statue of Liberty and another wondered if a specific actress lived in New York. These elaborations required prior knowledge.

Prior knowledge is so important that comprehension cannot occur without it. We cannot understand something new if we cannot connect it with something we already know. These connections help us to remember what we have read and to tie the content together.

Thus, you must make sure your students have adequate prior knowledge before asking them to read and comprehend. Building and/or checking prior knowledge should be a part of every reading activity. Suggestions for this are included in Chapter 7, though you probably also have many of your own ideas. The point here is to remind you of its importance.

A word about cultural differences is also in order here. Students from divergent cultural backgrounds often find that they lack the background knowledge assumed by the author of the text. This accounts for much of the comprehension difficulty experienced by some minority students. You have two options here, both of which you should use. One is to build the background of those students before asking them to read. The other is to look for reading materials that do not assume inappropriate background knowledge.

Remember that your culturally diverse students from minority cultures do not lack prior knowledge. They have lots of it. It is just that their prior knowledge does not match that assumed by the author. Use the prior knowledge that they do have to help them relate to the material. Lesson plans that encourage this can be found in Chapters 7 and 19.

Finally, even when you can assume that students have adequate prior knowledge somewhere in their heads, you will find that it is useful to bring it to the surface. Ask what they already know and get that information on the table. This sort of refresher also helps to catch their interest and get them on task. (See Chapter 7.)

Indeed, the second reader-related characteristic you must consider whenever you ask students to read and comprehend is motivation. Students can read and understand much more difficult material when they are truly interested. Certainly, they are much more likely to actively infer and elaborate. Suggestions for building general motivation and interest in reading are included in Chapter 8. Again, you probably know how to do this yourself. The point is that you should consider it with each reading activity you do. Asking students to read when they have no motivation and interest is counterproductive and results in an insufficient use of comprehension processes.

Finally, students cannot make sufficient use of comprehension processes if they are having trouble reading the words. We can pay attention to only one thing at a time. Thus, students who are trying to figure out words will be unable to devote attention to comprehension processes. All of the comprehension activities suggested in this book should be used with materials that are at or below the student's reading level.

THE TEXT

How do we determine whether materials are actually at a given student's reading level? This is a difficult question. Readability formulas are one kind of yardstick. Most publishers of reading materials base the approximate grade level of the materials on a mathematical readability formula. Most such formulas use measures of word difficulty (either word familiarity or word length) and sentence difficulty (usually determined by sentence length). (Some sources of specific formulas are listed at the end of the chapter.)

Unfortunately, these formulas do not measure everything you need to know. They do not address such matters as required inferences of assumed information, organizational simplicity, and assumptions of prior knowledge. Moreover, passages artificially rewritten according to formulas are often more difficult than the original.

Thus, you may want to assess more than just readability level. Figure 2-1 provides a checklist you can use when looking for materials. Though written for content area textbooks, it can be used with any reading material. Teachers who have used this checklist have said that it is effective and easy to use. Try it for a while until you become familiar with what to look for. Note that it asks you to consider such things as the prior knowledge and vocabulary knowledge being assumed, clarity of organization, number of inferences required, and motivational level. These things will affect your students' performance as much as readability level will.

Using this checklist will also help you to identify the deficits in the material that you will want to compensate for in your teaching. For instance, if, while using this checklist, you discover that the summaries are poorly written, you may decide to supply summaries yourself. If you find that the material assumes too much background knowledge, you may decide to provide background reading before using that material. If you find that the material is not very motivational, you may decide to use an especially motivational introduction. A thorough assessment of the reading material is

FIGURE 2-1 Readability Checklist

This checklist is designed to help you evaluate the readability of your classroom texts. It can be used best if you rate your text while you are thinking of a specific class. Be sure to compare the textbook to a fictional ideal rather than to another text. Your goal is to find out what aspects of the text are or are not less than ideal. Finally, consider supplementary workbooks part of the textbook and rate them together. Have fun!

Rate the questions below using the following rating system:

> 5 Excellent
> 4 Good
> 3 Adequate
> 2 Poor
> 1 Unacceptable
> NA Not applicable

Textbook title: _____
Publisher: _____

Copyright date: _____

UNDERSTANDABILITY

A. ___ Are the assumptions about students' vocabulary knowledge appropriate?

B. ___ Are the assumptions about students' prior knowledge of this content area appropriate?

C. ___ Are the assumptions about students' general experiential backgrounds appropriate?

D. ___ Does the teacher's manual provide the teacher with ways to develop and review the students' conceptual and experiential backgrounds?

E. ___ Are new concepts explicitly linked to the students' prior knowledge or to their experiential backgrounds?

F. ___ Does the text introduce abstract concepts by accompanying them with many concrete examples?

G. ___ Does the text introduce new concepts one at a time with a sufficient number of examples for each one?

H. ___ Is each definition understandable and at a lower level of abstraction than the concept being defined?

I. ___ Is the level of sentence complexity appropriate for the students?

J. ___ Are the main ideas of paragraphs, chapters, and subsections clearly stated?

K. ___ Does the text avoid irrelevant details?

L. ___ Does the text explicitly state important complex relationships (e.g., causality and conditionality) rather than always expecting the reader to infer them from the context?

M. ___ Does the teacher's manual provide lists of accessible resources containing alternative readings for the very poor and the very advanced readers?

N. ___ Is the readability level appropriate (according to a readability formula)?

LEARNABILITY
Organization

A. ___ Is an introduction provided for each chapter?

B. ___ Is there a clear and simple organizational pattern relating the chapters to each other?

C. ___ Does each chapter have a clear, explicit, and simple organizational structure?

D. ___ Does the text include such resources as an index, a glossary, and a table of contents?

E. ___ Do questions and activities draw attention to the organizational pattern of the material (e.g., chronological, cause-and-effect, spatial, and topical)?

F. ___ Do consumable materials interrelate well with the textbook?

Reinforcement

A. ___ Does the text provide opportunities for students to practice using new concepts?

B. ___ Are there summaries at appropriate intervals in the text?

C. ___ Does the text provide adequate iconic aids, such as maps, graphs, and illustrations, to reinforce concepts?

D. ___ Are there adequate suggestions for usable supplementary activities?

E. ___ Do these activities provide for a broad range of ability levels?

F. ___ Are there literal recall questions provided for the students' self-review?

G. ___ Do some of the questions encourage the students to draw inferences?

FIGURE 2-1 continued

H. ___ Are there discussions that encourage creative thinking?

I. ___ Are questions clearly worded?

Motivation

A. ___ Does the teacher's manual provide introductory activities that will capture students' interest?

B. ___ Are chapter titles and subheadings concrete, meaningful, or interesting?

C. ___ Is the written style of the text appealing to the students?

D. ___ Are the activities motivating? Will they make the student want to pursue the topic further?

E. ___ Does the book show clearly how the knowledge being learned might be used by the learner in the future?

F. ___ Are the cover, format, print size, and pictures appealing to the students?

G. ___ Does the text provide positive and motivating models for both sexes as well as for many racial, ethnic, and socioeconomic groups?

READABILITY ANALYSIS
Weaknesses

A. On which items was the book rated the lowest?

B. Did these items tend to fall in certain categories? Which?

C. Summarize the weaknesses of this text.

D. What can you do in class to compensate for the weaknesses of this text?

Assets

A. On which items was the book rated the highest?

B. Did these items fall in certain categories? Which?

C. Summarize the assets of this text.

D. What can you do in class to take advantage of the assets of this text?

Source: J. W. Irwin and C. J. Davis, "Assessing readability: The checklist approach," *Journal of Reading,* 24, (1980), 124–30.

TABLE 2-1 Examples of Typical School Reading Situations and Effective Reading Strategies

Type of Reader	Type of Reading Material	Purpose	Strategy
Kindergarten student	Picture book	For enjoyment	Look at the best picture. Make up a story.
First-grade student, average reading group, wants to succeed	Basal reader	To please teacher; to read aloud with perfect accuracy	Read slowly and carefully. Focus on every word; sound out unknown words.
Second-grade student, good reader, knows a lot about horses	Trade book about horses from school library; looks like easy reading	To give an oral report to the class about the book	Skip the boring parts. Read especially about the pictures so they can be shown. Read quickly, since most information is known already.
Third-grade student, interested only in baseball	First science textbook, section on the planets	To answer questions in the textbook	Look over the questions first. Read the section slowly, noting the subheadings. Use those to help locate the answers.
Fourth-grade student, average reader, generally does all right in math	Math text, section on multiplying fractions	Missed school; must read to do the homework problems	Read very slowly, making sure each sentence is completely understood. Study the examples in the text, step by step. Try practice problems when they are suggested.

TABLE 2-1 (cont.)

Type of Reader	Type of Reading Material	Purpose	Strategy
Fifth-grade student, below average reader, little interest in history	Social studies textbook on American history, chapter on Constitutional Congress	To pass test	Take each section separately. Use the context to figure out the vocabulary. For each section, write down the key idea. Find someone to listen while you tell him or her what the chapter was about.
Sixth-grade student, above-average reader, loves science, has chemistry set at home	Laboratory activity in science text on melting	To do lab the next day	Read each step while visualizing the activity. Make note of special warnings. Try to predict places where things could go wrong. Try to predict the results of each step.
Seventh-grade student, poor reader but very interested in this book	Adolescent novel	For enjoyment and for book report	Read straight through at your own pace in fairly long sittings. Let yourself "get into it"; worry about book report later.
Eighth-grade student, average reader but has little background in current events	Newspaper	To be able to discuss current events in social studies class the next day	Make a list of names, places, and vocabulary words that are causing you trouble. Get help with them from parents, friends, or the teacher the next day. For each major news item, make sure you understand the title and the first two paragraphs. Make a list of these as well. When possible, get background information from adults or older siblings.
Ninth-grade student, upper-level track, college-bound	*Moby Dick*, Chapter 1	To be able to discuss possible symbolism and potential themes	Read slowly circling figurative language and recurring images. Think about common themes in the images. What do they have to do with the action?
Tenth-grade student, lower-level track	*Auto Mechanics* magazine	To find new things to do with recently purchased "antique" car	Look at the ads and the titles of the articles. If anything seems "do-able," read carefully, picturing yourself doing it.
Eleventh-grade student, average reader, "C" student, not motivated in general	Chemistry textbook, a whole chapter	To understand what's going on in class	Use a systematic study system. Take notes, at least general ones. Keep a list of new vocabulary words. Find a friend to review the chapter with you. This may keep your interest up.
Twelfth-grade student, average reader, *no* interest in Shakespeare	Shakespearean play, one scene	For quiz	Read aloud, trying to use intonation. Try to visualize the action. If you can't tell what they are saying, think about what they might be saying and *then* see if that fits with the next part. Try to make it interesting by thinking about how it would be today.

Source: J. W. Irwin, *Teaching Reading Comprehension Processes* (Englewood Cliffs, N.J.: Prentice-Hall, 1986), pp. 131–33.

necessary if you are to provide the students with successful comprehension activities.

THE SITUATION

There are many other aspects of the reading situation that affect what students comprehend. Students must be aware of the purpose for reading a specific text, and the assessment task must match that purpose. Students must also be aware of how to read for that purpose. Examples of reading purposes and possible strategies are provided in Table 2-1. Note that the reader and text characteristics also affect what method is chosen. Think of some reading assignments you typically use. What purposes and strategies can be used for each?

Moreover, the social situation and classroom environment also affect what is comprehended. Students will recall differently in testing situations than in informal situations. They will recall differently for their peers than for the teacher. They will recall differently in an accepting atmosphere than in a critical one. They will recall differently according to the kinds of questions they are anticipating. You must take all this into consideration with each student in each situation!

SUMMARY

In Chapter 1 we discussed the comprehension processes. In this chapter we dealt with the factors that influence those processes. Each of the factors described in this chapter affects each of the processes described in Chapter 1.

For instance, we can look at how a reader's prior knowledge affects his or her ability to understand individual sentences, to make inferences, to understand the organization, to summarize, and to elaborate. We can look at how a reader's motivation affects his or her tendency to do these things. We can look at how poor decoding ability detracts from the reader's ability to use basic processes. We can look at how a poorly organized text affects summarizing, or how a boring text affects a student's elaborations. We can look at how a relaxed classroom environment encourages elaboration or how having a purpose determines the reader's ability to use flexible processes, and so on. The point is that the factors described in this chapter—the reader's characteristics, the text's characteristics, and the total situation—influence all of the processes described earlier. Thus, these factors must be taken into account regardless of which comprehension strategy you are trying to encourage.

BIBLIOGRAPHY

For readability formulas, see any reading methods text or:

DALE, E. AND J. CHALL. "A formula for predicting readability," *Educational Research Bulletin,* January 1948, 11–20, 28.

FLESCH, R. *How to Test Readability*. New York: Harper, 1951.

FRY, E. "Fry's Readability Graph: Clarifications, validity, and extension to level 17," *Journal of Reading,* 21, December (1977), 242–52.

FRY, E. *Reading Instruction for Classroom and Clinic*. New York: McGraw-Hill, 1972.

chapter 3

GENERAL CONSIDERATIONS FOR INFORMAL ASSESSMENT

Now that you have learned about the basic comprehension processes (Chapter 1) and the factors influencing them (Chapter 2), you are probably beginning to
realize that diagnosis is not as easy as it might once
have seemed. Standardized tests, for instance, do very
little to diagnose students' abilities to perform comprehension processes in real situations; because students
perform differently in different situations, the results
of these formal tests can tell you only how a student
performs in a testing situation. Moreover, standardized tests can tell you very little about what processes
a student is and is not using.

The purpose of this chapter is to suggest ways
that you can organize an informal look at each student's comprehension strategies in a variety of realistic contexts before coming to any conclusions about
appropriate teaching methods. You can combine these
observations with standardized test scores in making
instructional decisions.

Classroom teachers will not have the time to use
all of these procedures for all their students, but they
may wish to use the comprehension assessment checklist for a few students who are having problems. Also,

over a period of time the classroom teacher could use
the suggestions for informal diagnosis that appear
throughout the book.

If you are a remedial reading teacher, you will
probably begin with formal procedures learned elsewhere. We cannot begin to discuss all of these options.
Instead, we have included some new options for you
to consider adding to your usual diagnostic battery:
the free recall checklist, the comprehension assessment checklist, and systematic, multiple, informal observations.

THE FREE RECALL CHECKLIST

If you have had some training in using an informal
reading inventory, you may wish to begin your diagnosis of a student by using such an instrument. Reading
inventories are designed for diagnostic purposes and
should be used. (See the end of the chapter for a list of
informal reading inventories.) However, you may also
wish to adapt them to assess *free recall*. This is what
the student recalls when asked to recall what he or she

has read without any specific questions for guidance. Some believe that this recall can give a more accurate picture of the students' reading strategies than can guided questioning.

The first step in assessing free recall with reading inventories is to select a second passage at each reading level. Most published inventories supply alternative passages, so you can use these. Rather than asking the comprehension questions given in the inventory, ask the student to recall what he or she has read. Tape-record or write down the student's recall. Later, analyze the recall according to the checklist in Figure 3-1. This checklist encourages you to listen for each of the processes described in Chapter 1 and to consider all of the factors influencing comprehension

described in Chapter 2. It is this focus on specific processes and limiting influences that is missing in so many standardized procedures.

THE COMPREHENSION ASSESSMENT CHECKLIST

If you are a classroom or remedial teacher working with a student who is having a lot of trouble comprehending a given reading assignment, you may wish to use the checklist in Figure 3-2 to figure out why the student is having problems. This checklist encourages you to analyze the text and situational factors before you look at the student's abilities. This will help you to

FIGURE 3-1   Free Recall Processing Checklist

Answer each of these questions according to the following scale:

   5 Yes, very well
   4 Yes, more than adequately
   3 Yes, adequately
   2 No, not too well
   1 No, poorly
 NA Not applicable or can't tell

1. ____ Did the student recall a sufficient number of ideas?
2. ____ Did the student recall the ideas accurately?
3. ____ Did the student select the most important details to recall?
4. ____ Did the student understand explicit pronouns and connectives?
5. ____ Did the student infer important implicitly stated information?
6. ____ Did the student include the explicitly stated main points?
7. ____ Did the student create any new summarizing statements?
8. ____ Did the student use the organizational pattern used by the author?
9. ____ Did the student elaborate appropriately?
10. ____ Did the student know how to adjust strategies to the purpose given?

What effective comprehension processes were evident in the student's recall?

What comprehension processes were not evident, or seemed to be causing problems?

To what extent was the student's performance as just described affected by each of the following?

1. Limited prior knowledge or vocabulary

2. Limited motivation or interest

3. Cultural differences

4. Decoding problems

5. Difficulties in the text

6. The social context

7. Discomfort with the task

8. Other environmental influences

Source: J. W. Irwin, *Teaching Reading Comprehension Processes* (Englewood Cliffs, N.J.: Prentice-Hall; 1986), pp 170–71.

FIGURE 3-2 Comprehension Assessment Checklist

Name or Group _____
_____
Assignment _____
_____
Date _____

Directions: For each item, rate your student according to the scale below. A rating of 3 or lower indicates a need for remediation. Remember, you are trying to understand why there have been problems in a specific situation, so be sure to answer in terms of the specific student reading the specific material in the specific situation.

Student has:

5 no problems in this area.

4 only a few problems in this area.

3 some problems in this area.

2 many problems in this area.

1 very serious problems in this area.

N/A (not applicable: for instance, several items cannot be answered if the student read silently)

SITUATION–RELATED FACTORS

____ 1. Was the *physical environment* during reading quiet, well lighted, comfortable, etc.?

____ 2. Was the *teacher/student relationship* one in which the student felt comfortable?

____ 3. Was the situation one in which the *anxiety* level was at a minimum?

____ 4. Was the *purpose* of reading clearly stated?

____ 5. Did the *teacher expect* the student to be able to understand the material?

____ 6. Was the *teacher prepared* to assess the student's comprehension (e.g., familiar with passage, questions ready)?

____ 7. Was the student able to answer in the *format* for assessment (multiple choice, analogy, free recall, written short answer, etc.) that you provided? Consider the following:

a. Did the student have prior experience with the format?

b. Was there an extraneous skill being tested (e.g., talking in front of a group, writing, reasoning beyond the passage, using new equipment) that the student has not mastered?

____ 8. Were the questions and/or directions in the *assessment* themselves *understandable*? Consider the following:

a. Did the student understand exactly what was expected in the questions and/or directions?

b. Did the questions and/or directions meet the criteria in the text-related factors section? (see following)

TEXT–RELATED FACTORS

____ 1. Was the *readability* level appropriate for the student?

____ 2. Was the *vocabulary* in the passage sufficiently concrete and familiar to the student?

____ 3. Were any *sentences* unreasonably lengthy?

____ 4. Were the *relationships* between individual sentences stated explicitly?

____ 5. Was the *organization* sufficiently simple and explicit?

____ 6. If *new concepts* were introduced, was there a sufficient description and/or a sufficient number of examples provided for each?

____ 7. Was the *amount of material* to be remembered manageable (e.g., was the length of the passage appropriate)?

READER–RELATED FACTORS

Was the student:

____ 1. *healthy* and well rested?

____ 2. able to read the individual *words* accurately and easily?

____ 3. able to group the words into meaningful *phrases* and read with proper *intonation*?

____ 4. able to draw on adequate *prior knowledge* of this topic, including a knowledge of the general and specialized vocabulary?

____ 5. able to identify *main ideas* whether they were stated explicitly or not?

____ 6. able to *summarize*?

FIGURE 3-2 continued

____ 7. able to recall the *sequence* of important events?

____ 8. able to explain important *cause/effect relationships* whether they were stated explicitly or not?

____ 9. more likely to recall *important details* than unimportant details?

____ 10. able to identify *pronoun* referents?

____ 11. able to understand the *figurative language* in the passage?

____ 12. able to make *text-based inferences*?

____ 13. able to make *predictions* and/or draw *conclusions*?

____ 14. able to limit *elaborations* to those helpful in understanding and recalling the author's message?

____ 15. able to *adjust* his or her reading *strategies* to the purpose selected?

____ 16. able to read at an appropriate *rate*?

____ 17. able to *attend* to such a task for the required amount of time?

____ 18. aware when he or she had *not* understood something?

____ 19. *expecting* to be able to understand the material?

____ 20. *interested* in the material?

____ 21. *motivated* to try to understand and recall?

____ 22. free from *emotional* problems that might have interfered with concentration?

SUMMARY

Now, in general, what situation-related factors (if any) were causing problems?

Now, in general, what text-related factors (if any) were causing problems?

Now, in general, what reader-related factors (if any) were causing problems?

What can you do to alleviate these problems?

Source: J. W. Irwin, C. Pulver, and K. Koch, "A New Technique for Improving Reading Teachers' Diagnoses" (manuscript, Loyola University of Chicago, 1983).

get a balanced picture of which text and situational characteristics may be causing problems for this student, as well as what problems the student may have in his or her processing strategies.

To use this checklist, wait for a naturally occurring situation in which the student has problems. Then answer the questions in the checklist. You should then be able to identify the problem and avoid it in the future! After you have used this checklist a few times, you will see that it takes very little time and provides a lot of information.

INFORMAL DIAGNOSIS BY OBSERVATION

The main principle of diagnosis stressed in this book is careful, multiple observations of student strategies with a variety of texts and in a variety of situations. Each chapter in this book suggests some specific ways for you to observe whether students are using the appropriate processes and doing so effectively. These observations will be gathered over time, so you may wish to keep careful records of all aspects of the situation: the text, the task, and the strategies the student does and does not use effectively.

This last point is particularly important. Remember to listen for each student's strengths as well as difficulties. Because all the comprehension processes interact, students' strengths can be used to help them with new strategies. Every answer shows the use of some strategy, even if it is just guessing!

Of course, you may need to start teaching before you have observed a student enough times, but it is important for you to keep your diagnosis tentative until you have worked with the student for some time and observed his or her behavior in a variety of situations. You may find that the student seemed unable to do things at first because of anxiety or because he or she did not understand what you wanted. You may find that the student can do things with one kind of reading material, but not with another. You may find that the student is more effective in some situations than in others. Record all this information and use it when you are choosing instructional materials.

Whether you are a classroom or a remedial teacher, remember that you are always gathering diagnostic data. Whenever you are teaching reading comprehension through activities, questions, or discussion, you are gathering insights into students' comprehension strategies.

SUMMARY

Diagnosis of reading comprehension requires more than standardized and other formal diagnostic scores. It also requires careful observation of each student's processing strategies with a variety of texts and in a variety of situations. This chapter provided some checklists to help you do this.

Observational data can be gathered by using the informal techniques suggested in this book, by watching carefully while working with students, or by planning formal diagnostic sessions in which you insert the use of the free recall checklist or the more detailed comprehension assessment checklist. The important thing is to listen closely, to keep diagnoses tentative, to vary situations, and to understand which processes a student does and does not use effectively. Then, you can appropriately choose objectives for your instructional sessions.

BIBLIOGRAPHY

BURNS, P. C. AND B. D. ROE. *Informal Reading Assessment*. Rand McNally, 1980.

EKWALL, E. E. *Ekwall Reading Inventory,* 2nd ed. Boston: Allyn & Bacon, 1986.

JOHNS, J. L. *Advanced Reading Inventory*. Dubuque, Iowa: Wm. C. Brown, 1981.

SILVAROLI, N. J. *Classroom Reading Inventory,* 4th ed. Dubuque, Iowa: Wm. C. Brown, 1982.

WOODS, M. L. AND A. J. MOE. *Analytical Reading Inventory,* 3rd ed. Columbus, Ohio: Chas. E. Merrill, 1985.

chapter 4

GENERAL CONSIDERATIONS FOR TEACHING I: THE ACTIVE READER

The overall approach to teaching followed throughout this book is based on the principle that a good reader is an active reader. Look back over the comprehension processes in Figure 1-1. Notice how each requires that the reader do something actively: the reader must actively infer, actively connect, actively summarize, actively elaborate, and actively select strategies. A passive reader will not take the initiative to do these things. Thus, our teaching must focus on creating active readers who are actively creating meaning.

Recent research suggests that the methods most likely to develop active readers (1) define reading as always useful and meaningful, (2) teach conscious selection of reading strategies (metacognition), (3) involve discussions of the processes and strategies themselves, and (4) take place in an interactive classroom environment that empowers students. Let's look at each of these characteristics separately before giving a name to them as a whole.

MEANINGFUL COMPREHENSION ACTIVITIES

A basic requirement of all comprehension lessons is that the student expect the reading assignment to make sense and that the teacher expect the student to make sense of it as well. Research has indicated that many students become accustomed to isolated skill activities that seem like nonsense to them (see, for example, Anderson, 1984). We can hardly expect such students to try to actively understand.

Observers have also noted that teachers often give students meaningless shortcuts to answers, such as "the answer is a word in the first sentence" (see Durkin, 1978). These practices encourage passive reading strategies that lead to failure. In *What's Whole in Whole Language*, Ken Goodman points out that dividing language into parts and creating artificial reading activities make reading hard and can lead to frustration. He says that language is "easy" when it is "real and natural," "whole," "sensible," "interesting," "relevant," "part of a real event," and so on (Goodman, 1986, p. 8).

Teachers who realize that comprehension is best learned through real, meaningful reading tasks find that they integrate reading activities with the rest of the curriculum. They talk about study skills in terms of studying for a test in a specific subject; they talk about identifying with characters when students are reading their library books; they talk about comprehension monitoring when students are having trouble understanding meaningful reading assignments.

In talking about these things, they find that they use a mix of incidental discussion arising naturally during meaningful reading tasks and planned lessons built around specific strategies. (A general format for a planned lesson is included in Chapter 5.) They also often use both materials specifically designed to teach reading, such as basal series and other reading books, and other trade books and content-area materials that are being used for content lessons.

The activities suggested in this book encourage the use of specific strategies in meaningful reading situations. Though we have classified these activities by strategy, we are *not* recommending that you teach them in isolation from their use. In a few cases, we have included activities designed to introduce a strategy to students who are having problems. These isolated strategy lessons are marked with the symbol ☞ and the following warning: "This is a demonstration activity. Be sure to provide opportunities for application to meaningful reading tasks." Some isolated practice activities are included in selected areas, but they too are marked as such and should be used sparingly.

METACOGNITION

You may remember that one part of the comprehension process is to actively monitor whether one has understood and to select strategies that ensure success. This conscious control of the process is sometimes called *metacognition*. Though the term may not be important to you, the concept is. We believe it is one of the most powerful teaching ideas to emerge in the last twenty years. You will read about specific metacognitive processes in Chapters 23–26, but it is important now to understand how the concept of being aware of one's comprehension strategies pervades the approach used in this book.

Good readers actively look for meaning. Thus, if what they are reading is not making sense, they are aware of this. They are more likely than poor readers

to notice the problem and to know what to do about it. Similarly, readers who are actively in control will often choose strategies that will help them with the task at hand. For instance, they may choose to form a mental image during a description so that they can remember the details. They may choose to remember only main ideas when the details are not important to them, or they may decide to read slowly for details when they know they will need to perform a complicated task based on the written directions. In other words, good readers make active strategy decisions based on the demands of the task.

These active reading strategies, or processes, as they were called in Chapter 1, can be taught directly to all readers. Chapter 5 provides a format for doing this; the format includes explaining the strategy, modeling it, giving the students a chance to model it back, and then assigning the activity. All readers can learn to take conscious control over their own reading strategies through this approach. This conscious control is called metacognition.

TEACHING THE PROCESSES

When you begin to directly teach students about the processes they use to comprehend so that they can make metacognitive decisions, you will find that your reading discussion also changes in two ways. First, your responses to wrong answers improve. Instead of using the "one-right-answer" approach and responding to each answer as if it is either correct or incorrect, you can begin to give substantive feedback. For instance, suppose your student, Sally, gave you a wrong answer. You can try to figure out why Sally answered the way she did. Was she using the wrong prior knowledge? Was she forgetting to use prior knowledge? Did she fail to make a critical inference? Did she fail to understand the figurative language? And so on. You can explain to Sally the strategy you would have used to get the right answer. Then you can give her another chance to use the process correctly.

Second, the questions you ask will change. You will ask students about their strategies. Table 4-1 gives examples of the kinds of question you might ask. Note that you can ask students to describe any of the strategies discussed in this book. This is the best way to see if they know how to apply a particular strategy.

The result of directly instructing students in processes, responding substantively to their wrong answers, and questioning them about their processes will be a change in the focus of your classroom. Now you and the students will be talking about the *how* of reading comprehension. You will be developing their meta-

TABLE 4-1   Examples of Questions About Processes

Process	Sample Question
Selecting details	How did you know what was the most important idea here?
Interpreting figurative language	What word is being used in a new way?
Understanding pronouns	How did you know who "he" was?
Making connections	How did you know what caused it to happen?
Finding the main idea	How can you decide which sentence contains the main idea?
Summarizing	How should we go about writing a summary of this article?
Predicting	What did you already know that led you to predict this would happen?
Imaging	What part painted a picture in your mind?
Monitoring comprehension	What part made it hard for you to understand?
Adjusting strategies	How might you go about reading this in order to achieve your goal?

cognitive awareness. This can happen in both planned and incidental ways.

THE INTERACTIVE CLASSROOM

Finally, encouraging students to be active meaning seekers requires a classroom environment in which the students are active learners. In such an environment, teachers and students actively interact in their search for meaning. In a transmission environment, in contrast, the teacher simply tells the students what to learn and quizzes them to make sure they have done so. The latter creates passive learners who wait to be told what is important, how to do things, whether they are correct, and so forth.

In an interactive classroom, the teacher's role is that of collaborator. Students and teachers discuss their opinions, their strategies, their goals. Students sometimes select their own materials or reading purposes. Questions are often open-ended and the emphasis is on the use of valid processes rather than on correctness. These procedures encourage students to take an active approach to their learning. (In a transmission classroom, the teacher is a manager, test giver, and interrogator. This discourages students from taking an active role.)

In an interactive classroom, the activities are at a level of difficulty that the students can handle with success. Students are given the prior knowledge they need in order to read and understand. They are given help until they can function independently. This support may include direct instruction about which strategies would be useful. Knowing that assignments will be manageable encourages students to work actively.

SUMMARY

This chapter introduced a new approach to teaching active comprehending. This approach is sometimes called a *metacognitive* approach because it teaches students to be aware of their comprehension strategies, and it teaches them that comprehension is a set of strategies they can consciously choose to use in meaningful situations. Teachers using this approach teach comprehension in a variety of meaningful reading situations. They directly teach strategies. They respond to wrong answers with advice about alternative strategies. They regularly ask students about their reading strategies, and they work to establish an interactive learning environment, in which the student is an active participant. All of these procedures encourage the students to take control of their own comprehension processes and to make their own metacognitive decisions.

BIBLIOGRAPHY

ANDERSON, L. "The environment of instruction: The function of seatwork in a commercially developed curriculum," in *Comprehension Instruction: Perspectives and Suggestions,* eds. G. Duffy, L. Roehler, and J. Mason. New York: Longman, 1984, 93–103.

DURKIN, D. "What classroom observations reveal about reading comprehension instruction," *Reading Research Quarterly,* 14, 4 (1978–1979), 481–533.

GOODMAN, K. *What's Whole in Whole Language?* Portsmouth, N.H.: Heinemann Educational Books, 1986.

chapter 5

GENERAL CONSIDERATIONS FOR TEACHING II: THE PREPLANNED COMPREHENSION LESSON

Comprehension instruction takes many forms. As mentioned in Chapter 4, the best comprehension lessons are real, meaningful reading tasks undertaken for purposes that are relevant to the learner. However, sometimes you may wish to preplan a specific comprehension lesson. These lessons can be part of the meaningful reading tasks used in other situations.

Preplanned comprehension lessons usually involve selecting objectives and materials, preparing students, and directly teaching comprehension before, during, and/or after reading. Let's look at each of these steps separately.

SELECTING OBJECTIVES

The first thing to remember in selecting your objectives is that all the comprehension processes work together. Though you will sometimes choose lessons that address your students' weaknesses, you should also select activities that build on their strengths. Also, you will want to mix activities that focus on one strategy with activities that integrate all the processes. (See Chapter 26 for examples.) You may also want to consider your students' practical needs. A student who needs better grades in science might respond better to activities that directly address that need. Finally, you may wish to consider the students' attitudes and interests. As stated in Chapter 2, motivation can be a major factor in comprehension.

SELECTING MATERIALS

Use materials that cause students a minimum of word identification problems so that they can pay attention to their comprehension. You may wish to use materials for which students have a great deal of background knowledge, or you may decide to go ahead with materials that are unfamiliar. In the latter case, you can build prior knowledge yourself or help students see what they can do to build it.

If you are a classroom teacher, you may feel that you have little choice about the materials you use. In that case, you will want to use the checklist in Chapter 2 to assess the strengths and weaknesses of those materials so you can use them effectively. You may, however, decide that the materials you have are just impossible for some of the students to understand. In this case, you will want to find other materials for those students. You can "rescue" old textbooks discarded from lower grades. You can find trade books at easy reading levels on the same topics. You can bring in free materials gathered from real-world situations. You will find that taking the time to give students materials they can read is well worth it.

If you are a remedial teacher, you must decide whether to find your own materials or to use the materials available in the classroom. In our experience, it generally seems best to use the classroom materials, if students are able to read them with your assistance. Some classroom materials are so difficult that attempts to use them can be a waste of valuable time. In those cases, you may wish to find other materials that address classroom topics or, in extreme cases, select materials that directly address the students' reading interests without trying to relate those materials to classroom topics.

Many of the activities provided in this text use materials that the students might see or use in their daily lives. These activities are identified with the symbol 🏠 . We specifically looked for such activities because they allow students to learn active strategies in situations that seem relevant to them.

Many of the other activities we describe use content-area materials. These are identified with the symbol 🔬 . Content-area lessons provide a meaningful situation in which students can learn active strategies that are useful immediately.

PREPARING STUDENTS FOR READING COMPREHENSION

You can prepare students for each reading comprehension assignment by attending to all the factors that influence comprehension. In terms of the reader-related factors, you should make sure students have adequate prior knowledge about the topic, and you should bring that knowledge to the front of their minds with a brief prereading discussion. You will want to make sure that students are motivated and interested, and that they are familiar with important vocabulary. Ideas for doing these things are included in Chapters 6–8.

In terms of the text-related factors, you will want to explain important text characteristics to the students ahead of time. You may also want to supply things that are missing from the text, such as summaries or guiding questions.

You should also make the comprehension situation clear by telling the students what task you will be asking them to do after the reading and by making the purpose of the reading clear. They should be able to adjust their reading to this purpose and task, and you should encourage them to plan this before they read.

DIRECTLY TEACHING COMPREHENSION

Before-Reading Instruction

The prereading discussion also provides you with an opportunity to directly teach reading comprehension strategies. Research on current practices in reading comprehension instruction indicates that most teachers never tell students how to comprehend; they just tell them to comprehend.

Now that you know the processes involved in successful comprehension, you can directly teach them to the students when appropriate. At least three steps are involved: explaining the specific reading process, modeling that process, and having the students model it back to you.

Explaining. Explaining the process to the students and telling them why it is important would involve statements like the following:

1. "While you read this passage, you will need to think about how it relates to what you already know about X. Good readers always stop and think about what else they know. This helps them to remember and understand the new information. This is especially important when you are reading in social studies or science."

2. "When authors write, they often leave out information they think you can figure out for yourself. Therefore, it is very important for you to actively infer aspects of the situation that are not necessarily stated outright. This is especially important when you are reading a good story."

Notice that in this explaining step you are explaining strategies, not introducing the content of the passage. You are talking to the students about *how to comprehend* and telling them when a specific comprehension strategy should be used.

Modeling. So far your explanation is pretty abstract. Many students may be unable to understand exactly what you mean. Perhaps the best way to clarify your explanation is to model the process to the students. For the preceding explanations, the modeling would start something like this:

1. "For instance, let's read the first paragraph silently. [Students read.] Now when I read this paragraph about the climate in Alaska, I thought about what it was like when it snowed here last year. When the author referred to 'bitter' cold, I knew that he meant the kind of cold that makes you numb and tingly, like we get in January . . . ."

2. "Let me show you an example. [Teacher reads first part of story until coming to a required inference.] Now when I read that she stirred her coffee, I infer that she probably did this with a spoon. I also infer that it was sugar that she stirred in and that she was about to drink her coffee. This helps me to understand the next sentence . . . ."

The teacher uses the actual text and shows how he or she comprehends by using the process in question. Use your own judgment to determine when modeling is necessary.

Questioning. We call this step *questioning* because that is what it usually involves, but the essence of this step is having the students model the process back to you. You want to make sure they understand what you have explained, and you want to given them some guided practice. Examples of appropriate questions for this stage include:

1. "John, what do you already know that helps you to understand this paragraph?"
2. "What do the next two sentences have to do with each other? How do you know?"

Questions that ask students to talk about the processes they used can be called *process questions*. These questions focus on the *how* of comprehension. They often include "How did you know?" "Where did you find out?" "How can you find out?" (See Chapter 4 for more examples.)

During-Reading Instruction

Working with students while they are actually reading a passage provides an immediate way of having them model the processes you are teaching. You have two options for doing this, oral and silent.

If you would like to work with a student or group of students orally while they are reading, you can conduct a group discussion. In this format, students read small amounts of text and then discuss their reading with you. You can ask them to discuss their reading strategies, and you can give specific instructions on the use of the needed processes before they read on.

Your other during-reading option is to have the students complete study guides while they are reading. The questions in these guides can be designed to focus students' attention on the comprehension processes you have already explained and modeled. For instance, such guides can provide or request main ideas, summaries, prior knowledge inferences, and so forth, at selected points in the reading assignment. Numerous examples of activities in the study-guide format can be found in Chapters 17 and 19 and throughout this book.

AFTER-READING INSTRUCTION

This is the only part of comprehension instruction that has not been ignored in the past. After-reading activities should reflect your objectives and be preceded by some sort of explaining, modeling, and questioning, either before or during the reading. Use activities that require meaningful interaction between the reader and the material.

You will note that many of the activities recommended in this book involve writing. These are identified with the symbol ✎ . We specifically chose these activities because writing encourages the learner to actively interact with the material in a meaningful way. Activities that do not involve writing usually involve thoughtful discussion or some other active type of interaction. The symbol ✋ identifies hands-on activities—those that allow the reader to manipulate materials in an active way.

SUMMARY

The basic points of this chapter are simple. Though much of your instruction will occur incidentally during meaningful reading tasks, you may also wish to plan direct instruction in reading strategies. When you do so, choose objectives before you teach. Find materials the students can read. Select a situation that is meaningful to the learner. Prepare the students by attending to prior knowledge, motivation, purpose, and strategy. Teach them about the strategies they will need by explaining and modeling those strategies before you ask them to model them back and perform the activities. You can have students model the processes back to you in during-reading activities that are conducted orally or else silently with study guides. Use after-reading activities that encourage active, meaningful interaction with the ideas in the reading material. Do not forget to focus on the "how to" of reading comprehension before, during, and after the reading. Use the activities in this book within the context of such an approach.

BIBLIOGRAPHY

BAUMANN, J. "Implications for reading instruction from research on teacher and school effectiveness." *Journal of Reading,* 28, 1984, 109–115.

BAUMANN, J. "The direct instruction of main idea comprehension ability." In J. Baumann (Ed.), *Teaching Main Idea Comprehension,* Newark, DE: International Reading Association, 1986, 133–178.

PEARSON, P. D. AND GALLAGHER, M. C. "The instruction of reading comprehension." *Contemporary Educational Psychology,* 8(1983), 317–344.

ROEHLER, L. R. AND DUFFY, G. G. "Studying qualitative dimensions of instructional effectiveness." In J. V. Hoffman (ed.), *Effective Teaching of Reading: Research and Practice,* Newark, DE: International Reading Assn., 1986, 181–198.

VOCABULARY

Definition: *Knowledge of word meanings or the ability to infer those word meanings from information in the text*

RATIONALE AND INFORMAL DIAGNOSIS

In all the controversy over comprehension pedagogy, there is almost universal agreement that vocabulary knowledge is essential. Students must understand the individual words to be able to put them together into a meaningful whole. Moreover, understanding individual words involves at least four separate processes: (1) knowing the meaning of general vocabulary words, (2) inferring the meaning from the context, (3) inferring the meaning from word parts, and (4) knowing the meaning of the specialized vocabulary related to the specific content of the reading. Activities for each of these areas are provided in this chapter.

Learning General Vocabulary

Words must be meaningful to be learned. Research indicates that teaching words in isolated lists has only a limited value. If words are to be learned for the long term, they must be taught in meaningful contexts and in situations in which they can be used repeatedly.

Another way to teach vocabulary is to encourage wide reading of material at the students' reading level. This exposes students to words in meaningful contexts in which the complete connotation of the words can be understood. Similarly, writing exercises can provide useful incidental opportunities for teaching vocabulary: students tend to remember words they need in order to express a thought of their own.

As every teacher knows, however, getting excited about words is the key to learning vocabulary, and among the best times to teach vocabulary and foster this excitement are the unplanned moments during the school day when a new word surfaces during instruction. These moments have special value simply because they arise spontaneously and are relevant to the content being discussed. Use them whenever you can!

Activities for helping students to develop their general vocabularies are included in the first activity section of this chapter. Remember to use these activities to focus on concept development and on words that arise during tasks that are important to the learner.

Using Context Clues

It is not necessary for students to know every word before reading a passage. Some of the new word meanings can be inferred from the *context*. Indeed, inferring word meanings from the context is probably the most important vocabulary strategy, since it provides a way for students to continually learn new words.

Probably the best way to diagnose a student's ability to use context clues is to find examples in daily reading assignments. Ask questions to determine whether the student has inferred an appropriate meaning. You may also wish to develop a cloze instrument, which consists of sentences with critical words omitted. Students fill in the missing words, either from their own vocabulary or from a list supplied by you. They should be able to use the context to determine what words are missing.

In teaching context-clue use, you may wish to take the following approach: Explain the importance of context clues directly. Students should see the connection between any context-clue exercise and real reading. Extend lessons on the use of context clues back into meaningful reading tasks. Point out the author's use of context clues whenever the opportunity arises. Encourage students to guess the meanings of new words in low-risk situations. Try some of the activities included in activity section B of this chapter.

Using Word Parts

Knowledge of the meanings of frequently used word parts can also help students to become independent vocabulary learners. This chapter contains a useful list of prefixes (see activity C.1). A more extensive list of word parts is provided in Appendix A. Of course, these word parts should never be taught in isolation. Teach them in meaningful groups, and in situations where they will be useful for a real reading selection. Diagnosis should probably be informal: Ask students about the meanings of words that should be understandable from an analysis of their parts.

Learning Content-Specific Vocabulary

Problems in content-area reading often result from a lack of knowledge about basic content-area vocabulary. Authors of textbooks sometimes assume that students have more background than they actually do. If you find this to be the case, it doesn't mean that the students don't have any vocabulary knowledge. Their vocabulary has probably suited their purposes until this point. The problem is that their vocabulary does not match that of the text.

A related problem is that students may not realize that common words are being used in a new way. The *mouth* of a river and bacteria grown in a *culture* are just two examples.

If these are problems for your students, you will probably find this out very quickly through normal questioning procedures. Teach the words in meaningful groups and encourage their repeated use. You may also wish to use some of the activities supplied in the fourth activities section of this chapter.

GENERAL TEACHING SUGGESTIONS

1. Teach new vocabulary words when focusing on concept development. Never have students memorize definitions.

2. Use words that are relevant to the learners. Totally unknown and irrelevant words are much harder to learn.

3. Focus on the use of context clues and word-part clues as active strategies used by good readers. Give credit to students who get the gist by using the context.

4. Teach a love of words by modeling this yourself.

5. Limit the number of content-area words you choose to emphasize in a lesson. Do not try to teach so many that nothing is learned.

6. In defining words, use concrete examples and nonexamples whenever possible.

7. Words are learned through use. Provide ample opportunities for students to use new words in class discussion and written assignments.

chapter 6.   VOCABULARY
Activities

A.   TEACHING GENERAL VOCABULARY
    1.   The Frontier Vocabulary System   I J H A
    2.   Frontier Vocabulary Self-Assessment Inventory   I J H A
    3.   Vocabulary Self-Collection Strategy (VSS)   P I J H A
    4.   Which Meaning?   I J
    5.   Word Maps   P I J H
    6.   Vanity   J H A
    7.   What's in a Surname?   I J
    8.   Motor Imaging   P I J H A
    9.   Enough, Already!   I J H A
    10. Experience-Based Words   I J H A
B.   TEACHING USE OF CONTEXT CLUES
    1.   Context-Clue Types   I J H A
    2.   Possible Sentences   J H A
    3.   Intelligent Guessing   J H A
    4.   Bit by Bit   I J
C.   TEACHING USE OF WORD PARTS
    1.   Make a word   P I J H A
    2.   Wordo   I J
    3.   Affixionary   P I
D.   TEACHING CONTENT–AREA WORDS
    1.   Semantic Mapping   P I J H A
    2.   Student-Activated Vocabulary Instruction (SAVI)   I J H A
    3.   Not-So-Ordinary Words   I J H A
    4.   Mathematics Symbols and Words   I J
    5.   Computer Sight Vocabulary   I J

A.   TEACHING GENERAL VOCABULARY GROWTH

1.   The Frontier Vocabulary System*   I J H A

Developed by Johnson O'Connor, the Frontier Vocabulary System is an individualized approach to learning new words that is based on the learner's current vocabulary and interests. Words are divided into the three zones indicated in Figure 6-1.

Learning takes place at the frontier, in the twilight zone of words you may know how to pronounce, or have heard, or know a meaning for. These words are the easiest ones to master.

To find their frontier words, students should make a list of words that they recognize in reading or listening but do not themselves use. From these words they choose the ones that interest them.

Procedure: 1.   Explain to students the purpose of the activity—to have them increase their vocabularies using words they choose themselves and will need.

       2.   Demonstrate the first step of the process: On one side of a three-by-five card write a new word; on the other side write the sentence where it was found. Underline or otherwise highlight the word.

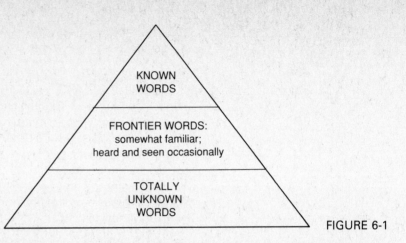

FIGURE 6-1

* From *How to Study in College, 3rd Ed* by Walter Pauk, p. 293. Copyright, 1984 by Houghton Mifflin, Co. Adapted by permission.

3. Give students the following instructions:

    a. After accumulating several cards, look up the words.

    b. Print the pronunciation of the word on the sentence side of the card. Practice saying the word out loud. This will make it easier to use. We don't use words we can't pronounce.

    c. On the back of the card write the prefix and root, if applicable.

    d. Write several definitions of the word, and put a star next to the one you used.

    e. Carry these cards in your pocket or purse so that you can practice them while you're waiting for a bus, appointment, etc.

    f. Place a dot over the words you don't define correctly, to remind you the next time you try.

    g. After you master this first set of words, file them and move on to others. Try to use these words in meaningful situations whenever possible.

    h. Test yourself occasionally.

Variation: Pairs of students can set themselves a number of frontier vocabulary words to learn each week. They then test each other, thereby doubling their learning.

* Pauk, 1984.

2. Frontier Vocabulary Self–Assessment Inventory   I J H A

Purpose: to assess students' knowledge of new vocabulary

Procedure: 1.   Before teaching a unit of study, give the students a list of words they will need in their reading. Have the students indicate the degree of their knowledge of the words by using the symbol system in Figure 6-2.

2.   After students have completed the instrument, have them share definitions of words they know, using them in sentences. Add any definitions needed for the material to be studied and give sentences using the words as examples.

FIGURE 6-2

NAME _____

DIRECTIONS: Look at the list of words.

Mark a * on the line if you know the word well.
+ on the line if you know the word somewhat.
− on the line if you've seen or heard the word
? on the line if you've never heard of the word.

____ feudal   ____ noble

____ knight   ____ chivalry

____ oath   ____ fief

---

3. Vocabulary Self–Collection Strategy (VSS)*   P I J H A

Purpose: to develop independent vocabulary-learning skills

Procedure: 1.   On Monday, tell students that they are each responsible for bringing to class the next day one or two words (depending on grade level) that they believe the entire class should learn. You will also bring in two words. The words should be ones they hear often, see on television, encounter in reading newspapers, etc.

2.   On Tuesday students write their words on the board when they enter the room.

3.   In class discussion, each student identifies the words he or she brought in, defines them, and states why the class should learn them. The emphasis should be on the context in which they were found, and on why they are needed by the students.

4.   The class narrows the list down to a predetermined number of words by eliminating duplications, words most students already know, and words not often used. The list they choose is composed of high-frequency words.

5.   The originator of each word in the final list gives the definition again. Lead a discussion to clarify, refine, and extend the definitions.

6.   Students record the final list of words and definitions in their notebooks, keeping in a separate list any extra words they choose.

7.   Reinforce word meanings with puzzles, sentence writing, skits, research on word history, and meaningful reading assignments during the week.

8.   If you wish, on Friday give an informal quiz on the words in the final list.

Caution: Haggard notes that this procedure takes longer than you'd expect (twelve students could not settle on a word list in thirty minutes), because of the enthusiasm generated and because it was a new instructional procedure. But she recommends that you stay with it, so that word searching becomes a weekly habit.

Variations: 1.   *Content area:* Instead of preteaching a vocabulary word for a new unit, have the students preview the reading assignment and choose one or two words they feel are important. These words form the basis for the VSS procedure.

2.   *Large class:* Have half of the class bring words one week, the other half the next week. Or have each student bring in only one word.

* Haggard, 1982.

4.   Which Meaning?   I J

Purpose: to develop the ability to recognize multiple meanings

Procedure: 1.   Select several words with multiple meanings from the text.

2.   Have students fold a piece of paper into four columns and write the words in the left-hand column.

3.   In the next fold they write the predicted meaning.

4.   After reading the text, they put a check in the third column if they were right, or write down the correct meaning if they were wrong.

5.   In the right-hand column students write the context clue words that determined the meaning. (See Figure 6-3.)

5.   Word Maps*   P I J H

Purpose: to teach students how to understand and use definitions

Procedure: Day 1

A.   Explain the purpose of the activity and why it is important.

B.   Show students a word map (see Figure 6-4) and tell them it is a diagram they can use to remind themselves of what they must know to really understand a word.

C.   Demonstrate the use of the first part of the word map. Use familiar material. A very general word is needed for "What is it?" For example, if *television* were the word to be defined, *machine* would apply (it would also apply to many other words.)

D.   Demonstrate the next step in the procedure by having the students give details for "What is it like?" (It has a picture screen, sound, controls for stations, etc.) These details should tell how a television is different from other machines.

E.   Complete the procedure by eliciting examples: "What are some examples?"

F.   Provide supervised practice with a list of selected words.

FIGURE 6-3

WORD	PREDICTED MEANING	AFTER READING	CLUE WORDS
seal	animal	official wax imprint on a paper	document, legal, king, ring
root	part of a plant that takes in water	source, original form, and language of a word	origin, word form, Latin

Day 2

    A.   Review the procedure.

    B.   Demonstrate the procedure with a word from a current textbook. Use the context, the glossary, a dictionary, your own prior knowledge, and even an encyclopedia if not enough examples are provided.

    C.   Provide supervised practice with current textbook words.

    D.   Have students work independently on relevant words.

Day 3

    A.   Demonstrate writing definitions without looking at a word map. Students should learn to use it only as a mental guide for following the procedure just outlined.

    B.   Provide supervised practice in writing definitions. Have students share definitions; place a check mark on the board for each component of the word map that is given.

    C.   Use this procedure regularly with new words.

Variations: Make word maps of synonyms and antonyms.

* Adapted from Schwartz and Raphael, 1985.

6. Vanity*   J H A

Purpose: to enable students to recognize word connotations

Materials: work sheets
dictionaries

Procedure: 1. Present examples of Bertrand Russell's "conjugation" of an irregular verb:

I am firm.
You are obstinate.
He is a pig-headed fool.

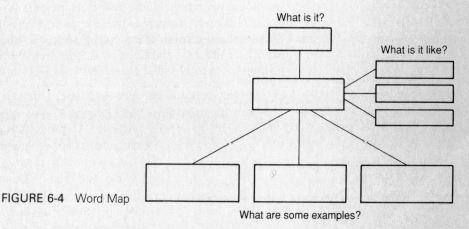

FIGURE 6-4 Word Map

Source: Schwartz and Raphael, 1985, p. 201. Reprinted with permission of Robert M. Schwartz and the International Reading Association.

This was presented on a BBC radio program called "Brains Trust" and resulted in a contest sponsored by *The New Statesman* and *Nation* for similar "irregular verbs." Some of the published entries were:

> I am sparkling. You are unusually talkative.
> He is drunk.
> I daydream. You are an escapist.
> He ought to see a psychiatrist.
> I am righteously indignant. You are annoyed.
> He is making a fuss about nothing.
> I am beautiful. You have quite good features.
> She isn't bad-looking, if you like that type.

2.   Ask students to provide their own conjugations for statements such as:

   a.   I am slender.
   b.   I am a little irritable today.
   c.   I don't swim too well.
   d.   My room is a little messy.
   e.   I am careful with money.

3.   Have students create their own conjugations for statements they themselves suggest. Focus on positive as well as negative attributes in the conjugations.

☞   This is a demonstration activity. Be sure to provide opportunities for application to meaningful reading tasks.

* Hayakawa, 1972.

7.   What's in a Surname?*   I J

Purpose: to arouse students' interest in vocabulary and word origins

Procedure:

1.   Provide some background about surnames, which developed as population increased and a need for them arose. Surnames in the Western world follow the given name (e.g., James Brown); in some Asian countries such as China or Korea, however, surnames precede given names (e.g., Mao Tse-tung).
Surnames arose from several logical sources—locations, relationships, and occupations or offices—and from nicknames derived from such things as colors, animal names, and physical characteristics. Here are some examples.

   a.   Locations: Brook, Stone, Hill, Berg ("hill" in German), Glen
   b.   Relationships: MacDonald (son of Donald; Scottish)
                     Adamczyk (son of Adam; Polish)
                     Adamson (son of Adam; English)
                     Cohen (priestly family; Hebrew)
                     O'Donnell (son of Donnell; Irish)
   c.   Occupations: Sawyer (lumber) Smith (blacksmith)
                     Mason (brick) Baker
                     Dufour (baker; French) Cooper (barrelmaker)
                     Berger (shepherd; French)

d.   Nicknames: Bruno (brown; Italian) Stalin (steel; Russian)
Reid (red hair; Irish) Rosen (rose; Yiddish)
Savage, Young, Armstrong

2.   Instruct the students to use their school library or the public library to find information about their surnames.

3.   Display these facts on posters around the classroom.

4.   Have students copy or create coats of arms.

Variations: 1.   Students find information about three or four of their friends or people of their own choosing.

2.   Students are asked to pretend that they have no surname, only a given name. Their task is to choose an appropriate surname based on the four categories. Students share surnames with the class.

3.   Name-Match Game

a.   Objective: to match surnames with their correct classification
b.   Procedure:

(1)   Divide the class into two groups.

(2)   Print four classifications on large strips of paper and attach them to a bulletin board.

(3)   Print some surnames on small pieces of paper and place them face down on a table.

(4)   The groups take turns drawing a name from the pile.

(5)   The group selects what it thinks is the proper classification for the name.

(6)   If the placement is correct, points are earned.

(7)   Extra points are earned for giving the meaning of the surname.

(8)   If the group fails to classify the name correctly, it is placed at the bottom of the pile.

Sources to Use in Re-   CHUKSORJI, OGONNA. *Names From Africa*. Chicago, IL: Johnson Publishing, 1972.
searching Surnames: DILLARD, J. L. *Black Names*. Hawthorne, NY: Mouton, 1976.

HAKIM, DAWUD. *Arabic Names With Their Meanings*. Philadelphia, PA: Hakim's Publishing, 1970.

SMITH, ELSDON. *American Surnames*. Radner, PA: Chilton Book Co., 1969.

SMITH, ELSDON. *Treasury of Name Lore*. New York: Harper & Row, Pub., 1975.

WAGNER, RUDOLPH, AND WAGNER, MARNEY. *New Dictionary of Family Names*. Portland, ME: J. Weston Walch, 1977.

* Source: Miller and Thompson, 1984, p. 357. Reprinted with permission of Harry Miller and the International Reading Association.

8. Motor Imaging*   **PIJHA**

Procedure: 1.   Explain to students that they are going to learn a strategy that will help them learn and remember new words. They will be learning new words from a selection that they will read.

2.   Write a word on the chalkboard or overhead, pronounce it, and tell its meaning.

FIGURE 6-5 Examples of Motor Imaging (See Casale, 1985)

NEW WORD	LANGUAGE MEANING	MOTOR MEANING
1. appropriate	right or fit for a certain purpose	both palms together, matching perfectly
2. woe	great sadness or trouble	one or both hands over the eyes, head slanted forward

3. Ask the students to *imagine* a simple pantomime they could use to show someone what the word meant.

4. When you give the signal, students all do their pantomimes simultaneously.

5. Select the most common pantomime they have used. Have someone show the pantomime to the other students, who then *say* the word while doing the pantomime. (See Figure 6-5).

6. Repeat this procedure with the other new words.

7. Students read the selection containing the new words they have just pantomimed. They are encouraged to apply this technique in other reading tasks.

* Casale, 1985.

9. Enough, Already!   I J H A

Purpose: to practice using synonyms for overused words

Procedure: 1. Read to students a short selection that overuses a common word, such as *said*. Ask why the selection is boring.

2. Discuss overused words, which fail to communicate exact meaning because they are so general. For example, *big* can mean tall, wide, immense, gargantuan, giant, and so on.

3. Explain the purpose of the activity—to find synonyms for overused, tired words.

4. Divide students into groups.

5. Give groups a list of "tired words." Their task is to write down in five minutes as many synonyms for each word as they can think of.

6. At the end of the assigned time, call on each group in turn to give a synonym for a word you mention. The group must give a synonym that has not been mentioned before. Each synonym given counts for one point. Begin with a different group for each new word.

7. The group with the most points wins.

8. As a class, rewrite the selection from (1) using the new words.

Variation: Have students use their synonyms to revise stories they wrote earlier in the year.

10. Experience–Based Words* (five strategies for introducing new words)   I J H A

Procedure: Strategy 1: Synonyms and Examples

1.   Choose an important word you wish to teach, find a simple synonym for it, find several familiar examples that can illustrate the word, and write a sentence containing the word. For example:

   a.   New word: *notorious*

   b.   Synonym: *infamous*

   c.   Examples: Adolf Hitler, Attila the Hun, Caligula

   d.   Sentence: If you can manage to steal one million dollars and get away with it, you'd be *notorious*.

2.   Write the word on the board, pronounce it, and have students pronounce it. Define the word: *Notorious* means famous for doing something bad; it means infamous. For example, Adolf Hitler is notorious for . . . (have students respond).

3.   Use other examples and then have students supply examples.

4.   Have students copy the word and write down the name of the person they think of when using it. This will help them remember the word.

Strategy 2: Positive and Negative Instances

1.   Select your word, decide on the definition, and think of positive and negative instances of the word. For example:

   a.   New word: *apathy*

   b.   Definition: disinterested

   c.   Positive instance: Friday afternoons at 1:35 I feel great *apathy* about school and schoolwork.

   d.   Negative instance: when our team is tied in the final minutes of a championship game I don't feel *apathy*.

2.   Follow the procedure for strategy 1.

Strategy 3: Example and Definition

1.   Select an important new word and write a two-sentence paragraph in which the first sentence contains the word and the second is the definition. For example: Jane was a *pyrotechnical* expert. She could make better fireworks than anyone.

2.   Display the word, pronounce it, and have the students pronounce it. Then display the paragraph and ask what the word means. Elicit through discussion a description of what the word means.

Strategy 4: Definition and Use

1.   Select several important new words and develop definitions for each. Create a sentence fragment for each word. For example:

   a.   *loquacious:* talkative
        My sister is so loquacious that she . . . .

b. *satiated:* full, having eaten enough
I felt satiated after I ate . . . .

c. *irate:* angry
My mother was irate when . . . .

Put all this material on a work sheet and distribute it to the students.

2. Have students look at the first word and pronounce it. Then ask them what the definition is.

3. Have students read the incomplete sentence and suggest possible completions.

Strategy 5: Synonym and Antonym

1. Select an important new word, decide on a simple definition, and choose a synonym and an antonym. Create examples and nonexamples of the word. For example:

a. New word: *bizarre*

b. Synonym: unusual

c. Antonym: ordinary

d. Examples: dyeing your hair green, wearing vampire teeth

e. Nonexamples: dressing conventionally

2. Show students the word, pronounce it, and have them pronounce it. Give them examples of the word and have them provide examples.

3. Similarly, give them the antonym, providing and eliciting examples.

Variation: Have the students select the words!

* Duffelmeyer, 1980.

B. TEACHING USE OF CONTEXT CLUES

1. Context–Clue Types*   I J H A

Procedure: 1. Ask students what they do when they come to a word they don't know in their reading. Lead a discussion focusing on the availability of several strategies: using the *context,* analyzing the *structure,* and using the *dictionary,* the last of these being the most disruptive to reading.

2. Tell students that they will learn several strategies for using context as an aid in figuring out word meanings so that they can read more efficiently. Using overheads or handouts, present the following examples of the strategies:

A. LINKED SYNONYMS AND/OR APPOSITIVES: almost like little dictionary definitions supplied by the author. For example:
"*Democracy,* rule by the people, was developed by the Greeks."
Clues: commas, dashes—usually in pairs
B. CONTRAST: to tell you what it *is,* the author tells you what it *isn't.*
For example:
"Instead of his usual air of despondency, today he seemed quite *elated.*"
Clues: *instead of, unlike, rather than,* etc.

C.   DIRECT DESCRIPTION: the author actually creates a picture for you. For example:

"The *gargoyle* on the corner of the church, with its ugly face, flapping wings, and extended claws, was a frightening piece of sculpture indeed."

Clues: *that is, in short, in summary, thus,* etc.

D.   CAUSE–EFFECT: the author explains the reason for or result of the word. For example:

"Because she wanted to impress all her dinner guests with the food she served, she carefully studied the necessary culinary arts.

Clues: *because, since, therefore, thus, so,* etc.

E.   LANGUAGE EXPERIENCE: the reader uses prior knowledge to figure out the meaning. For instance:

"She walked away from her closet and quickly slipped a *jersey* over her head. She smoothed it into place over her hips, added a belt, glanced at the mirror, and left for work."

Clues: *The reader* is the clue, using his or her prior knowledge.

FIGURE 6-6   Sentences for Demonstrating Context Clues

---

1.   Mortimer, a *pyrotechnical* expert, made better firewords than anyone.
   Meaning: _____ Clue: (appositive) _____

2.   Eating four Big Macs, three orders of french fries, and two milkshakes made me positively *satiated*.
   Meaning: _____ Clue: (cause–effect) _____

3.   He didn't seem to want to make friends; unlike the outgoing college students, he was positively *introverted*.
   Meaning: _____ Clue: (contrast) _____

4.   Mozart was a *prolific* composer, composing 104 sonatas, over 40 symphonies, several operas, and many concertos.
   Meaning: _____ Clue: (direct description/example) _____

5.   Knowledgeable sports fans receive greater pleasure from watching basketball games than do *neophytes*.
   Meaning: _____ Clue: (contrast—*than*) _____

6.   Beethoven's deafness began to *manifest* itself as early as 1798, and grew steadily worse until by 1820 it was practically total.
   Meaning: _____ Clue: (combination) _____

7.   The Australian Aborigines like to play the *didgeridoo*.
   Meaning: (a musical instrument) _____ Clue: (use of *the*) _____

(Items 8–12 are nonsense words. The context easily determines their meaning.)

8.   I *janifle* cats, although my mother loves them.
   Meaning: _____ Clue: (contrast—*although*) _____

9.   The *manixophylic* behavior of the team made us all laugh.
   Meaning: _____ Clue: (cause–effect) _____

10.   My *lanixious* uncle, who has every penny he ever earned, is coming to dinner tonight.
   Meaning: _____ Clue: (appositive) _____

11.   She was so *magniventrous* that we have to be sure that she sat in a sturdy chair.
   Meaning: _____ Clue: (cause–effect—*so–that*) _____

12.   I need some *marmanile* to put on this bread, please.
   Meaning: _____ Clue: (prior knowledge) _____

F. COMBINATION METHODS: students use all these strategies to figure out the word. For instance:

"The balloon sank lower and lower. The flyer nodded his head towards the edge of the basket. '*Jettison* everything we don't need!' 'Get rid of the heaviest stuff first. We will float better if the basket is lighter. Start tossing.' "

Clues: the reader and his or her experience and prior knowledge.

3. Practice with the students, using handouts or an overhead projection. You can demonstrate that context clues work by using nonsense words in the sentences. (See Figure 6-6.)

4. Have students work independently on sentences and discuss the reasons for their choices in class.

5. Finally, have students provide meanings for selected words in content-area textbook assignments. Discuss these in class!

6. Reinforce context-clue skills when introducing new content-area words.

* Dulin, 1979.

2. Possible Sentences*   J H A

Procedure: 1. Select from a passage key words that are adequately defined by the context. Write these words on the board and pronounce them for the students.

2. Ask a student to choose any two of the words and use them in a sentence. Write the sentence on the board. Continue this procedure with other students until all the words have been used.

3. Have the students read the passage and check the accuracy of their sentences.

4. Students make corrections and additions and write the revised sentences in their notebooks.

* Mangieri and Corboy, 1984.

3. Intelligent Guessing*   J H A

Procedure: 1. Give students a sheet containing five columns: *Chapter Number, Page Number, Vocabulary, Intelligent Guess, Meaning.* The first three columns will be filled in with the chapter numbers, page numbers, and vocabulary words from the material to be read.

2. Students find these words *after* reading the assigned text, and make an "intelligent guess" about their meaning.

3. The next day, discuss the guesses in class. If the students' guesses were correct, they can draw an arrow from the guess column to the meaning column. If the guesses were incorrect, have the students write down the correct meaning, which either you or other students can supply. Have students keep track of their percentage of correct guesses and try to improve their records.

4. Be sure that the discussion in step 3 focuses on the clues the author gave for the meanings of the words.

* Sodano, 1984.

4. Bit by Bit   I J

Procedure: 1. Develop a title that contains an unfamiliar word from the content to be studied—for instance, "Marsupial Reproduction."

2. Using an overhead projector, flash the title on the screen. Ask students for predictions about the meaning of the word *marsupial.*

3. After the students have made their predictions, show them one sentence from the material to be read. Have them verify, modify, or correct their definitions.

4. Continue one sentence at a time until the entire selection is read.

C. TEACHING USE OF WORD PARTS

1. Make a Word   P I J H A

Procedure: 1. Explain to students that learning suffixes, prefixes, and roots is a useful vocabulary activity, as it gives them "mileage." They will encounter prefixes in many words, and once they learn them they will be able to figure out word meanings more easily. (See Figure 6-7 for a list of prefixes.)

FIGURE 6-7 Frequently Used Prefixes

a–not (amoral)	maxi–large (maximum)
ante–before (antecedent)	mini–small (minimum)
anti–against (antisocial)	mono–one (monotony)
auto–self (autonomous)	
	neo–new (neolocal)
bi–two (bicycle)	
bio–life (biology)	omni–all (omnivorous)
circum–around (circumnavigate)	pan–all (pantheon)
contra–against (contradict)	poly–many (polygon)
cum (com, col, con)–with (collaborate)	post–after (postnatal)
	pre–before (prefix)
di–two (dicotyledon)	pro–forth, for (propose)
dis–not (disagree)	pseudo–false (pseudonym)
duo–two (duet)	
	semi–half (semicircle)
ex–out of, from (excommunicate)	sub–under (submarine)
	sui–self (suicide)
geo–earth (geology)	syn–with, together (synonym)
hemi–half (hemisphere)	tri–three (tricycle)
homo–same (homogeneous)	
hyper–above, more than (hyperactive)	uni–one (unified)
in (il, im)–not (impossible, illogical)	
in–into, within (inmate)	
inter–between (intermediate)	
intro–into (introduce)	

2.   Teach only one prefix at a time, and teach word families and extensions of the word if appropriate. For example, once you have explained the prefix *mono,* meaning "one," have students create a word family list—for example, *monophony, monotony, monocycle, monocle, mononucleosis.* Extensions of the word *monocycle* might include *bicycle, tricycle,* etc.

3.   Develop original words with the students. For instance, one-headed would be *monohead,* one boyfriend would be a *monoboyfriend,* many-headed would be *polyhead,* two-faced would be *bifaced.*

4.   Have students create their own new words and illustrate them. Create a class *Our Own Words* dictionary.

5.   Another way to reinforce the value of this activity is to give extra points on vocabulary tests for creating and defining new words.

☞   This is a demonstration activity. Be sure to provide opportunities for application to meaningful reading tasks.

2.   Wordo*   I J

Procedure:

1.   Give students blank Wordo sheets (see Figure 6-8).

2.   Write on board or overhead several word families, each of which has a prefix in common. For example, *illegal, impossible, illogical, impertinent, intolerable, inhuman.* Use from four to six families.

3.   For each family, have each student write on several small pieces of paper the prefix that all members of the family have in common.

4.   Now have students write in random order twenty-four of the base words in the spaces on their Wordo sheets (see Figure 6-8). For example, if one of the words listed in step #2 were "illogical" they would write "logical" on their sheet.

5.   The point of the game is to match the base words with the prefixes. Give a clue for each word students must form. For example:
"The baby was not happy . . . not happy." (Students cover *happy* with a slip with *un* on it.)
"The man was not honest . . . not honest." (Students cover *honest* with a slip with *dis* on it.)

6.   The first person who gets five in a row wins Wordo.

☞   This is a demonstration activity. Be sure to provide opportunities for application to meaningful reading tasks.

* Burmeister, 1978.

logical	appear	human	like	fair
happy	honest	correct	trust	loyal
sphere	cycle	FREE	lock	do
possible	certain	please	turn	seat
agree	paid	formal	reliable	marine

FIGURE 6-8   Sample Wordo Sheet

3. Affixionary*   P I

Procedure:

1. Explain to students that prefixes and suffixes are important clues to the meanings of words. To help themselves learn the skill of using these word parts—called *affixes*—they can create their own affix-dictionaries (affixionaries) for the affixes they use.

2. One method of making an affixionary is to fold several sheets of white typing paper in half. The number of pages will depend on the number of affixes to be learned.

3. Add a heavy paper cover, for the student to decorate.

4. Page one will be a table of contents.

5. Each page will contain one affix at the top. Beneath the affix is written its definition. (See Figure 6-9.)

6. The rest of the page is composed of two columns, the narrow one on the left containing examples of words using the affix, the broader one on the right containing sentences using the examples.

7. Students may want to illustrate the example word.

8. The book may list suffixes and prefixes together or be divided into a suffix section and a prefix section. In either case, the entries should be arranged alphabetically.

☞ This is a demonstration activity. Be sure to provide opportunities for application to meaningful reading tasks.

* Lindsay, 1984.

D. TEACHING CONTENT–AREA WORDS

1. Semantic Mapping*   P I J H A

Procedure:

1. Select a word that is central to the topic to be taught.

2. Write the word on the chalkboard, overhead, or tablet.

3. Have the students brainstorm words related to the selected word. List these new words by category on the board, overhead, or tablet. (See Figure 6-10).

4. Have students work independently for a few minutes, trying to think of as many words as they can that are related to the central word. Then have them list these words by category on a piece of paper.

FIGURE 6-9 Un-

THE PREFIX *UN*- MEANS "NOT".	
unhappy	I was unhappy when I lost my dog.
untied	I fell when my shoelace became untied.

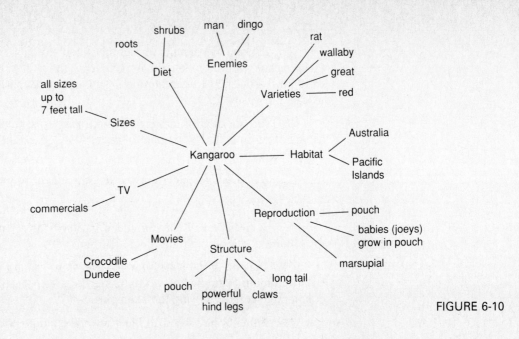

FIGURE 6-10

5. Have students share their lists orally. Then add their words to the class map in the proper categories.

6. Ask the students to suggest labels for these categories. For example, category labels for kangaroos could include *habitat, diet, enemies, structure, varieties,* and also kangaroos in *books,* in *movies,* on *television,* as popular *toys,* etc.

7. Discuss the categories and words on the map. Help students become aware of new words (*marsupial*), acquire new meanings for old words (*joey, mob*), and focus on relationships among the new and old words.

8. This procedure works well as both a pre- and a postreading strategy.

9. After the material is read, students can add words and categories to their map copies.

Variation: Use a semantic map as a prewriting strategy to help students organize information for a story or report.

* Johnson, Pittelman, and Heimlich, 1986.

2. Student–Activated Vocabulary Instruction*   I J H A

Procedure: 1. Identify five to ten words in the new material that are outside the students' vocabularies.

2. For each word make three cards. On one card, write the word's phonetic spelling (an tip a thee). On the second card, write the word and its definition (*antipathy:* a feeling of dislike or hatred). On the third card, use the word in a sentence rich in context clues. (When my brother borrowed my car without my permission and dented the fender, I felt great *antipathy* towards him.) *Note:* use definitions and sentences that are meaningful to your students.

3. Shuffle the cards and give one to each student.

4. Students must move around the room to find the students who have the accompanying cards. Each group of three then sits together.

5. Each group then creates a list of words that are related in some way to the new word. For example, for a noun or adjective, group members would list attributes and nonattributes of their word. For verbs, they write synonyms, antonyms, and words that are not related to their word. When first using this strategy, model the attributes and nonattributes of a word. For example, for *antipathy* model fondness, hatred, attraction, sympathy, aversion, etc.

6. Students put their lists on transparencies, the board, or duplicating masters.

7. To teach a word, you or a member of the corresponding group can present the word, definition, attributes, and nonattributes.

8. The class responds to the attributes and nonattributes by identifying each as one or the other.

9. A less time-consuming alternative to steps 5–8 is to give students copies of each group's cards and have them make the accompanying lists as homework.

10. The next day, put the words and definitions on the board and ask yes–no questions about the attributes. For example: "Would you feel antipathy for a hijacker?" "Do you have antipathy for [name a famous TV star]?"

11. The new words can be used in writing. Read the students the beginning of a story and have them complete it using two of the new words. Five to ten minutes later students exchange stories. Have each student in turn continue his or her classmate's story, using two of the new words not found in that story.

12. Completed stories are handed in. You can then use them in a cloze procedure, either reading them aloud and having the students supply the new words, or duplicating them.

☞ This is a demonstration activity. Be sure to provide opportunities for application to meaningful reading tasks.

* Ryder, 1985.

3. Not–So–Ordinary–Words   I J H A

Procedure: 1. Explain to students that very ordinary words can have different meanings in different subjects. Use as an example the word *division* in mathematics and social studies or the word *cell* in science and history. Elicit other examples from students.

2. With the students, go through a short textbook selection you have chosen and find other uses of these words.

3. Students can then work in groups on a textbook assignment, or on different content-area textbooks, to create lists of these words.

4. Have the students combine their words into a class chart, possibly like the one provided in Figure 6-11.

FIGURE 6-11

MATH	SCIENCE	HISTORY	ENGLISH
division	reduce	division	colon
difference	base	mouth (river)	period
product	culture	class	appendix
times	graft	article (law)	article
sign	mouth	sentence (law)	tense
reduce	class	cabinet	romance
power	matter	race	act
root	sound	bill	style
base	iron	duty	scene
		left	

4. Mathematics Symbols and Words*   I J

Procedure: 1.   Explain to students that the mathematics vocabulary is composed of two languages—word symbols and verbal symbols. Students can practice reading both types of symbols using the same strategies they use in reading, such as knowing sight words, using context clues, using structural analysis, and looking words up in the dictionary.

2.   Demonstrate each of these strategies (see Figure 6-12). Provide supervised practice with relevant text material.

3.   Regularly assign work with these strategies when introducing or reviewing mathematics material.

* Ciani, 1981.

FIGURE 6-12

A. *Sight words*
  1.   Write the correct mathematical symbol for:
       a.   and _____   b.   sum of _____   c.   divided by _____
       d.   multiplied by _____   e.   take away _____

  2.   On the line next to the mathematical symbols, write another way of stating the operation.

       a.   a + b + c   <u>a plus b plus c</u>
       b.   10 − 5   _____
       c.   4 × 5   _____

  3.   Match the verbal symbols in column A with the correct mathematical symbols in column B.

	A	B
a.	equals	+
b.	greater than	<
c.	plus	=
d.	less than	>

FIGURE 6-12   continued

B. *Context clues*
1. After reading pages 18–24, find these words in your text and supply your own definition.

    a. *binomial* _____

    _____

    b. *prime* _____

    _____

2. The following words were taken from Chapter 7. Draw the mathematical shape the word represents. Record the number of times the word or the shape is found in the chapter.

    a. square _____   _____
    b. angle _____   _____

C. *Structural Analysis*
1. Each of the following words contains either a prefix or a suffix attached to a root word. Separate the words into the proper categories.

Prefix	Root	Suffix

    a. binomial
    b. polygon

2. Each of the following words has four syllables. Separate the words, placing a syllable in each column.

1	2	3	4

    a. binomial
    b. tetrahedron

D. *Dictionary*
1. Write the guide words and page number where the following words are located.

	Guide Words	Page Number
a. polyhedron	polygon; polyps	
b. tangent		

Source: Adapted from Ciani, A. *School Science and Mathematics*, p. 374–376, with permission.

5. Computer Sight Vocabulary*   I J

Procedure: 1.   Present words early in classroom instruction, preferably in the context of phrases used in computer programs—for example, "Loading . . . please wait. Press spacebar to continue."

2.   During instruction, alert students that the same terms may show up in different forms in various programs. For instance, command-key names may be written in capital letters (for example, RETURN), within brackets ([RETURN]), abbreviated (esc), or highlighted on the screen. (See Figure 6-13.)

* Dreyer, Futtersak, and Boehm, 1985.

FIGURE 6-13 Essential Words for Computer-Assisted Instruction for Elementary Grades (based on a sample of thirty-five programs)

activity	description	lesson	ready
adjust	different	letter	regular
again	directions	level	remove
another	disk	list	repeat
answer	diskette	load	return*
any	display	loading*	[rewind]
arrow*	document	match	rules
audio	down	memory	save
bar	drive	menu*	score
before	edit	[module]	screen
begin	effects	monitor	select
bold	end	move	selection
button	enter*	name*	sound*
[cartridge]	erase	need	spacebar*
[cassette]	escape, esc*	no	speed
catalog	exit	number*	start
change	find	off	team
choice	finished	on	text
choose*	follow	options	then
colors	format	paddle	try
column	game*	password	turn
command	good	picture	type*
compete	help	play	up
complete	hit	player	use
computer	hold	please*	video
continue*	incorrect	point	wait
control, cntrl	incorrectly	practice	want
copy	indicate	press*	which
correctly	instructions	problems	word
cursor	joystick	program*	work
delete	key*	quit	yes
demonstration	keyboard	rate	your

Bracketed words do not appear in any of the thirty-five programs. Starred words are present in ten or more of the thirty-five programs.

Source: Dreyer, Futtersak, and Boehm, 1985, p. 14. Reprinted with permission of Lois G. Dreyer and the International Reading Association.

BIBLIOGRAPHY

BURMEISTER, L. E. *Reading Strategies for Middle and Secondary School Teachers.* Reading, Mass.: Addison-Wesley, 1978.

CASALE, U. P. "Motor imaging: A reading-vocabulary strategy," *Journal of Reading,* 28, April (1985), 619–21.

CASSELL, B. C. "Stump-the-Teacher: A word game," *Journal of Reading,* 27, January (1984), 365–66.

CIANI, A. J. "Mastering word and symbol language in mathematics," *School, Science, and Mathematics,* 81, May–June (1981), 373–76.

DEMETRULIAS, D. A. M. "Gags, giggles, guffaws: Using cartoons in the classroom," *Journal of Reading,* 26, October (1982), 66–68.

DREYER, L. G., K. R. FUTTERSAK, AND A. E. BOEHM. "Sight words for the computer age: An essential word list," *Reading Teacher,* 39, October (1985), 12–15.

DUFFELMEYER, F. A. "The influence of experience-based vocabulary instruction on learning word meanings," *Journal of Reading,* 24, October (1980), 35–40.

DULIN, K. "Using context clues in word recognition and comprehension," *Reading Teacher,* 23, February (1970), 440–45, 469.

HAGGARD, M. R. "Vocabulary Self-Collection Strategy: An active approach to word learning," *Journal of Reading,* 26, December (1982), 203–7.

HAYAKAWA, S. I. *Language in Thought and Action,* 3rd ed. New York: Harcourt Brace Jovanovich, Inc., 1972.

JOHNSON, D. D., S. PITTELMAN, AND J. E. HEIMLICH. "Semantic mapping," *Reading Teacher,* 39, April (1986), 778–83.

LEHMAN, J. AND R. WRIGHT. "Multiple meanings and science reading," *Reading Teacher,* 37, October (1983), 100.

LINDSAY, T. "The affixionary: Personalizing prefixes and suffixes," *Reading Teacher,* 38, November (1984), 247–48.

MANGIERI, J. N. AND M. CORBOY. "Reading in content fields: Realistic strategies," *NASSP Bulletin,* 68, February (1984), 18–21.

MILLER, H. B. AND C. THOMPSON. "What's in a surname?" *Reading Teacher,* 38, December (1984), 357.

PAUK, W. *How to Study in College.* Boston: Houghton Mifflin, 1984.

RYDER, R. J. "Student activated vocabulary instruction," *Reading Teacher,* 39, December (1985), 254–59.

SCHWARTZ, R. M. AND T. RAPHAEL. "Concept of definition: A key to improving students' vocabulary," *Reading Teacher,* 39, November (1985), 198–205.

SODANO, F. M. "Context clues and vocabulary," *Journal of Reading,* 28, December (1984), 272.

PREREADING PRIOR KNOWLEDGE

Definition: *Background knowledge about the topic of the reading passage possessed and recalled by the student(s) before reading the passage*

RATIONALE

One of the central findings of recent research on reading comprehension is that there can be little comprehension without prior knowledge. Prior knowledge of the content enables students to interpret ambiguous words, make necessary intersentence inferences, and make important predictions and elaborations. Indeed, research indicates that much of what is labeled a comprehension problem is actually a lack of prior knowledge.

For example, suppose your students are reading about someone going to a movie and the author mentions something white and crunchy on the floor. Most students would use their prior knowledge to infer that this was popcorn, so they would understand any references to popcorn later in the text. But suppose a student had never been to the movies. Such a student might be quite baffled: would the crunchy white substance be snow or ice, perhaps? And later, when the children are discussing popcorn, this student wouldn't know why popcorn had come up.

Prior-knowledge problems can arise for at least three reasons. First, students may simply not possess the important prior knowledge assumed by the author. In this case, it is the teacher's responsibility to build that prior knowledge with prereading activities such as those suggested in the first section of this chapter. Second, students may fail to recall or activate their prior knowledge, or may activate the wrong prior knowledge before reading. For instance, in our example, a student thinking about movies in the classroom rather than movies in a theater might erroneously infer that the white substance on the floor was paper wads. To avoid this, teachers can conduct prereading activities designed to activate the appropriate prior knowledge. Such activities are provided in the second part of this chapter.

Finally, students can forget to use the appropriate knowledge during and after reading. Activities that encourage the use of prior knowledge during and after reading are included in Chapter 19.

INFORMAL DIAGNOSIS

Of course, asking students what they already know about the topic of a passage will give you a lot of information. Also, many of the activities suggested in the second section of this chapter will let you know if there is a problem. Activity B.4, suggested by Langer (1981), is specifically designed to diagnose prior-knowledge levels. Langer suggests that rather than dividing students into those who have the appropriate knowledge and those who don't, teachers should divide them into at least three categories: those who have much prior knowledge about the topic, those who have some, and those who have almost none. Activity B.5 also provides a way to divide students into these three categories.

Over time you may see that some students consistently lack the necessary prior knowledge about the topics they are reading about in school. For those students, you could begin a systematic plan for building school-related prior knowledge by using many of the activities suggested in this chapter. Remember, however, that these students bring much prior knowledge with them to school, even if it is not about the topics you are discussing.

GENERAL TEACHING SUGGESTIONS

This was a very difficult chapter to assemble, in the sense that it is almost impossible to entirely separate prior knowledge from vocabulary and motivation—the other two reading prerequisites. Vocabulary activities completed before reading will activate and build prior knowledge. You may wish to refer especially to the activities in section D of Chapter 6. These provide techniques for building content-area vocabulary knowledge. Also, the activities suggested in this chapter will often lead to discussions of specific vocabulary words. This is as it should be. Moreover, building background knowledge almost always increases motivation, because it is much easier to be interested in something you already know a little about.

Here are some other useful suggestions:

1. Use activities for building prior knowledge when you believe that your students' prior knowledge is inadequate.

2. Use activities for activating prior knowledge when you believe that the students probably already know enough about the topic. Remember that prior knowledge of a situation doesn't guarantee that it will be used for comprehension. It must be activated in the students' minds.

3. Before reading, ask questions that encourage students to relate the topic to their own experience. This should be done in the content areas as well as during reading group.

4. During prereading discussions, be sure students know that it is okay to use their own experiences to answer questions. "Using your own life" is a phrase coined by children to describe this. (Hansen and Pearson, 1985)

5. Use analogy to develop prior knowledge. For example, have students read a passage about baseball. Then have them read a passage about cricket that contains analogies to baseball.

6. Use firsthand experiences to develop prior knowledge. Field trips, guest speakers, experiments, audiovisual aids, and other such class activities can provide this experience.

7. Reading aloud daily, at least in the primary grades, is a technique that develops background knowledge and exposes students to material and language beyond their reading ability.

8. Find related trade books and encourage students to know when reading can be used to build necessary prior knowledge. This can become a useful habit for students throughout their school and professional lives.

chapter 7.   BUILDING PRIOR KNOWLEDGE
Activities

A. BUILDING PRIOR KNOWLEDGE

1. Easy First   P I J H A

Procedure: 1.   Assemble a library of books at various reading levels containing information on the topic about to be studied. Sample textbooks are an excellent source of material.

2.   Mark the relevant pages in the books.

3.   Write on the board, "True or False: Your past experience with the subject matter in a textbook will affect your comprehension."

4.   After tabulating student responses, lead a discussion about how prior knowledge about a subject (or lack of it) can affect comprehension. Use as an example someone knowing nothing about a football. Which kind of book should that person read, one containing statistics, discussions of techniques, and so on, or a beginner's book with diagrams of the field, definitions of terms, and so forth? Have examples of these books to show the students.

5.   Having established the importance of prior knowledge in comprehension, explain to students that filling in their background knowledge before they read about a topic will help them understand the topic. Show them the library of books you have collected, explaining that all of these books contain information about the new topic they are going to study. Suggest that they browse through the collection and choose a book to read to fill in their background knowledge.

6.   In a class discussion summarize on the board the new knowledge students have learned before beginning the assigned text.

7.   Continue creating a class library for each new topic.

2. Guided Reading Strategy*   I J H A

Procedure: 1.   Have students survey an assigned section of a text chapter, reading only the chapter title, subtitles, graphs, charts, maps, vocabulary lists, and chapter questions.

2.   Have students close their books and orally state everything they can remember from this preview.

3. Record verbatim on the board all the students' information.

4. Have students check the chapter for any information not included, and add this to the summary on the board.

5. Discuss the results of this text survey. Organize the information into a topical outline on the board.

6. Have students read the text silently.

* Bean and Pardi, 1979.

3. Science Language Exercise*   P I

Procedure: 1. Choose a new unit of study in a science textbook or workbook, or create one of your own.

2. Assemble manipulatives related to the subject. For example, if the subject is mealworms, provide mealworms and containers with chambers so that students can observe the worms in their different growth stages. (One teacher also provided orange juice, vinegar, pickle juice, salt, and sugar.)

3. Ask questions about the manipulatives to encourage discussion and experimentation. For example: "Do all mealworms have the same number of segments? How do they react to . . . ? Do they like to be alone or together?"

4. Have students record their observations. Depending on the students's ages, these can be recorded by the students themselves or dictated individually or in a group to the teacher.

5. Have students illustrate the observations. (You may want to have younger students draw before writing their observations.)

6. Have students exchange observations and read them. A class book can be "published."

7. Students then read the text assignment.

* Barrow, Kristo, and Andrew, 1984.

4. The Coming Attraction*   P I J

Procedure: The procedure involves reading a preview, or script, to the students immediately before they read a short story. Use this procedure primarily with students needing a great deal of support.

1. Components of the preview

a. several rhetorical questions to arouse the students' interest and build a bridge between a familiar topic and the topic of the story

b. questions to facilitate students' discussion of the story's theme or topic

c. description of the characters, setting, and point of view

d. description of the story up to the climax

2. How to write the preview

a. Read the story until you are thoroughly familiar with it.

b.   Decide what link you will develop between the topic of the story and something familiar and relevant to the students.

c.   Write the rhetorical questions and the discussion questions.

d.   Decide if understanding the material requires background knowledge that some or all of the students may not have. If so, write a brief section that will provide this knowledge.

e.   Write a synopsis describing the characters, setting, point of view, and summarizing the plot up to the climax.

f.   Write directions for reading the story. Consider including a suggestion to look for an outcome. You might also want to include suggestions for a general approach to reading. For example, if there is a flashback in the story, you would want to alert the students to this time variation.

3.   How to present the preview

a.   Tell the students what you're doing—introducing their new reading selection.

b.   Read to the students the first few sentences of the preview.

c.   Spend two to three minutes on the discussion questions.

d.   Read the rest of the preview to the students.

e.   Have students begin reading the selection as soon as you've finished reading the preview. This previewing procedure should take five to ten minutes.

Variations: 1.   List only the characters on the board.

2.   Use only the interest-building part of the preview.

3.   Provide only the background information.

4.   Have students write and/or videotape previews as their book report format.

5.   Videotape a preview for use with small groups.

* Graves, Prenn, and Cooke, 1985.

5.   60 Minutes   P I J H A

Procedure: 1.   Arrange for a guest speaker to address the class on a topic about to be studied.

2.   Tell the students about the speaker, and ask them to formulate some questions they want him or her to answer. Write these questions on the board. Remind the students that they will be interviewing the speaker, like on television—so they will want to ask questions that have to be answered with more than a yes or a no.

3.   Guide the students in developing questions that will focus on analogies to their prior knowledge. For example, have them ask a television personality if preparing for a TV show is like anything they do in their daily lives.

4.   Depending on the age of the students, either have them ask the ques-

tions after you have given the speaker a copy, or simply present the questions on paper to the speaker.

5. Make a sheet with the questions and room for the answers, and give each student a copy. Tell them they will check off the questions as they are asked. Depending on the speaker and the age of the students, you may want to have the students write the answers as they interview the speaker.

6. After the speaker has left, discuss with the class the answers to the questions.

7. Then do the reading related to the topic!

B. ACTIVATING PRIOR KNOWLEDGE

1. Comprehension Weave*   P

Materials: gray construction paper, cut to look like a human brain
colored slips of paper
scissors

Procedure: 1. Explain to students that when they read something new, it is important for them to use their own knowledge to help themselves understand what they have read.

2. "To make sure that this knowledge is used, let's make a bank of it here on the chalkboard."

3. Lead a thorough discussion to find out what prior knowledge the students have about the subject to be studied.

4. Write all their contributions on the chalkboard.

5. "Taking a look at all this information you have put into our bank of knowledge, what predictions do you think you could reasonably make about our reading assignment in the text?"

6. Write down some of the students' expectations on the board.

7. Ask students to choose two or three of their own expectations and write them on the colored paper, one to a slip.

8. Students then weave these strips into the gray brain, showing that their predictions are interwoven with the knowledge they already have in their heads, and that all of this knowledge is woven together as they read the text.

9. Have the students read the text.

* McIntosh, 1985.

2. Prethinking for Success*   PIJHA

Procedure: 1. Read the book or story students will be reading and decide on two to four important ideas that represent the theme, the moral, the basic problem of the main character, or a key event, action, or feeling.

2. For each of these key ideas, write two questions like, "Have you ever . . . ?" or "What do you think X will do?" and so on.

3. Before the students begin reading, take a few minutes to discuss each of the two questions you wrote for each key idea.

4. (optional) After the students have read the story, discuss the predictions that were made and the differences and similarities between them and the actual events.

5. Somewhere along the way discuss why you are asking them to prethink.

* Pearson, 1985.

3. Personal Meaning Guide*   I J H A

Procedure: 1. Read the material the students will be reading and select the most important ideas.

2. Choose one of these ideas and phrase six to eight statements about it.

3. Write these in a prereading guide, asking for students' agreement or disagreement (see Figure 7-1).

4. After students have completed this guide, structure small-group discussions or a class discussion so that students may share their reactions and reasons with each other.

5. After students have read the assignment, they can discuss how their opinions have or have not changed because of their reading. Ask them to indicate what parts of the text were relevant to each prereading statement.

* Macklin, 1978.

4. Prereading Plan (PReP)*   I J H A

Procedure: 1. Examine the text to be read and choose key words, phrases, and pictures that will arouse group interest and stimulate discussion. For example, if feudalism were being studied, you might choose the words *chivalry* and *knights* and a picture of a medieval castle.

FIGURE 7-1

DIRECTIONS: Here are seven statements that deal with the concept of change. Place a "+" by those you agree with and a "−" by those you don't agree with. Leave blank those statements that affect you neither way. Feel free to add your own statements about change and how you feel about them. Be prepared to discuss the reasons for your choices.
____ 1. It takes time for change to be felt.
____ 2. The effects of change are often felt by those not directly involved in change.
____ 3. Change is generally hard to stop.
____ 4. Change needs the support of the majority in order to occur.
____ 5. Fortune smiles on those who change.
____ 6. The greater the degree of change, the more resistance there is to that change.
____ 7. Change guarantees growth.
____ 8. _____

Source: Macklin, 1978, p. 214. Reprinted with permission of Michael D. Macklin and the International Reading Association.

2.   Tell students they will be studying feudalism, and begin the three phases of PReP:

Phase a: Initial associations with the concept. "Tell me anything that comes to your mind when you hear the word 'feudalism.'" Jot all responses on the board. For example:

knights
lords, ladies
kings
armor

Phase b: Reflections on the initial associations. "What made you think of . . . ?" Answers to this might be "I saw knights in a movie," "I think all the people wore armor then," "Isn't *King Arthur* about chivalry?" "I think they carried shields with coats of arms on them." Students have the chance to listen to each other's ideas and to modify their own.

Phase c: Reformulation of knowledge. "Before we read the assignment, and based on this discussion, do you have any new ideas about . . . ?" Students have a chance to elaborate their prior knowledge, based on the class discussion. For example, a student might say, "I think all the knights had to be faithful to their king."

3.   Write these new ideas on the chalkboard. Ask the students to set purposes for their reading: what will they want to find out or confirm when they read? Have each student write down several questions and then read.

4.   After the students finish reading, have them share their questions and the answers they found.

Variations: You can also use this activity to assess students' prior knowledge. Langer (1981) suggests using the students' responses to classify them into three levels:

Level 1.   *Much prior knowledge*. Students with much prior knowledge can supply:
   a.   definitions—e.g., "A dictator is a ruler with absolute authority."
   b.   analogies—e.g., "Cricket is a ball game like baseball."
   c.   superordinate concepts—e.g., "A rodent is a mammal."

Level 2.   *Some prior knowledge*. Students with some prior knowledge have trouble with level 1 questions but can supply:
   a.   examples—e.g., "Aren't squirrels rodents?"
   b.   attributes—e.g., "Rodents have gnawing teeth."
   c.   defining characteristics—e.g., government: dictatorship; government: makes laws.

Level 3.   *Little prior knowledge*. Students with little or no prior knowledge can probably supply only:
   a.   morphemes (prefixes, suffixes, roots)—e.g., binary, bicycle.
   b.   words that sound like a stimulus word—e.g., gerrymander: salamander; Iran: Iraq.
   c.   firsthand, irrelevant experiences—e.g., Iran: news on television.

Students at level 3 will need help in reading the text and instruction in relevant concepts.

* Langer, 1981.

5. Word–Association Prior Knowledge: WAPK*   P I J H A

Procedure: 1.   Choose a key word or phrase that encompasses the main idea of the topic about to be studied. For example, if you are studying China, the phrase might be "natural resources of China"; if liquids and gases found in sedimentary rock, the words might be "fossil fuels."

2.   Tell students that you want to give them a "test" to see how many words they can think of and write down in a short time. Demonstrate for the students using a stimulus word, such as *emperor,* and writing down as many words as you can that you associate with that word. Brainstorm words or phrases, emphasizing that any idea, no matter how many words, is acceptable.

3.   Have students use practice sheets to brainstorm word associations with familiar words such as *transportation* or *television*. Students write one word or phrase on each line of the sheet. Set a time limit—three minutes works well—for the task.

4.   During practice and during the actual task, remind the students:

a.   that they don't have to fill in *all* the spaces, but should write as many words as they can.

b.   to think back to the key word after each idea, because the goal is to see how many other ideas the key word brings to mind.

c.   to repeat the key word or phrase over and over to themselves.

5.   Share ideas in class and clarify any questions.

6.   Have students use this process for the key words selected in step #1.

7.   Students then read the original selection.

* Zakaluk, Samuels, and Taylor, 1986.

BIBLIOGRAPHY

BARROW, L. H., J. V. KRISTO, AND B. ANDREW. "Building bridges between science and reading," *Reading Teacher,* 38, November (1984), 188–92.

BEAN, T. W. AND R. PARDI. "Guided reading strategy," *Journal of Reading,* 23, November (1979), 144–47.

GRAVES, M. F., M. C. PRENN, AND C. L. COOKE. "The coming attraction: Previewing short stories," *Journal of Reading,* 28, April (1985), 594–98.

HANSEN, J. AND P. S. PEARSON. "Poor readers can draw inferences," *Reading Teacher,* 37, March (1984), 586–89.

LANGER, J. "From theory to practice: A prereading plan," *Journal of Reading,* 24, November (1981), 152–56.

MCINTOSH, M. E. "What do practitioners need to know about current inference research?" *Reading Teacher,* 38, April (1985), 755–60.

MACKLIN, M. "Content area reading is a process for finding personal meaning," *Journal of Reading,* 22, December (1978), 212–15.

PEARSON, P. D. "Changing the face of reading comprehension instruction," *Reading Teacher,* 38, April (1985), 724–38.

ZAKALUK, B. L., S. J. SAMUELS, AND B. M. TAYLOR. "A simple technique for estimating prior knowledge: Word Association," *Journal of Reading,* 30, October (1986), 56–60.

chapter 8

MOTIVATION

Definition: *The desire to complete a specific reading activity or the desire to read in general*

RATIONALE

The importance of motivation cannot be overstressed. Research indicates that students can comprehend materials at a higher readability level when they are sincerely motivated to comprehend. Ideally, this motivation takes the form of genuine interest, but there are other factors that can influence motivation.

Dulin (1978) has suggested that the motivation to read a specific assignment can be viewed in terms of a ratio:

$$\text{Motivation} = \frac{\text{expected reward}}{\text{expected effort}}$$

Students can be motivated by the expectation of a reward. They can also be turned away if the effort looks too great. Since this relationship between reward and effort is a ratio, motivation can be increased *either* by increasing the reward *or* by decreasing the effort. Everything that affects motivation affects one of these factors. Table 8-1 gives some examples, but there are many others.

As a teacher you must attend to motivation with every reading assignment you give. The time this takes varies with the situation, but you will almost always have to give your students a motivating purpose for reading. This might involve preparing for a debate or guest interview, solving a problem, or answering an interesting question. Never just say, "Read pages . . . ." Who can be motivated by that?

The other prereading activities mentioned throughout this book affect motivation by reducing the amount of effort required (see Table 8-1). For instance, reviewing students' background knowledge and tying the new content to something they already know are mentioned in Chapter 7, but they also influence motivation. Similarly, finding students material they can read is discussed in Chapter 5, but is definitely related to motivation in terms of the students' expected reward.

A second aspect of motivation is the students' desire to read in general. There are many reasons people choose to read. For instance, Waples (1967) has suggested that people read for (1) useful information, (2) prestige, (3) reinforcement of an attitude, (4) vicarious aesthetic experience, and (5) respite. For the purposes of this chapter, we have reduced this and other

TABLE 8-1 Sample Procedures for Increasing
Motivation

Increasing Expected Reward:
    Provide regular praise.
    Provide interesting activities.
    Write fair tests.
    Provide high-success tasks.
    Involve students in a purpose setting.
    Involve students in questioning.
    Use meaningful reading tasks.
Decreasing Expected Effort:
    Provide background information.
    Give a specific purpose.
    Preview the assignment.
    Preview vocabulary.
    Discuss reading strategies and skills.
    Divide a long chapter into shorter assignments.

Adapted from J. W. Irwin, *Teaching Reading Comprehension Processes* (Englewood Cliffs, N.J.: Prentice-Hall, 1986).

lists of reasons for reading to the categories of (1) usefulness (instrumentality, prestige) and (2) fun (attitude reinforcement, aesthetic experience, respite). We have also added the category of communication, because we believe that students' attitudes improve when they realize that reading is a social act. Thus, this chapter contains activities designed to help students develop a lifelong habit of reading by focusing on these three reasons for reading. The final activity section suggests ways to involve parents in motivating their children to read.

INFORMAL DIAGNOSIS

Of course, you can informally assess your students' motivation on specific assignments by asking direct questions and/or by observing their behavior. Most students are willing to let you know how they feel. You can also assess your students' attitudes toward reading in general by using one of the instruments provided in any reading methods textbook. Then you can begin to provide experiences that help them along the scale from negative to positive. Remember that the negative attitudes have often taken years to develop and will take some time to change.

GENERAL SUGGESTIONS FOR MOTIVATION ON SPECIFIC ASSIGNMENTS

1. Never give a reading assignment without thinking about how to motivate students.
2. Never present reading as a chore or a punishment.

3. As much as possible, increase the reward and decrease the effort (see Table 8-1).
4. Give students some control over what and why they read.
5. Follow reading assignments with activities that allow the students to use what they learned while reading.
6. Make all reading assignments relevant, meaningful, and useful by giving the students an interesting purpose for reading.
7. When possible, use reading materials that are related to the students' interests.
8. When possible, show the students how the material might be useful to them in the future.
9. Show that you are also interested in the material.
10. Make sure that each student has a chance to succeed.

GENERAL SUGGESTIONS FOR IMPROVING STUDENTS' ATTITUDES TOWARD READING

1. Buy enough copies of the same paperback so that you and the students can all read the same book and discuss it together, sharing one another's enjoyment and views about the characters and plot.
2. Read the lyrics of favorite songs and sing along with the record. Song lyrics make excellent adult reading material because students are probably already familiar with the words.
3. Use the local newspaper as material for reading. The International Reading Association (IRA) has published an excellent source of strategies—*Teaching Reading Skills through the Newspaper* by Arnold B. Cheyney (1984).
4. Bring in a guest to give testimonials on how reading for work and pleasure has benefited him or her.
5. As an alternative to book reports, have students make their own card catalog of books. On each card they write the author, the title, and a short summary of the book with their own evaluation of who would like (or not like) the book and why.
6. Every day read books of high interest to your students, thus modeling pleasure in reading and exposing students to language patterns and vocabulary. This procedure can be used until junior high level.
7. Use *TV Guide* as reading material. Have students choose programs and read synopses.
8. Tape students reading children's stories. These tapes can be used with family members or given

to a school or community library. Story synopses written to accompany the tapes give additional reading and writing practice.

9. Establish the importance of reading in your classroom from the first day of school. Set out books, write on the board "Welcome! Browse through the books, choose a book, and read until class begins," and continuing the classroom procedure that students read the first thing upon arriving at school every day.

10. One of the better ways to encourage reading is to model it. Always have a book on your desk and always read during the daily silent reading period.

11. Use brochures that help parents encourage their children's interest in reading. Reading Is Fundamental (RIF) has published four such brochures in response to the questions most frequently asked by parents:

Choosing Good Books for Your Children
TV and Reading
Reading Aloud to Children
Upbeat and Offbeat Activities to Encourage Reading

The cost to booksellers is fifty cents each, or fifteen dollars for 100 of each title. Order from:
Reading is Fundamental
600 Maryland Avenue S.W.
Suite 500
Washington, D.C. 20560

chapter 8. MOTIVATION
Activities

A.	READING IS USEFUL	
	1. Where in the World?	I J H A
	2. Potential Parenting	H A
	3. Alphabet Time	P I J H A
	4. Chain-Letter Reading	I J H A
	5. A Balanced Diet	I J
	6. Super Spending	P I J
	7. Athletic Reading	H
B.	READING IS FUN	
	1. Thin-Book Reading	P I
	2. Oral Book Reports	I J H A
	3. Circle of Books	P I
	4. Video Book Talks	P I J H A
	5. Reading Clubs	P I
C.	READING IS COMMUNICATION	
	1. Language Experience	P I J H A
	2. Computer Language Experience	P I
	3. Peer Reading	P I J H A
	4. One-Page Surefire Book Report	I J H A
	5. Organizing Your Classroom Library	P I J H A
D.	INVOLVING PARENTS	
	1. Suggestions for Parent–Teacher Conferences	
	2. Parent Self-Help Checklist	

A. READING IS USEFUL

1. Where in the World?   I J H A

Procedure: 1.   Assemble a group of reading materials from all aspects of life. Include such things as cereal boxes, rules-of-the-road booklets, travel folders, medicine labels, and driver's license applications.

2.   Discuss with students the need for reading in their daily lives. Show them the material you have collected, and ask them to brainstorm other places where they might find reading material.

3.   Assign students the task of finding reading material outside of school and bringing it in or noting what it was and where it was found.

4.   Have students report on their search. The class may find it interesting to note the most unlikely places where reading material was found (for example, on a golf ball); the most interesting reading material; the most difficult reading material (and why it was difficult); and the easiest reading material (and why it was easy).

2. Potential Parenting*   H A

Materials: favorite books for young children
basal readers
reading tests

Procedure: Session A

    1.   Explain to students that the goal of this activity is to show them how they, as potential parents, can help their children learn to read.

    2.   Lead a discussion of favorite childhood books. Brainstorm suggestions about how parents can provide a nurturing climate for reading.

Session B

    1.   Have a primary teacher explain to students *reading readiness* and some common reading problems in young children.

    2.   Lead a discussion on how these children learned to read.

    3.   Have students browse through the basals and reading tests.

Session C

    1.   Discuss with students the importance of parents reading to children. Hand out and discuss the following checklist of the six key components of the parent–child reading episode:

    a.   words spoken by the child

    b.   questions asked by the child

    c.   questions answered by the child

    d.   warm-up questions asked by the parents

    e.   poststory evaluative questions asked by the parents

    f.   positive reinforcement by the parents

(Flood, 1977)

    2.   Have students watch a videotape of a parent reading to a child or observe a primary teacher reading to a class, either in person or through a videotape.

    3.   Discuss what your students saw in terms of the six components of the reading episode.

    4.   Ask students to read to younger children and to mark off their behaviors on the checklist. Have students discuss their experiences in class. (If no younger children are available, perhaps primary schools or day-care centers could be used.)

Session D

    1.   Have the elementary librarian present a brief lesson on the history of children's literature. Let the students browse through children's books.

    2.   For homework have students choose three pieces of children's fiction and one of children's nonfiction and read them. For each book, each student must then:

    a.   design three warm-up questions;

    b.   design two questions for a parent to ask after reading;

    c.   state whether the illustrations are appropriate or inappropriate;

    d.   list the author, title, publisher, date of publication, and illustrator.

Session E

    1.   Students list the interests and abilities of a real or imaginary five-year-old.

2.   Students choose one of the following magazines as a subscription gift for the child: *Chickadee, Owl,* or *Ranger Rick's Nature Magazine.* They base their choice on the child's interests, the variety of articles and activities in the magazine, and the visual appeal and cost of the magazine. Students write an explanation of their choice.

3.   Students then choose one article and one activity from each of the magazines and:

a.   state the name and issue of the magazine;

b.   design one warm-up question for each article or activity;

c.   rate the articles and activities on a scale of 1 (lowest) to 3, giving reasons.

Session F

1.   Review parents' role in giving their children a head start in school—reading to their children and being an informed consumer of children's books and magazines.

2.   Discuss the idea of *safety* in reading:

a.   "Hard" books (those with more words and fewer pictures) are dangerous for children because they make reading less fun. Encourage them to read easier books.

b.   Don't let your children criticize *anyone's* reading matter.

c.   Read aloud to your children.

d.   Have books and magazines at all reading levels around the house.

e.   Model reading behavior by reading easy and hard books.

f.   Set aside time each day, if possible, for quiet reading.

(also see Bellica, 1984)

Extensions: 1.   Students write and illustrate their own stories for children.

2.   Students write and illustrate nonfiction books for younger children or beginners—for example, a cookbook or a guide to the city. These books should be saved for their own children.

3.   Students write and illustrate parodies of familiar children's stories—for example, "The Three Little Rock Stars."

4.   Students write modern versions of old favorites. The story of Little Red Riding Hood, for instance, could be rewritten with the wolf a member of the Mafia.

* Smale, 1982.

3. Alphabet Time   P I J H A

Procedure: 1.   Lead a discussion about the alphabet, concluding that knowing the alphabet seems to be one of the most important skills for a child entering school.

2.   Have students think of a particular preschool child (or make one up) and think about how they could create an ABC book that would interest this child.

3. Students write and illustrate, using drawings, photographs, magazine pictures, or any other media, an ABC book for that child.

4. Students share completed books with the class, then read them to the target children—or to younger classes in the school.

4. Chain-Letter Reading   I J H A

Materials: all types of useful reading materials: travel folders, train schedules, recipe books, newspapers, magazines, appliance booklets, TV guides, store catalogs, etc.: each has stapled to it a piece of paper with a question, space for an answer, and room for other questions

Procedure: 1. Discuss with students the many times they have had to get information by reading material such as you've assembled. Brainstorm the types of questions that might lead you to these sources—for example, when a train is due or where a movie is playing.

2. Tell the students that they will be reading these materials in the manner similar to that of a chain letter: they will read to find the answer to a question, write the answer down and initial it, and then create another question for the next reader to answer.

3. Distribute the materials, or have the students choose their own. Set a time limit for the procedure.

4. When time is up, have students share in a class discussion the questions and answers on the reading materials.

5. A Balanced Diet*   I J

Procedure: 1. Tell students that they are going to find out how balanced their reading diet is: they will find out how much the books they have read reflect or extend the reality of their own lives. Discuss with them what they will look for in checking the content of their books:

    a. physical attributes of characters:
        gender
        skin color
        hair color
        color of eyes
        height

    b. language used:
        familiar expressions
        style, dialect
        vocabulary

    c. activities:
        active
        passive
        types of games
        types of work

    d. extent to which the characters:
        look like them
        do similar things

have similar opinions
have a similar family situation
have similar living conditions

    e. opinions about the characters:
what they liked about them
what they disliked about them

2.   Create a questionnaire and have the students discuss it and then fill out one for each of the books. Adapt the questions to the students' level. For example, "Is there a character in this story who looks just like me (is as old as I am/who does the same kind of work my mother or father does/etc.)" Be sure students know that they do not have to answer yes to all the questions; there are no right or wrong answers. Instruct students to circle "yes" or "no" on the questionnaires.

3.   A student committee collates the information on the questionnaires and shares it with the class.

4.   Conduct a class discussion focusing on whether the students have a balanced reading diet or whether they need other books that would better reflect the reality of their lives and extend it.

5.   Students look in the school library and outside for books that meet specific deficiencies detected in the survey.

Extension: Students write stories that will fill in the deficiencies and give the stories to the school library.

* Zimet, 1983.

6. Super Spending   P I J

Procedure: 1.   Lead a discussion about what students do with their spending money. Are they getting value for it? How do they know if a movie, toy, or whatnot is worth the money it costs?

2.   Suggest that as consumers students can write evaluations of their current purchases for their classmates. Sharing this information would be worthwhile for everyone.

3.   Have students keep track and write evaluations of the movies, toys, clothes, and other things they have spent money on. Develop with the class the different items to be included in the evaluations.

4.   Set aside a time for students to read their reviews in class.

5.   Publish these reviews in some form (as in a newspaper or on the bulletin board) so that others can benefit from the advice.

7. Athletic Reading*   H

Procedure: 1.   Get weekly "tip sheet" scouting reports from one of the school's coaches. Use these as reading material for your athlete students, who have to learn the numbers of the opposing team members, their positions, and the way they play.

2.   Get copies of the coaches' play books. Use these as reading material for vocabulary and comprehension.

3. Some coaches give written tests on opponents' plays. If available, use these to teach comprehension and to diagram reading.

4. Clip newspaper stories about the team and its opponents to use as high-interest reading material.

* Bland, 1981.

B. READING IS FUN

1. Thin–Book Reading*   P I

Materials: old basal readers: cut out and staple together short selections

Procedure:

1. Tell students that because not many people like to read *thick* books, you are going to have them help make a class library of *thin* books.

2. Have students browse through the basal selections to find stories that interest them.

3. As soon as students are able to read their chosen stories aloud (to you or to the group), they may create a cover for each story. Students put their names on the covers as Cover Illustrator. Students may take their books home to read to their families.

4. This process continues through the year as students create a class Thin Book Library.

* Criscuolo, 1983.

2. Oral Book Reports*   I J H A

Procedure:

1. Explain to students that although the best way to learn how to read well is to read often, many people don't like to write reports about what they have read. Therefore, in order to encourage book sharing, you have created a system of oral book reports.

2. Create a comprehensive book list with the librarians, labeling each book easy, average, or difficult. Preface the list with a note that (a) not all books are recommended for all students, as they have differing interests, and (b) these are not the only books that are good or recommended.

3. Set aside time each week to listen to oral reports while other pupils do assigned work. Students bring their books to your desk and answer questions. (This could also be done in a small group format.)

4. If you have not read the book, skim paragraphs from the beginning, middle, and end and ask questions based on that material. As the student begins to talk about the book, information is revealed which leads to other questions.

5. Reviewing a short book will take about five minutes; a long book will require fifteen. You will find it an enjoyable experience, but guard against spending too much time.

6. Students will recommend books to each other, so that you will eventually become familiar with the books.

7. For each student, keep a large file card with spaces for name, year, book title, author, reporting date, number of credits earned, and teacher's initials.

8.   If it seems that a student has not read the entire book, suggest that he or she review it. If this doesn't work, formulate some written questions. If the student can't answer the questions but insists the book has been read, he or she may have a reading problem.

* Schlessinger, 1984.

3.   Circle of Books*   P I

Materials: five-by-seven cards with a hole in one corner
two-inch looseleaf ring

Procedure: 1.   At the beginning of the year give each of the children an index card on a ring. This is their Circle of Books title card, which they decorate and identify with their names.

2.   Each week students get another card, on which they will tell something about a book they have read that week during independent reading or at home.

3.   On one side of the card children record the title of the book, the author, their name, the date, and a drawing of an original cover for the book.

4.   On the other side students write the week's activity (see Table 8-2). Pick activities that require the children to focus on one aspect of the book. Keep the activities brief.

5.   When the Circles are not in use, display them on hooks near the class library area so that everyone can read them.

* Krouse and Hamlin, 1986a.

4.   Video Book Talks*   P I J H A

Procedure: 1.   Have students videotape short book reports. The following format is useful:

a.   Student holds book to camera, shows cover, and says name of author, title of book, own name as reviewer.

b.   Student mentions one interesting aspect of the book.

TABLE 8-2   Sample Circle–of–Books Activities

1.   Write to a friend, telling why he or she would like this book.
2.   Divide your card in thirds. Tell about something interesting that happened in the beginning, middle, and end of the book.
3.   Write a thank-you note to your book, telling why you enjoyed it.
4.   Write a poem to or about a character in your book.
5.   Choose one character and write five sentences describing him or her.
6.   Tell another way the book might have ended if . . . .
7.   Tell five new facts you learned from a nonfiction book you read.
8.   Choose a character and tell why you would like that character as a brother, sister, or friend.
9.   Write a note to a character in your book.
10.   Imagine what would happen if there were another chapter in this book. Write the first five or six sentences of this chapter.

Adapted from Krouse and Hamlin, 1986a.

    c. Student reads a short section of the book—preferably one with conflict.

    d. Student ends by telling viewers they need to read the book to find out what happens.

    2. An alternative format is to have students work in pairs, one as an interviewer and the other supplying information about the book.

* Frager, 1985.

5. Reading Clubs*   P I

Procedures: A. BOOK–A–DAY CLUB

1. Select students who read below grade level, lack confidence in reading, or have difficulty selecting books to read independently.

2. Send each a letter (see Figure 8-1) inviting them to join the Book-a-Day Club.

3. Students sign and return the Book-a-Day agreement (see Figure 8-2), or decline to join.

4. Meet with club, decide on meeting times, set rules. Students choose from collection of short, easy books you've chosen.

5. Students read a book every day and keep records of each.

6. Have students attend meetings regularly. Structure these to meet their needs: discuss books, read favorite parts, and so on.

7. After the club has been active for a few months, you and the students may want to change its emphasis or choose another way of developing independent reading habits.

FIGURE 8-1 Sample Invitation

Dear _____ ,

This is a VERY SPECIAL invitation for you to join a VERY SPECIAL CLUB— the Book-a-Day Club. This is a new club organized for people just like you— who can read, but who want to read more. You will read books that are interesting, exciting—and can be finished in ONE DAY!

WHAT WILL MEMBERS OF THE BOOK–A–DAY CLUB DO?

1. They will read at least one book every day.
2. They will keep a record of all books they read.
3. They will attend a Book-a-Day Club meeting two times a week.
4. BEST OF ALL, they will become readers who really read many books!

The first meeting of the Book-a-Day Club will be _____ .

DON'T PASS UP THIS FANTASTIC OPPORTUNITY
TO BECOME ONE OF THE WORLD'S FANTASTIC READERS!

Sign the attached agreement and return it to _____ .

Source: Melvin, 1986, p. 484. Reprinted with permission of Mary P. Melvin and the International Reading Association.

FIGURE 8-2 Sample Agreement Form

I wish to become a member of the Book-a-Day Club.

I understand that the club leader will help me select books that I can easily read in one day.

I promise:

1. to read a book each day.
2. to keep a record of all the books I read.
3. to attend meetings twice a week if possible.

_____

Signature   Date

Source: Melvin, 1986, p. 484. Reprinted with permission of Mary P. Melvin and the International Reading Association.

B.   READING GIANTS

1.   Make a tall paper giant for the bulletin board.

2.   Students mark a chart next to the giant to show progress as they read a designated number of books.

3.   A Reading Giant pin is awarded to those who complete the full number of books.

C.   100–MINUTE CLUB (younger students)

1.   Make a brightly colored train that extends over a large bulletin board. Use twenty squares, each representing 5 minutes of reading, to make up the train.

2.   Students choose reading coupons worth 5, 10, or 15 minutes, and read for that amount of time.

3.   Students turn in credits so that they can move their own markers along the display. The markers can be small train-shaped badges that will become a student's prize for completing 100 minutes of reading.

D.   500–MINUTE CLUB (older students)

1.   Organize a club called A Circus of Disney Stars.

2.   Students move Disney characters from tent to tent after each 100 minutes of reading.

3.   Reading coupons are worth 10, 20, or 30 minutes.

4.   As each tent is reached, award a small prize, such as a pencil or sticker.

5.   Certificates are presented for 500 minutes of reading.

E.   SMURF READING CLUB

1.   Color-code each classroom book according to level of reading difficulty. Use color values of one, two, five, and ten points.

2.   Display four Smurf houses on the bulletin board. Students can move a Smurf(ette) marker from one to the next upon earning ten points.

3.   Prizes (e.g., Smurf stickers) can be awarded at each house. The last house has the biggest prize.

* Melvin, 1986; Malkames, 1984.

C.   READING IS COMMUNICATION

1.   Language Experience*   P I J H A

Procedure: 1.   Discuss with student the idea that he or she can write a story. (This activity works best in a one-to-one situation.)

2.   Explain that to avoid any spelling problems, which might limit the vocabulary used, you will write down the story as the student dictates it.

3.   If needed, provide some prompts for starting the story—questions about the student's interests, his or her daily life, current events, television programs, and so on.

4.   Write down the story as the student dictates it, using carbon paper so that you both will have a copy.

5.   As the student dictates, ask questions to keep the narrative flowing. Don't change the grammar, but use correct spelling.

6.   Read the story to the student, pointing to each word.

7.   Reread the first sentence. Have the student then read the first sentence. Supply any words causing difficulty.

8.   Have the student take the story home.

9.   Type or word-process two double-spaced copies of the story. Prepare practice exercises for the troublesome words if needed.

Variations: 1.   Students create their own books of stories.

2.   Students dictate letters to friends, recipes, directions for a familiar task (such as changing a baby or a tire), and so on.

3.   Students dictate character sketches of friends and family members for a *Notebook of Important People.*

4.   Students dictate descriptions of childhood experiences for an autobiographical sketchbook.

* Johnston and others, 1975.

2.   Computer Language Experience*   P I
(used with remedial reading students in grades 1, 2, and 3)

Procedure: 1.   Sitting at the keyboard with two or three students, type in the story as one student dictates.

2.   Students not dictating act as proofreaders. Make several mistakes (leave out a word, etc.) to maintain interest.

3. Ask each student to type in several words on the computer.

4. Ask students to correct some of the errors on the screen.

5. Student author reads completed story aloud.

6. Help student with any errors.

7. When story is ready, have student author hit the command keys for the printer.

8. Students silently read printout, checking for errors.

9. Repeat these steps with other groups of two or three until all students have a printed story.

10. Students can then look for someone to listen to their story. School staff members are often receptive.

11. These stories can be printed out and placed in the classroom library.

* Kramer, 1986.

3. Peer Reading*   P I J H A

Procedure: 1. On a bulletin board create a section called A GOOD READ. Place an envelope with a supply of index cards in it.

2. Students use a card to recommend a book they have read. They list their name, the title of the book, the author, the library call letters, and a brief summary of the story. They should also include a short critical reaction to the book. Students who complete cards get credit for a book report.

3. Have students compile a Super Summer Reading List of these and any other titles they may recommend.

* Walsh, 1984.

4. One–Page Surefire Book Report Form*   I J H A

Procedure: Have students use the one-page form illustrated in Table 8-3 in writing book reports. The completed form will usually contain about fifteen sentences, and will thus be feasible for students and easy to read and grade. (This activity has been used successfully with remedial, average, and gifted students.)

* Robbins, 1981.

5. Organizing Your Classroom Library*   P I J H A

Materials: colored paint tape
cardboard boxes covered with adhesive plastic
index cards
library book pockets

Procedure: 1. Make a color chart explaining the five divisions of subjects. Hang this in the class library.

2. Mark the lower spine of each book with a strip of tape denoting its subject. For example:
Blue: history and biography

TABLE 8-3 Book Report Form

> DIRECTIONS: Write each answer in a complete sentence.
>
> 1. What book did you read? Include title and author.
> 2. Who are the most important characters?
> 3. In what place or what kind of place does the story happen?
> 4. Who is the main person—the hero/heroine—in the story?
> 5. What is the main problem or conflict in the story?
> 6. How does the main character change? (In what way is s/he different at the end of the story?)
> 7. What causes the main character to change?
> 8. What is the most important event? Why is it the most important event?
> 9. Why do you think the author wrote this book?
> 10. Would you recommend this book to other readers? Why or why not?

Source: Robbins, 1981, p. 166. Reprinted with permission of Louise S. Robbins and the International Reading Association.

Yellow: science
White: other nonfiction
Red: "Red Light Books"—harder fiction that will take longer to read
Green: "Green Light Books"—easier fiction that can be read quickly

   3.   Be sure to tell the students that the fiction choice depends on the reader's mood; red books are not "better" than green books, but simply require more time to read.

   4.   Glue a library book pocket to the inside front cover of each book. Place an index card with the book title on it in the pocket.

   5.   Make a chart of library book pockets, one for each student with his or her name printed on it. Students remove the cards from the books they borrow and put them in their book pockets.

   6.   Mark the edges of the cardboard boxes with the appropriate color of tape and set them on their sides on the classroom shelves as containers to keep the books easily arranged.

   7.   Make a Librarian's Supply Box for scissors and extra colored tape, book pockets, and cards. The student classroom librarian is responsible for managing the library, preparing new books, replacing cards, straightening shelves, and so on. The job of classroom librarian can be rotated or handled by a team.

   8.   If desired, alphabetical book lists in each category can be kept for quick reference.

* Krouse and Hamlin, 1986b.

D. INVOLVING PARENTS

1. Suggestions for Parent–Teacher Conferences

Parent–teacher conferences provide an opportunity to suggest strategies for helping younger readers. Among the many suggestions available are the following:

   1.   Set up note centers in the home where information is exchanged; the

refrigerator or telephone are good locations. Write notes to the young child there. Stick-on notes are useful.

2. Give the child a note pad so that he or she can leave notes for you.

3. Write directions for the child—how to get to a friend's house, where the cookies are hidden, and so forth.

4. Buy an attractive hard-cover blank book for the child and have him or her dictate a story to you. Continue until eventually the child can write the story unaided.

5. Use stick-on notes to label items in the home so that the child can learn new spelling words.

6. If the child likes TV, buy or borrow books about TV series or programs.

7. Use reading as a reward. (If you do X, I'll read to you.)

*8. Have the child help you in the supermarket by:

a. writing part of the grocery list.

b. reading items from the list and telling you the major food group they belong to. This teaches the child location and allows him or her to practice classification.

c. checking the prices and weights of different brands and deciding which is the best buy.

d. arranging grocery items in the cart so that the heaviest are on the bottom, and helping you put the groceries away (organization).

e. exploring words that are the same (*row, aisle,* etc.) and words that are opposite (*sweet/sour, solid/liquid*). Explore shapes and sizes of containers and other objects. (vocabulary)

f. following specific two- and three-step directions involving directional words (*right, left, first,* etc.). For example: "Walk to the dairy-food case and get me one container of milk from the right-hand side."

9. Give books as gifts—for the child and for the family. (Have your librarian give you a book list.)

10. Be sure to have many kinds of reading materials on hand in the home.

* Thompson, 1986.

2. Parent Self–Help Checklist*

Procedure: 1. Give the parent a copy of the Self-Help Checklist (Table 8-7) and discuss the points on it, explaining their value in encouraging reading in a child.

2. Have copies of different types of books and other reading materials for the parents to look at and for you to use as reference and examples.

Variation: Hold an after-school or evening meeting with parents and go over the checklist.

* Smith, 1984.

TABLE 8-4

PARENT SELF-HELP CHECKLIST

	Yes	No
1. I read aloud to my child every day.	____	____
2. If my child asks for it, I'll read the same book aloud repeatedly.	____	____
3. When I read aloud, my child sits on my lap or very close beside me and is in a position to follow along in the book.	____	____
4. My child has seen me read frequently.	____	____
5. My child has seen a man and a woman reading.	____	____
6. There are books, magazines, and newspapers in our home.	____	____
7. My child has books of his/her own and a place to keep them.	____	____
8. Books and magazines are an important part of my gift-giving for each child.	____	____
9. Our conversations go beyond daily functions like eating, dressing, bathing. For example, we talk about what happens in our family and neighborhood, and why things are done the way they are.	____	____
10. I give my child opportunities to express himself/herself through art, play, and talking.	____	____
11. I am a concerned and interested listener, showing my child that his/her feelings and interests are important to me.	____	____
12. My child knows I value reading as much as I do watching television.	____	____
13. I control the amount of time my child spends watching TV, and the types of programs.	____	____
14. I provide many interesting and varied experiences for my child, such as visits to parades and fairs, restaurants, cities and towns of different sizes, concerts, church, beaches, mountains, lakes, rivers, nature walks.	____	____
15. I provide plenty of paper, pencils, and crayons or a chalkboard for play activities.	____	____
16. We play games that help my child see differences and likenesses in objects in our home.	____	____
17. My child has a library card and has a chance to use it regularly.	____	____
18. I transmit a positive attitude towards schools and teachers.	____	____
19. My child's hearing and vision are checked regularly.	____	____
20. I am sure my child receives a balanced diet.	____	____

Source: Smith, 1984, p. 670. Reprinted with permission of Nancy J. Smith and the International Reading Association.

BIBLIOGRAPHY

BELLICA, A. H. "Making safe reading environments," *Reading Teacher,* 38, October (1984), 119–20.

BLAND, J. J. "Got any athletes in your reading lab?" *Journal of Reading,* 25, November (1981), 165.

CHEYNEY, A. *Teaching Reading Skills through the Newspaper.* Newark, Del.: International Reading Association, 1984.

CRISCUOLO, N. P. "Meaningful parent involvement in reading," *Reading Teacher,* 36, January (1983), 446–47.

DULIN, K. "Reading and the affective domain," in *Aspects of Reading Education,* ed. S. Pflaum-Connor. Berkeley, Calif.: McCutcheon Publishing Co., 1978.

FLOOD, J. "Parental styles in reading episodes with young children," *Reading Teacher,* 31, May (1977), 864–67.

FRAGER, A. M. "Video book talks," *Reading Teacher,* 38, March (1985), 712.

JOHNSTON, J. P., AND OTHERS. *The Language Experience Approach: Application for Tutoring Adults in Reading.* University of Georgia (ED 120 343) Instructional Concept Guide No. 8. Athens, 1975.

KRAMER, C. J. "Language experience stories on the computer in remedial reading class," *Reading Teacher,* 39, March (1986), 741–42.

KROUSE, S. S. AND N. G. HAMLIN. "It's better than a book report!" *Reading Teacher,* 39, February (1986a), 613–14.

KROUSE, S. S. AND N. G. HAMLIN. "Organizing the classroom library," *Reading Teacher,* 39, January (1986b), 481–43.

MALKAMES, R. M. "Reading clubs motivate remedial readers," *Reading Teacher,* 37, April (1984), 796–97.

MELVIN, M. P. "Book-a-Day Club," *Reading Teacher,* 39, January (1986), 483–84.

ROBBINS, L. S. "A way out of the book report dilemma: Making individualized reading feasible in the content areas," *Journal of Reading,* 25, November (1981), 165–67.

SCHLESSINGER, J. H. "Outside reading and oral reports: Sure-fire reading motivation," *Journal of Reading,* 28, December (1984), 228–31.

SMALE, M. "Teaching secondary students about reading to children," *Journal of Reading,* 26, November (1982), 208–10.

SMITH, N. J. "Parent Self-Help Checklist," *Reading Teacher,* 37, March (1984), 669–70.

THOMPSON, L. L. "Reading skills go to the supermarket," *Reading Teacher,* 39, January (1986), 488.

WALSH, R. W. "Peers and reading motivation," *Reading Teacher,* 38, November (1984), 251–52.

WAPLES, D. *What Reading Does to People,* Chicago, IL: Univ. of Chicago Press, 1967.

ZIMET, S. G. "Teaching children to detect social bias in books," *Reading Teacher,* 36, January (1983), 418–21.

CHUNKING WORDS INTO PHRASES

Definition *The process of automatically grouping words into meaningful phrases while reading*

RATIONALE

Assuming that readers can read and understand the individual words, their next task is to group those words into meaningful phrases. Research indicates that the syntactic phrase and the clause are basic units for good readers (Hurtig, 1977).

Research also indicates that some poor readers may benefit from chunking assistance (Mason and Kendall, 1978). Word-by-word reading does not result in adequate comprehension. It may be caused by too little practice with fluent reading of easy materials, by a concept of reading as word identification, or by an overemphasis on accurate oral decoding.

Thus, the activities in this chapter are designed to (1) encourage students to read in phrases, (2) teach students to identify phrases for themselves, (3) encourage students to focus on phrase meaning rather than on word identification, (4) provide practice in combining words into phrases and phrases into sentences, and (5) help students use chunking to improve oral reading (and to use oral reading to improve chunking). Word-by-word readers may benefit from the games and activities, with the possible exception of those in section B, which require readers to identify phrases for themselves. This process may be too difficult to comprehend for readers in the early stages of learning.

Research also indicates, however, that even older readers who are not obviously hesitating while reading may not have reached an automatic level in their chunking skills and may benefit from direct practice (Stevens, 1981). This is especially true for students who read slowly or who have a difficult time comprehending. These students can be asked to chunk for themselves as suggested in section B, and they should probably work on these activities rather than on the easier games in the other sections. Moreover, older students who are self-conscious about their oral reading may wish to work on the exercises in section E.

INFORMAL DIAGNOSIS

Primary and Intermediate Reading Levels

A. Use oral reading with materials that students can decode easily. The following may indicate a word-by-word style that could be improved with chunking exercises:

1. choppy, word-by-word hesitations
2. lack of normal intonation
3. missed punctuation
4. pointing to each word

B. You may also wish to try a flashed presentation of sentences. Put sentences with several phrases on cards. Let students see each sentence briefly, just long enough for them to read about half of it. Have students recall what they read. Students whose recall ends in the middle of a phrase may be reading in a word-by-word fashion.

Junior and Senior High Reading Levels

Use silent reading with material students can decode easily. Look for slow rate or poor comprehension. Then have students read an unchunked passage and a passage you have chunked by putting slashes between phrases. Compare their rate and comprehension on these two passages. Ask if they found the chunked material easier to read. If so, then they should work on the activities in section B of this chapter.

GENERAL RECOMMENDATIONS FOR TEACHING

1. Always make sure that chunking exercises use materials at the students' independent reading level.

2. Always focus on meaning during chunking activities. The purpose of chunking is to derive meaning from phrases. (For older students, more efficient chunking may also lead to increased rate.)

3. Throughout all other instructional sessions, stress phrases rather than words. Have students identify words in phrasal contexts, pause for discussion only at phrasal or sentence boundaries, and so on.

4. Help students transfer their awareness of natural phrase boundaries from oral language to written material. To do this, design activities in which you and the students orally read with expression (see section E).

5. Activities in which the material is printed with one phrase to a line may help younger and beginning students (see A.1).

6. Activities in which the material is chunked with slashes between phrases may help older or more fluent readers (see section B).

7. Activities in which students identify phrases in sentences or combine phrases to make sentences will improve their phrase awareness (see section D).

8. None of the aforementioned activities will ensure that students automatically chunk when they read. Wide reading of chunked and unchunked material that can be decoded easily is necessary for fluency.

chapter 9. CHUNKING WORDS INTO PHRASES
Activities

A. READING IN PHRASES

1. Reading Machine*   P I

Materials: story at students' independent reading level, separated into chunked phrases, one phrase to a line
paper attached together to make a continuous roll
cardboard or construction paper 8½-by-11 with two slits cut in the center so that the paper roll can be threaded through (see Figure 9-1)

Procedure: 1. Students pull the paper through, reading the series of phrases orally.

     2. Students practice reading the story in this manner until they can pull the paper through quickly.

Variations: 1. Have students time themselves (or each other, if they are working in pairs) in reading the story, so that they can see how they improve their speed.

     2. Set up speed contests (if appropriate).

     3. Have students create chunked sentences and stories for each other.

     4. Replace the last phrase on the roll with a question mark. Students guess what phrase comes next and write their answer down in phrase form. The correct answer is found further along on the roll. For example:

FIGURE 9-1

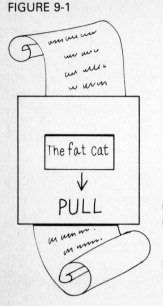

Source: Irwin, 1986, p. 20.

The little red hen
laid three little eggs.
She sat
on the three little eggs
for three little days.
Finally
the eggs hatched
and out came
?

three little chicks.

5. (intermediate level only) Students write stories in chunked fashion to be used in lower-grade classrooms. The pieces of cardboard or construction paper used to hold the rolls are decorated to accompany the stories.

6. (intermediate level only) Students create greeting cards, such as a heart shape to thread a Valentine message through, or a pumpkin for Halloween.

* Irwin, 1986.

2. Words or Chunks?   P I

Materials: Two sets of flash cards, one of single words, one of words in phrases; color the backs of the cards two different colors; words should be at students' independent reading level

Procedure:

1. Ask for a student volunteer to read three cards.

2. Student picks three cards from the same deck.

3. The student reads the cards aloud, with expression.

4. Student chooses three cards from the other deck and reads.

5. Continue as long as desired. Then ask students, "Which deck was more fun to read? Which deck was more fun to listen to? Which deck seemed to make more sense when you read it?"

6. Develop the concept that reading words in phrases has more meaning than reading words separately.

7. Give students two or three single-word cards and make each of them into a chunk card. Students read their cards aloud, giving the word and then the chunk that they created.

Extension: Students choose their own words from a list and make chunk cards.

☞   This is a demonstration activity. Be sure to provide opportunities for application to meaningful reading tasks.

B. IDENTIFYING PHRASES

1. Slashing for Comprehension: Student Writing   I J H

Procedure: 1.   Using a piece of student or teacher writing, demonstrate how to slash the material into meaningful phrases for comprehension. For example:
Today/ is/ the first day/ of the fall season./ Soon/ the leaves/ will be falling/ to the ground./ Is that why/ we call it/ fall? Explain that the slashes separate meaning units, and that students should use this strategy to organize their thoughts when they are reading.

2.   Students slash their own writing to make it easier to read, and to insure proper expression if it is to be read orally.

Variations: 1.   Students work in pairs, exchanging and slashing each other's compositions. Then they discuss the writing in order to get agreement on the divisions.

2.   Students create a ''talking book,'' making tapes of selections that they read from slashed scripts. To facilitate their oral reading, students enlarge chunks to include other chunks.

2. Slashing for Comprehension: Student Texts   I J H

Procedure: 1.   Using an overhead projection of a page in a book the students are reading, demonstrate how to read words in phrases, not word by word, in order to focus on the meaning of what is being read. Slash the text at appropriate places to show the procedure. Explain that the slashes separate meaning units.

2.   Explain that using these phrase boundaries to organize their thoughts when they are reading may improve their comprehension.

3.   Have the students help you slash another selection on the overhead. Mention that there may be different ways to slash a selection. For example, ''My brother Jack/ is always looking/ in the refrigerator/ for food'' can be slashed as indicated, or in several other ways. For instance, ''looking/ in the refrigerator'' could be chunked into a single phrase.

4.   Distribute copies of current text selections and have students slash several paragraphs, focusing on meaning units.

5.   Have students read each other's selections to see if they are easier to understand when chunked.

Variation: 1.   Provide students with other short articles that have been slashed for easy reading by their peers.

2.   Have students practice reading these articles each day, keeping track of any improvements in reading rate. (You will need the approximate number of words in each article.)

3.   After students have read, have them describe their article to a partner so that you can check their comprehension as well.

C. FOCUSING ON PHRASE MEANING RATHER THAN WORD IDENTIFICATION

☞ *Note:* This section consists of three games to be used for *practice only*. Use them only with students who need this practice, and show how they can be applied to their real reading tasks!

1. Paraphrase Concentration   P I J

Materials: set of 3-by-5 cards of phrases; each phrase is matched by a paraphrase on another card; for example, ''Alice ate the hamburger'' and ''The hamburger was eaten by Alice''

Procedure: 1.   Shuffle the cards and arrange them face down in rows.

2.   Follow rules for Concentration given in Appendix B.

2. Go Fish a Phrase   P I

Materials: deck of pairs of paraphrase cards, as in activity C.1; cards should be written across the shorter side to make reading easier

Players: three or more

Objective: to get the greatest number of pairs of paraphrases

Procedure: See directions for Fish in Appendix B.

3. Odd Person Out   I J

Materials: deck of paraphrase cards, as in activities C.1 and C.2 but also including one ODD PERSON OUT card

Players: three or more

Objective: to get rid of all cards as quickly as possible

Procedure: See directions for Odd Person Out in Appendix B.

D. COMBINING WORDS INTO PHRASES AND PHRASES INTO SENTENCES

☞ These four activities are for demonstration and practice only. Tie this strategy back to meaningful reading tasks.

1. Sentence Anagrams*   P I

Materials: cards of words that create a sentence; one word per card

Procedure: See Figure 9-2.

1.   Mix up the cards.

2.   Model the procedure for creating a sentence, selecting cards in this order: verb, helping verb, subject, prepositional phrase.

FIGURE 9-2

> "Well, let's see: I've got the cards 'boy,' 'store,' 'the,' 'the,' 'was,' 'to,' 'going.' The verb is 'going,' so we'll start with that: GOING (placed on the table).
>
> "Are there any helping verbs? Yes, 'was' is a helping verb. Let's tape these together: WAS-GOING Now, I can ask, *Who* was going? Well, it was either the boy or the store . . . probably BOY, and THE goes with it, so I'll tape THE to BOY and put it in front of my other phrase: THE-BOY WAS-GOING (two taped phrases placed next to each other).
>
> "Now, what words are left? STORE THE TO (left on table) Can I make a phrase from those? Yes, and I'll tape those together: TO-THE-STORE (taped together). Does this go with the rest? Yes, at the end": THE-BOY WAS-GOING TO-THE-STORE.

Source: Irwin, 1986, p. 21.

3. Indicate that the best way to solve sentence anagrams is to find the action word first and then to ask "wh" questions to find the other phrases.

4. Initially, have students work with easy sentences.

5. As the students become more proficient, create longer and more complex sentences.

* Irwin, 1986. See also Weaver, 1979.

2. Chunking Dice   P I

Materials: dice

two sets of eleven cards, numbered on the back from two to twelve, consisting of:
two cards with a subject and modifiers (e.g., "the lazy dog," "the black cat")
two cards with a verb and modifiers (e.g., "ran quickly," "chased")
one conjunction (e.g., "and")
six cards with prepositional phrases (e.g., "over the sink," "with black whiskers," "into the kitchen")

Number of Players: two

Objective of Game: to be the first player to create a sentence of five or more phrases

Procedure:
1. Spread out cards face down in front of each player.

2. First player throws dice, turns over the card matching the number rolled, and reads it aloud.

3. Second player does the same.

4. A player who rolls a number he or she has already rolled, must pass to the other player.

5. A round ends when one player has assembled a sentence of five phrases or more.

6. The winner of a round gets one point for each phrase in his or her sentence.

7. The first person to get thirty points wins the game.

Variations: 1. A player who rolls the same number again must put back the corresponding card.

2. Primary: Make a card numbered 1, and use only one die and six cards.

3. Use only one set of cards. Each player takes the card corresponding to the number rolled, even if it has already been taken by the other player.

4. Students make their own sets of cards.

5. Killer 7: A player who rolls a seven has to turn over all his or her cards and start again.

6. Wild 7: Sevens are wild, and can be any phrase needed.

7. (intermediate level only) Students make sets of cards for younger classes, using sentences from the stories of readers that the younger students are using. Backs of cards can be decorated as well as numbered. Students teach the game to younger class.

3. Sentence Sense*   **P I J**

Materials: a selection, divided into sentences, of expository prose or narrative at the students' independent reading level

Procedure: 1. Cut the sentences into phrases, and label phrases from the same sentence with the same letter on the back. For example, all the phrases of sentence 1 could have C on the back; sentence 2, A; sentence 3, G; and so on.

2. Give each student one phrase.

3. Students' first task is to get together in groups—all A's together, all B's together, and so forth—and re-create their sentences.

4. The next task is for each group to read its sentences aloud.

5. The final task is for the class to reassemble the sentences in the proper order.

Variations: 1. Individual work: Give the scrambled phrases to the student, who then assembles the sentences and puts them into the proper order.

2. Content area: Cut up a chapter summary into sentences. Use material with which the student is familiar. The student reassembles this material as a review as well as to gain chunking practice.

3. Math: Scramble problems about a familiar process, and demonstrate to the student the procedure to follow in unscrambling them.

* Cunningham and Cunningham, 1984.

4. Chunking Rummy   I J

> *Materials:*   deck of chunking cards:
>
>> five subject cards
>> five verb cards
>> two conjunction cards (*and* works best)
>> five phrase cards beginning with *with* (for example, "with blue eyes")
>> twenty prepositional-phrase cards
>> five adjective-phrase cards beginning with a participle (for example, "holding a balloon")

> *Number of Players:*   two or more

> *Objective of Game:*   to have all cards in one's hand create one meaningful sentence

> *Procedure:*   See directions for Rummy in Appendix B.

E.   USING CHUNKING TO IMPROVE ORAL READING AND VICE VERSA

1.   Reader's Theater*   P I J H A

> *Materials:*   any story, poem, nursery rhyme, newspaper article, advertisement, set of directions, or other selection at the readers' independent reading level, divided into numbered sections and dittoed

> *Procedure:*
>> 1.   Give each student a section of the selection.
>>
>> 2.   Students read silently and then practice reading orally with expression.
>>
>> 3.   When all students are ready, they read their sections aloud, as dramatically and meaningfully as they can.

> *Variation:*   Tape the final reading for a classroom oral library. To give additional practice and variety, have students reread the selections with different emphases, tape, and compare readings.

> * Pikulski, 1983.

2.   Three–Way Oral Reading*   I J

> *Procedure:*
>> 1.   Have students read assigned textbook selection silently. They can take it home and practice it before the activity.
>>
>> 2.   Tell students that they will be reading orally, to improve their oral-reading skills. Explain the variations that you will use for oral reading of the selection:
>>
>>> a.   The *order* may vary, and students will be called on randomly.
>>>
>>> b.   The *number* of people reading will vary. Sometimes one person will read, sometimes two, sometimes three, sometimes the whole group.
>>>
>>> c.   The *style* of reading will vary, changing at random points in the

selection, and not necessarily at the ends of paragraphs. For example, students may be asked to read the selection as a speech, to read angrily, to read sorrowfully, to read as if telling a secret, and so on.

3.   Describe and demonstrate the three types of oral reading:

paired reading: either the teacher and a student read together, or two or more students read together.

choral reading: the teacher and students read together, with the teacher setting the tempo and dropping out eventually.

imitative reading: the teacher reads, exaggerating the style if appropriate, and the students imitate.

* Wood, 1983.

3.   Verse Choir*   P I J H

Procedure: 1.   Explain to students that they are going to be a verse choir, an activity that will help them improve their oral reading and enable them to perform for some specified occasion.

2.   Group the students according to voice—either boy/girl or light/medium/ dark. (Have them say their names to you to decide this.)

3.   Use a poem or speech of interest to the students. Work on the seven variables of speech (pitch, power, phrasing, tempo, voice quality, number of voices, and bodily movement) to paint a "sound picture" of the selection.

4.   It is not necessary for all the students to be able to read the selection; learning to perform it together will help them read it when they feel sufficiently familiar with it.

5.   Have the students practice and perform, and enjoy their success and new interest in reading aloud.

* Povenmire, 1977.

4.   Multipaired Simultaneous Oral Reading*   P I

Procedure: 1.   Have children choose a partner to read to. Children should choose different partners each time they do the activity, so that they do not become dependent on each other. Monitor the pairs, and if you notice that a pair doesn't work well together, ask the two children to change partners.

2.   Each pair sets its own rules about the length of the material it reads (one paragraph, two paragraphs, one page, or more).

3.   Let children read their selection to each other at their own rate.

4.   Monitor regularly and make suggestions as needed. For example, suggest alternating the reading more often if one member of a pair is a more halting reader than the other.

5.   When a pair finishes reading their selection, give each member a comprehension work sheet. This can be something you make or a work sheet that accompanies the basal.

6.   When everyone has finished their selection and the work sheet, lead a discussion of the story or stories read.

7. As children become accustomed to this procedure, you will find that they enjoy assuming responsibility for their own reading performance, and that the temporary rise in classroom noise will not disturb the class.

* Poe, 1986.

5. Friday Read–Aloud*   **P I**

Procedure: 1. Set up a time on Friday afternoon for students to read aloud to their classmates.

2. Students must sign up in advance. You may find you will have a waiting list.

3. The time limit for reading aloud is five minutes.

4. Students select their own pages to read aloud, and practice at home during the week. If a student is unprepared at the assigned time of reading, he or she sits down and must practice some more the next week before getting another opportunity.

* Ross, 1986.

BIBLIOGRAPHY

CUNNINGHAM, P. M. AND J. W. CUNNINGHAM. "The hidden agenda of sequencing," *Clearing House,* 56, April (1984), 362–63.

HURTIG, R. "The validity of clausal processing strategies at the discourse level," *Discourse Processes,* 1, January–March (1977), 195–202.

IRWIN, J. W. *Teaching Reading Comprehension Processes.* Englewood Cliffs, N.J.: Prentice-Hall, 1986.

MASON, J. AND J. KENDALL. *Facilitating reading comprehension through text structure manipulation,* Center for the Study of Reading, University of Illinois. Technical Report No. 92. Urbana-Champaign, IL., 1978.

PIKULSKI, J. "Reader's Theatre," *Reading Teacher,* 37, November (1983), 223–24.

POE, V. L. "Using multipaired simultaneous oral reading," *Reading Teacher,* 40, November (1986), 239–40.

POVENMIRE, E. K. "Advantages of verse choir for reading," *Reading Teacher,* 30, April (1977), 761–65.

ROSS, E. P. "Classroom experiments with oral reading," *Reading Teacher,* 40, December (1986), 270–75.

STEVENS, K. "Chunking material as an aid to reading comprehension," *Journal of Reading,* 25, (1981), 126–29.

WEAVER, P. A. "Improving reading instruction: Effects of sentences organization instruction." *Reading Research Quarterly,* 15, Fall (1979), 129–46.

WOOD, K. D. "A variation on an old theme: 4 way oral reading," *Reading Teacher,* 37, October (1983), 38–41.

chapter 10

SELECTING
THE IMPORTANT
DETAILS

Definition: *Selecting the important information from individual sentences*

RATIONALE

Even as we read single sentences, we must decide what parts to remember as we read on. We cannot recall every detail from every sentence, so good readers select certain parts of each sentence to retain. This decision is based on the content of the passage and the purpose for reading. Readers select the information they will need for upcoming interpretations.

For instance, in the following sentence, a good reader would remember the color of the man's hair if that were important for remembering which man was involved. But if there were only one man, the reader might not think that hair color was important information.

> The yellow-haired man sincerely believed that the only solution was to move out of the brick house in which he had been raised.

This sort of choice is constantly involved in content-area reading as well. It is clearly impossible to remember every fact in a content-area text; indeed, some facts are put there simply for embellishment. Good readers effectively choose the important information

to remember. Research indicates that poor readers are often less able to do this.

This strategy is clearly related to finding main ideas (Chapter 15) and summarizing a passage (Chapter 16). Indeed, selecting the important facts in individual sentences is the first step toward an appropriate summary. Reporting the important details of a passage is an extension of selecting those details while reading each sentence and the ability to find main ideas and summarize a passage is based on the ability to do these things. Thus, this chapter contains activities designed to teach students to select important details from sentences and passages. These activities should probably be followed by activities from Chapters 15 and 16, in which selection of important details is combined with strategies for finding main ideas and summarizing passages.

INFORMAL DIAGNOSIS

Of course, you can diagnose students' abilities in this area by asking them to select important details from individual sentences or from short passages. You can also ask for free recall of short passages to see if students recall the important facts.

GENERAL TEACHING SUGGESTIONS

1. When students are reading long sentences, pause at the end of each and ask the reader to tell you what was the most important information in that sentence.

2. Avoid giving picky tests that focus on unimportant information. This encourages bad reading habits.

3. When possible, use the activities in this chapter along with meaningful reading assignments. If you are a remedial teacher, try to use these activities to help your students with their content-area assignments. They will be interested in the strategy when they see that it can help them in practical ways. (Of course, you may need to let the classroom teacher know that this is something you are emphasizing.)

4. After students have selected important details, ask them to defend their selection.

5. Explain to each student the importance of selecting the important details.

6. Model this process to the students before asking them to perform it independently.

7. Begin with easy materials for which the students have a lot of background knowledge. Then gradually move to more difficult materials.

8. Discuss the clues that content-area authors might use to highlight important facts. These might include format changes such as highlighting or underlining, or specific expressions like "the important thing is . . . ," "the point is . . . ," or "it is important to know . . . ." Check the text!

9. If you encourage students to underline in their readings, be sure that they learn to do this *selectively*.

chapter 10: SELECTING THE IMPORTANT DETAILS
Activities

A. SELECTING DETAILS TO REMEMBER FROM A SENTENCE

1. Which Words?   P

Procedure: 1. Write on the board (or say) a sentence such as "The little cat came to the house."

2. Tell students that you have to condense this sentence into just two or three words. They will help you choose the most important words. These words will probably be the ones that can help you picture the sentence in your head.

3. Read the sentence aloud. Then reread it, stopping at each word and having the students help you decide if it is important.

4. After choosing *cat, came,* and *house,* work with students on several other sentences.

5. Practice this procedure when working on other material.

6. Reinforce the procedure when reading to the students.

2. Newslead   I J H A

Procedure: 1. Give students copies of a local newspaper and the work sheet illustrated in Figure 10-1.

2. Students choose a headline from the newspaper and complete the answer sheet.

3. If the answer to a category is not contained in the headline, students write "Not in Headline" and read the article to find the answer.

FIGURE 10-1 Answer Sheet for Newslead

WHO?	WHAT?	WHERE?	WHEN?	WHY?	HOW?
____	____	____	____	____	____
____	____	____	____	____	____
____	____	____	____	____	____
____	____	____	____	____	____

4. If the answer is not found in the article, students write "Not Given."

5. Class shares results, determining which headlines contained the most information, which were the most provocative, and so on.

Variation: Use this procedure for the first sentence of content-area texts, stories, or other selections. Students compare and discuss answers.

3. What's the Question?   P I J H A

Procedure: 1. Read the textbook chapter to be studied.

2. Select important details students should learn.

3. Create a reading guide that lists these details and asks students to create questions that will elicit these facts as answers (see Figure 10-2).

4. Math Word Clues*   P I J H A

Materials: paper and colored pencils for students to use for "visual doodling" during class modeling and instruction sessions

Procedure: A. Teacher Preparation

1. Read story problem.

2. Ask yourself *how* you know the correct problem-solving procedure.

3. Select the words in the problem needed for its solution.

4. Read only the selected words.

5. Decide whether there are some other words you could delete and still solve the problem.

FIGURE 10-2   Question Guide to Chapter 8 in *Exploring History* (fictional text)

Directions: Listed below are the *answers* to questions about important information in Chapter 8 in your textbook. Next to each answer write the question that should be asked to get this answer. Be very specific in your question: include who, what, when, where, and why, if possible. The first question is done for you. We'll choose the best questions tomorrow in class.

ANSWER	*QUESTION*
	where? what?
1. Henry VIII	*Who* was the *English* king who *started a church*
	when?
	in the *16th century* in order *to*
	why?
	marry again and have a son?
2. John Cabot	
3. Francis Drake	
4. Armada	
5. King Philip of Spain	

6. Ask yourself if any of these essential words or symbols are difficult vocabulary or concepts.

7. Make sure the class understands these words and concepts.

8. Visualize the problem, trying to think of a way to solve it visually; e.g. is it possible to visualize a.m. and p.m. hours around 12 if you are using a digital clock?

B. Direct Instruction

Provide a direct explanation of how to solve a problem; model your strategies (see Figure 10-3).

C. Follow-Up

1. Go through the problem a second time. Give students time to work on

FIGURE 10-3   Modeling a Strategy for Solving a Math Problem

SAMPLE PROBLEM: Mrs. Jones is planning to buy carpeting that costs $14.95 a square yard. Her living room measures 8 by 5 yards. How many square yards of carpeting will Mrs. Jones need?

1. Use the SQ3R strategy (survey, question, read, read, review). *Survey* the problem aloud, reading the question sentence first. "Well, since I see the words 'carpeting' and 'square,' I'm probably going to have to multiply. And 'square' and 'carpeting' are usually associated with area, and when I have to find area, I usually multiply."
2. Draw a square on the board. "It's easier to work if I can *see* what I have to do. Here's the carpet."
3. *Question:* "What is it they *want* in this problem? What's the purpose of this problem?"
4. *Read:* "Okay—find how many square yards of carpet. How many does not mean how *much*—that usually refers to money, and that would be another problem. Well, what do you think would be the correct process to use here?"
5. *Read* the room-measurement information from the problem. Write the numbers on the diagram.
6. Complete the problem: $8 \times 5 = 40$ square yards. Draw these in on the diagram.
7. *Review:* Model your strategy for checking the problem, using the QAER formula (question, answer, evidence, reasoning).
   a. Question: "What process did I use here to find the square yards of carpet?"
   b. Answer: "Multiplication."
   c. Evidence: "What was my evidence for deciding to use this process? 'Room,' 'carpet,' '8 by 5,' and 'how many square.'"
   d. Reasoning: "8 and 5 were given as measurements of the room. Therefore, one number is probably width and one is probably length. Carpets cover floors—so we need to find the area of the floor. The formula for finding area is length times width, so I multiplied 8 times 5."

Source: Adapted from Kresse, 1984, p. 600.

the problem and draw visualizations. Ask the inference question (step 3 in Figure 10-3) and supply the answer.

2. Students find evidence and explain their reasoning.

3. The third time through the problem, ask the inference question and have the students answer. Give the evidence and have students explain the reasoning.

4. Have students draw and reason one problem for each assignment. Mix previous story problems in present assignments to check on comprehension.

5. The fourth time through, ask the inference question and have students do the rest.

6. Finally, have students do all the operations independently.

* Kresse, 1984.

5. Beginning Underlining IJHA

Procedure: 1. On an overhead or the board, show a long sentence, such as "John and Mary, the happy-go-lucky Smith twins who live across the street, just won $1000."

2. Model selecting the main idea of the sentence (John and Mary won $1000) and underline it in red.

3. With the students, practice selecting the main idea from a sentence. Use relevant content-area material.

4. Students work on sentences on their own, using felt pens to underline.

5. Discuss sentences and responses.

6. Using content-area texts, have students work independently, choosing one sentence per paragraph and writing down the part of that sentence that they would underline.

6. Key Words in Test Directions* IJHA

Procedure: 1. Mention to students that one of the problems test examiners have encountered in marking tests is that many students don't answer the essay question asked—they write another answer entirely. Ask why these questions could be a problem for students.

2. Discuss the possibility that such students have not read the question correctly. They might not have understood the key words or read carefully. Ask students if that has ever happened to them.

3. Provide examples of test questions and student answers that were off the mark or incomplete—for example, the question "List the two types of sedimentary rock and give examples of each" and a student answer that names the two types of rock but gives examples of only one kind.

4. Have students select the key words in questions. In our example these would be *List, two types, sedimentary rock, and examples.*

5. List the five categories of exam words on the board, give examples of each, and have students supply possible questions using these words.

a. FACTS: who, what, where, when, define, describe, list, show, tell, write, identify, enumerate, outline

b. UNDERSTANDING: what is the cause (effect), compare, contrast, distinguish, explain, show how, show why, discuss, relate, review, state

c. ANALYSIS (understanding the parts): analyze, classify, distinguish, compare, contrast, categorize, trace, outline, illustrate, examine

d. SYNTHESIS (understanding the whole): create, make up, suggest, infer, summarize

e. EVALUATION: decide, select, evaluate, judge, what is your opinion, what would you do if, what would have happened if, suppose, justify, prove, assess

6. Brainstorm facts from a recent lesson. Write the facts on the chalkboard and label and categorize them. For instance, for the topic *mammals,* "live in deserts," "live in forests," "some live in oceans," and so on, would be classified *habitats.*

7. Ask "What sorts of questions could we ask about this information?" After several questions are suggested, say "Maybe the best way to make up a question is to *start* with the information you want supplied, and *then* create the question. For example, if you want the student to give you the characteristics of mammals, what category of question words would you use?"

8. Work through the five types of question words, creating questions for each. See Pauk (1984) and Kesselman-Turkel and Peterson (1981). You may want to spend one lesson on each type of question word.

9. Reinforce this skill by having students make up questions for textbook reading assignments.

* Adapted from Balajthy, 1984.

7. Selective Paraphrasing*   I J H A

Procedure: 1. Demonstrate a short paraphrase of a long sentence. For example, "John ran, panting with fear, down the alley, chased by the tall man in the blue uniform" can be paraphrased "John ran away from the policeman."

2. Work with the students making short paraphrases of long sentences.

3. Have students work independently in pairs or teams, trying to make the shortest paraphrases of a series of long sentences.

4. Share results in class. If appropriate, have the class choose the best paraphrases.

☞   This is a demonstration activity. Be sure to provide opportunities for application to meaningful reading tasks.

* Irwin, 1986.

B. SELECTING DETAILS TO REMEMBER FROM A SELECTION

1. Selection Guide*   I J H A

Procedure: 1. Read chapter to be studied by the students.

2. Select the main points of the chapter.

3. Create a study guide that identifies these main ideas and asks the students to find the important details related to them (see Figure 10-4).

* Irwin, 1986.

FIGURE 10-4   Study Guide for First Section of Physical Science Chapter on Matter

As you read, complete the following:

I.   Here are the main points of this chapter. For each, list five related details that would be important to remember.
   A.   Matter can be classified in several ways.
       1.
       2.
       3.
       4.
       5.
   B.   In a chemical change, new substances are formed.
       1.
       2.
       3.
       4.
       5.
   C.   A chemical equation describes chemical changes.
       1.
       2.
       3.
       4.
II.   In the following list of details, put a star (*) by the four most important.
   A.   Compressed air becomes a liquid below −201.
   B.   An element is a substance that cannot be broken down into simpler substances.
   C.   Seawater is a mixture.
   D.   The three forms of matter are solid, liquid, and gas.
   E.   Chlorine is a dense, greenish yellow gas.
   F.   Water is the same compound whether it is liquid water, vapor, or ice.
   G.   The formation of dew is a chemical change.
   H.   Sodium is soft enough to be cut with a knife.

Tomorrow in class, we will discuss why you thought the starred details were important.

Source: Irwin, 1986, p. 59

2. Which One?*   **I J H A**

Procedure: 1.   Divide students into pairs or small groups. Have them read a section of a textbook or story in short segments.

2.   Each student writes down the *one* most important thing to remember from each segment.

3.   Students in each team compare choices. The team must select one choice as its entry.

4.   If appropriate, compare team answers for the whole class.

5.   Test items can be selected from team choices.

* Irwin, 1986.

BIBLIOGRAPHY

BALAJTHY, E. "Using student-constructed questions to encourage active reading," *Journal of Reading,* 27, February (1984), 408–11.

IRWIN, J. W. *Teaching Reading Comprehension Processes.* Englewood Cliffs, N.J.: Prentice-Hall, 1986.

KESSELMAN-TURKEL, J. AND F. PETERSON. *Test-Taking Strategies.* Chicago: Contemporary Books, Inc., 1981.

KRESSE, E. C. "Using reading as a thinking process to solve math story problems," *Journal of Reading,* 27, April (1984), 598–601.

PAUK, W. *How to Study in College.* Boston: Houghton Mifflin, 1984.

chapter 11

UNDERSTANDING FIGURATIVE LANGUAGE

Definition: *Understanding the intended meaning of metaphors, similes, and idioms*

RATIONALE

Metaphoric language uses a comparison between two dissimilar things to make a point about what they have in common. With similes, the comparison is stated with *like* or *as:* "My heart sank like a stone." (Both are heavy, etc.) With metaphors, the comparison is implicit: "All the world's a stage." (Both involve actors, etc.)

Children may have trouble understanding a metaphor if they know nothing about the terms involved. In this case, direct vocabulary instruction is probably needed. Students may also misunderstand a metaphor or simile because they don't know how it works and attempt to respond to it literally. If this is the case, activities that explain the purpose of such language are useful (see activities A.3 and A.4), as are games that require appropriate interpretations (see activity B.3).

FIGURE 11-1 Idioms for Charades

He's waiting on tables.
He cracks me up.
Time marches on.
He's a wise guy.
She slays me.
You turn me on.
He's a chip off the old block.
He kicked the bucket.
I've got cold feet.
Don't bank on me.
I'm all washed up.
She's got a chip on her shoulder.

He gave me the brush.
Don't hang your head.
They were pulling his leg.
She's over the hill.
He's lost his marbles.
I finally saw the light.
He wants to break the ice.
Cut it out!
That's out of sight.
I'm in the dark.
I don't see the point.

Source: Foerster, 1974.

FIGURE 11-2 Humorous Idioms for Illustration

I'm burned up.
He's a big wheel.
I'm an egghead.
She's a real jewel.
She flew off the handle.
He's off his rocker.
She hit the ceiling.
He's a shady character.
She gave him the gate.
It was a hair-raising experience.
Don't get your wires crossed.
He'll talk your arm and leg off.
I'll bet her ears are burning.
He's low man on the totem pole.
They're head over heels in love.

Source: Foerster, 1974.

Similarly, idioms represent one concept in terms of another, but their meaning is more fixed and they are based on local customs. Although they are disruptive and sometimes ambiguous to the naive reader, they are also interesting and colorful, and they can often communicate more clearly than purely literal prose. The meaning of idioms can neither be inferred grammatically nor always understood from the surrounding information. Therefore, idioms have to be learned by explanation, definition, and memorization. Figures 11-1 to 11-4 list some common English idioms.

Bilingual students have the most difficulty with idioms because they try to translate them directly into their own language. This usually causes misunderstanding, because by definition an idiom must be understood as a whole. Often, the only solution is to teach these expressions as if they are new vocabulary

FIGURE 11-3 Idioms for Classification

COLORS
She's in the pink.
He's feeling blue.
Don't be yellow.
I'm in the red.
She's green with envy.
He was purple with rage.
There's too much red tape.
He was caught red-handed.
This is a red-letter day.

ANIMALS
Don't make a hog of yourself.
She's top dog.
He's a sourpuss.
He's a rat.
Don't count your chickens before they're hatched.
It sounds fishy.
She's playing possum.
I'm not chicken.
She's a clothes horse.
He's a wolf in sheep's clothing.
We're eating high on the hog.
He's no spring chicken.
Things are just ducky.
Quit horsing around.
Get off your high horse.
He's a stool pigeon.
He's a fat cat.

FOOD
I'm in a stew.
Don't put all your eggs in one basket.
She's some tomato.

She's the salt of the earth.
That's sour grapes.
She brings home the bacon.
You're full of baloney.
Everything's in apple-pie order.
He's top banana.
I'm in a pickle.
She's feeling her oats.
That's pure corn.
She's full of beans.
It's a piece of cake.
He can't cut the mustard.
She's a peach.
Don't spill the beans.
They were just chewing the fat.

PARTS OF THE BODY
Get off my back.
Lend me your ears.
He's a busybody.
Don't run off at the mouth.
I've got my eye on you.
She has a sharp tongue.
Better shake a leg.
I gave him a tongue lashing.
I have a nose for news.
I can't stomach him.
He's a heel.
Lend me a hand.
They're pulling his leg.
She's a pain in the neck.
That's a second-hand store.

Source: Figures 11-1, 11-2, and 11-3: Foerster, L. M. "Idiomagic!" *Elementary English,* 51, 1974, 125–127. Copyright © 1974 by the National Council of Teachers of English. Reprinted with permission.

FIGURE 11-4 Figurative Language from Sports

Idiom/Metaphor/Simile	Origin
start from scratch	first Olympic Games, 776 B.C.: line scratched in dirt for starting point of race
kick off	*soccer*
get the ball rolling	
right off the bat	*baseball*
off base	
can't get to first base	
go to bat for	
in there pitching	
ballpark figure	
southpaw	original term for a left-handed pitcher, because home plates in early ballparks faced west so that the batter wouldn't have to face the afternoon sun. As a result, when a pitcher faced the plate from the mound, his left hand would be on the south side. Eventually, "south paw" came to refer to any lefty.
huddle	*football*
Monday morning quarterback	
All-American	
a low blow	*boxing*
below the belt	
on the ropes	
down for the count	
saved by the bell	
throw in the towel	
put up your dukes	derived from "put up your Duke of Yorks", old Cockney rhyming slang for "forks", which meant the fingers of one's hands, eventually coming to mean the fists
tee off	*golf*
stymied	(when another ball is between the player's ball and the cup; before 1951 the player had to putt with it in place, as it could not be removed)
below par	
up to par	
butterfingers	*cricket*
	(poor fielders who dropped the ball)
fast one	(fast ball)
stonewalling	(to bat defensively, trying to protect the wicket like a stone wall)

Source: Considine, 1986. Copyright © 1986 by The New York Times Company. Reprinted by permission.

words. See Chapter 6 for vocabulary activities that you might wish to use for teaching idioms. The practice activities provided in section B of this chapter would also be useful for bilingual students.

INFORMAL DIAGNOSIS

Of course, you will learn the most during discussions of reading materials that use idioms and metaphoric expressions. Students will generally know some idioms but not all. Keep a record of idioms with which they have trouble. The other thing you will wish to diagnose is whether students know that idioms and metaphoric expressions cannot be interpreted literally. Do they actively infer the meaning intended by the author, or do they just read without expecting these expressions to make sense?

GENERAL TEACHING SUGGESTIONS

1. Students may have difficulty identifying statements as figurative rather than literal language if they lack the specific word knowledge required. Therefore, exercises that focus on differentiating literal from figurative language will have little instructional value for these students. Instead, in teaching students to identify metaphors and similes teachers should:

a. identify the metaphors and similes the students will encounter in their assignments;

b. decide the vocabulary needed to comprehend the selected phrases;

c. teach that vocabulary to the students.

(Readence, Baldwin, and Rickelman, 1983)

2. Arouse interest in idioms and figurative language by using them yourself and asking students to tell you what you really mean. For example, tell them they'll be "in the doghouse" for some reason, or that you will have to "play it by ear."

3. Discuss the literal meaning of an idiom and elicit the actual meaning from the students or supply it yourself. Ask them how they know the literal meaning is not appropriate—that it doesn't make sense. Tell them that knowing that something doesn't make sense—that "something's wrong"—is the clue that they should read the expression not literally but in some other way.

4. Demonstrate to the students that looking up the words of an idiom, metaphor, or simile in a dictionary will not usually help in figuring out the meaning of the expression.

5. Discuss why people use idioms and metaphors so often, pointing out how these expressions not only make language more colorful but also manage to convey meaning exactly.

6. Provide opportunities for students to use the new idioms. Charades of literal interpretations of idioms can be acted out by teams, who score points only by correctly identifying the actual meaning of the idiom. See Figure 11-1 for suggestions.

7. Have students illustrate favorite idioms. The funnier the idiom, the better. See Figure 11-2 for suggestions.

8. Create a dictionary of idioms and add to it throughout the year.

9. Classify idioms by colors, animals, actions, food, and other categories. Create a chart for each category. See Figure 11-3 for suggestions.

10. Keep a list of idioms heard on TV, on radio, or in conversations or seen in reading. Figure 11-4 lists idioms related to sports.

11. Use idioms as starters for creative writing. For example, have students write stories or plays containing speculations on the actual origin of an idiom.

12. Read aloud to the students books using idioms. Books like *Amelia Bedelia* (Parish, 1963), contain idioms, homonyms, homophones, and homographs presented in a humorous and interesting manner.

13. Use writing activities that encourage students to create their own metaphors.

chapter 11. UNDERSTANDING FIGURATIVE LANGUAGE
Activities

A. DEVELOPING AN AWARENESS OF FIGURATIVE LANGUAGE

1. Idiom Charades*   P I

Materials: slips of paper with an idiom on each
envelopes
objects (if needed) for acting out literally certain idioms, such as a button for "button your lip"

Procedure: 1. Ask: "Did you ever get in trouble for doing what you were told *not* to do?" (hands)

"Did you ever get in trouble for *not* doing what you *were* told to do?" (hands)

"Did you ever get in trouble for doing *exactly* what you *were* told to do?" (hands)

2. Tell the students examples of children who did get in trouble for doing exactly what they *were* told to do. For instance, when told not to track mud over the clean kitchen floor, a student went in the front door and got mud on the rug—and got in trouble.

3. Tie this into idioms by telling of a girl who was told not to let the cat out of the bag, and proceeded to put her cat in a bag and tie it up. *She* was following directions exactly, too. The problem is that our language contains colorful phrases that people use to make their meaning clear but that are not meant to be taken literally—for example, "pain in the neck" or "break the ice."

4. Tell students that they are going to have a chance to show how well they can read expressions literally. Give each student an envelope. Each must open the envelope when called on and do *exactly* what the directions say. Examples of possible idiom directions and materials:

Envelope with a piece of tape: Find a friend and stick to him or her.

Stone in envelope: Chip on your shoulder, chip off the old block.

Empty envelope: Walk on air.

5. The group must try to identify what the student is doing.

This is a demonstration activity. Be sure to provide opportunities for application to meaningful reading tasks.

* Lorenz, 1977.

2. Common Ground   P I

Procedure:
    1.   Identify metaphors and similes that the students will be reading in their texts.

    2.   Decide what vocabulary students will need to understand these statements. For example, to understand "proud as a peacock" students must know what a peacock is and what its attributes are.

    3.   Teach the needed vocabulary before the reading assignments.

    4.   Explain to the students that many figures of speech, such as metaphors and similes, make language more interesting and colorful—but can also make it more difficult to understand. The key to understanding these expressions, such as "busy as a bee" or "slow as molasses," is to figure out what the two words compared (*busy* and *bee; slow* and *molasses*) have in common.

    5.   Demonstrate on the overhead or chalkboard how to figure out the meaning of an expression such as "the fog was like pea soup." Make a list of the words that come to mind when thinking of pea soup (*liquid, green, thick*) and ask which of these words could also apply to fog (*thick*). Therefore, thickness is the quality of pea soup that also describes the fog.

    6.   Have students practice this procedure with several expressions you have selected. Discuss the results with them.

    7.   Have students use this strategy on material in their textbooks. For example, a social studies text might have the sentence "Coffee was king in Brazil." Their task would be to discover what coffee in Brazil had in common with kings.

3. What's Missing?*   P I J

Procedure:
    1.   Use an overhead projection to show a pair of sentences, one a metaphorical statement and the other nonexplicit. For example:
       a.   My cat is as fierce as a tiger.
       b.   My cat is a tiger.
Point out that in both sentences two things are being compared.

    2.   Explain that the two sentences are alike except that in sentence *b* the word *fierce* is missing. A sentence such as this is called a metaphor. To understand such sentences we have to search our minds to find a missing word that would create a match between the two things being compared in the metaphor.

    3.   Present students with a new metaphor without giving its explicit equivalent—for example, "My love is a red rose." Ask students to guess the missing word.

    4.   Model how to do this by demonstrating that many words are really a "series of lists" in our minds. Use the example of a rose and show how the reader can generate a list of attributes associated with roses (fragrant, thorny, colorful, beautiful, etc.).

    5.   After solving the new metaphor, present students with some other words, such as *winter,* and have them generate lists of associated words.

    6.   Provide supervised practice in figuring out what's missing in selected metaphors.

FIGURE 11-5 What's Missing?

Directions: In the following sentences some words are missing. Supply the missing words and explain the metaphor. The first one is done for you.

WHAT'S MISSING?

1. That student is a clown.

as funny as—the student likes to make jokes and fool around

2. Her heart is ice.
3. He's a real hippopotamus!
4. Her desk is a garbage dump.
5. Her eyes are saucers.

7.   The next day, review and practice the procedure. Have students supply some metaphors for discussion.

8.   Have students work with a series of novel metaphors, writing their own interpretations of them and supplying what they think are the missing words (see Figure 11-5).

9.   Reinforce this skill in textbook assignments and when reading aloud with and to the class.

* Readence, Baldwin, and Head, 1987.

B. PRACTICE ACTIVITIES

Note: The following three activities are isolated from real reading. Use sparingly!

1. Idiom Baseball*   I J

Procedure:
1.   Divide students into two teams or into pairs.

2.   Each team or member of a pair has a list of idioms that have been studied.

3.   The "pitcher" from one team calls out one of the idioms.

4.   The "batter" on the other team scores a hit by correctly giving the meaning of the expression.

5.   Three "outs" and the other team (pair member) is up.

* Foerster, 1974.

2. Draw an Idiom*   P I

Procedure:
1.   Write idioms on small pieces of paper, fold them up, and put them in a bag or box.

2.   Children take turns drawing an expression from the box.

3.   Give children sheets of paper on which to illustrate their idioms.

4. When finished, children take turns showing their illustrations to class-mates and having them guess the idiom.

Variation: This can be played as a team game like charades.

* Foerster, 1974.

3. Idiom/Metaphor Concentration   P I

Materials: deck of idiom and metaphor cards, one idiom or metaphor written on each match-ing number of cards with the literal meanings of the idiom or metaphor; for example:
in the pink—feeling well
in the doghouse—in trouble

Procedure: Follow the rules for the game of Concentration (Appendix B). The object of the game is to get the most pairs of matching idiom/metaphor and literal-meaning cards.

BIBLIOGRAPHY

BROMLEY, K. "Teaching idioms," *Reading Teacher,* 38, December (1984), 272–76.

CONSIDINE, T. "Starting from scratch," *New York Times Magazine,* July 27, 1986, pp. 6–8.

FOERSTER, L. M. "Idiomagic!" *Elementary English,* 51, January (1974), 125–27.

LORENZ, E. K. "Excuse me, but your idiom is showing," *Reading Teacher,* 31, October (1977), 24–27.

PARISH, P. *Amelia Bedelia,* New York, Harper and Row, 1963.

READENCE, J. E., R. S. BALDWIN, AND M. H. HEAD. "Teaching young readers to interpret metaphors," *Reading Teacher,* 40, January (1987), 439–43.

READENCE, J. E., R. S. BALDWIN, AND P. J. RICKELMAN. "Instructional insights into metaphors and similes," *Journal of Reading,* 27, November (1983), 109–12.

chapter 12

UNDERSTANDING PRONOUN REFERENCE AND OTHER SUBSTITUTIONS

Definition: *Understanding that certain words or terms in one sentence refer to or replace certain words or terms in another sentence*

Examples: John ran home. *He* was late.
(pronoun reference)
He bought an apple. *The fruit* was red.
(substitution of a term)

RATIONALE

Writers often use words in one sentence to refer to words in another sentence; this is called *anaphora*. Anaphora helps to link sentences together and to provide variety. Readers, however, must understand these referents in order to understand the writer's message.

There are many types of anaphora, and they are probably not all equally difficult. The most common type of referent is the pronoun. This includes the personal pronouns—*I, me, we, us, he, him, she, her, it, you,* and *they;* demonstrative pronouns, such as *this, that, these,* and *those;* locative pronouns, such as *here* and *there.* Proverbs, such as *does, can, will,* and *have,* which can be substituted for verbs, are also common referents.

Anaphora also vary in terms of what is being replaced. Sometimes a noun is replaced, sometimes a verb, and sometimes a whole phrase or clause. Examples of these are provided in Table 12-1.

Finally, the referent sometimes comes before the term being replaced, as in the first of the following three examples. This structure is often more difficult for students than the more common order in which the referent comes after the term being replaced as in example 2. Also, one or more sentences sometimes come between the referent and the term being replaced, as in example 3. This can also be difficult, because students must remember from an earlier point in the text.

Example 1. She was really happy. Sally loved the snow.

Example 2. Sally was really happy. She loved the snow.

Example 3. Sally was really happy. The weatherman had not predicted snow, but here it was. It was white and soft and beautiful. She loved the snow.

When teaching anaphora, you may be tempted to

TABLE 12-1 Some Types of Anaphora

Item Being Replaced	Example
Noun	I liked the *apple*. *It* was green.
Verb	Jack *went* to the store. So *did* Sally.
Clause	*They all passed the test. This* pleased me.

use a lot of work sheets and isolated skill activities. Indeed, many of the ideas in this chapter are just that. Overuse of such activities, however, can teach students that reading is meaningless and boring. Whenever possible, use portions of real books and stories that they are reading for other purposes. Whenever you can, teach the skill in the context of real tasks. Students must be shown how the skill applies to their own independent use of comprehension strategies!

INFORMAL DIAGNOSIS

First of all, every reader can sometimes have trouble when referents are ambiguous. Here is an example. Who is "he"?

John told Michael that he needed a new car.

Thus, a mistaken anaphoric inference is not always a sign that remediation is needed. However, if you find that a student is not inferring referents regularly, some remediation is probably in order. *Do not use the isolated practice activities in this chapter unless you have reason to believe that the student is having trouble comprehending pronouns and other substitutions.*

GENERAL RECOMMENDATIONS

1. Remember that anaphora includes proverbs, locative pronouns, demonstrative pronouns, and substituting terms as well as personal pronouns.

2. Look out for ambiguous anaphora in reading assignments. Discuss these with the students.

3. Point out the use of anaphora in all of the content areas—not just on reading work sheets.

4. Collect examples of anaphora from your textbooks and use those for class discussion.

5. Tie anaphora activities back to real reading tasks by showing students how they can apply their understanding of anaphora in content-area texts and other school reading assignments.

6. Tie anaphora activities to writing tasks by showing the students how they can use different types of anaphora in their writing.

chapter 12.   UNDERSTANDING PRONOUN REFERENCE AND OTHER SUBSTITUTIONS
Activities

A.   INITIAL INSTRUCTION IN IDENTIFYING ANAPHORIC TERMS

1.   Tie It Together*   P I J H

Procedure: 1.   Construct pairs of sentences that illustrate a personal pronoun replacing a noun, the simplest type of pronominal anaphora. For example:

Jack went to the store.
He bought some candy.

2.   Set the purpose for the lesson (see Figure 12-1).

3.   Show on an overhead projection or chalkboard sentences or pairs of sentences such as the following:

    a.   Mary ate a cookie. *It* was good.
    b.   Robert was late. *He* missed the bus.
    c.   My sister fell down. *She* broke her leg.
    d.   Joe and Fred play soccer. *They* are on the soccer team.
    e.   "Miriam, will *you* come to my party?" said Alice.

4.   Demonstrate on the overhead or board the following marking procedure:

My sister fell down. *She* broke her leg.

5.   Provide supervised practice using selections they are reading.

6.   Provide practice using current content area textbooks.

7.   Reinforce the skill when students are reading orally or when you are reading to them.

Variations: 1.   (I J H) Use questions about pronoun referents in study guides for content-area material.

2.   (P I J H) Have students go on a "pronoun hunt" and find pronouns and referents in text material.

3.   (P I J H A) Have students find pronouns and referents in their own writing.

FIGURE 12-1   Explaining Anaphora

"Today you are going to learn a strategy that will help you comprehend what you read. Let me show you how it works. Look at this pair of sentences:

John ate the ice cream.
He got sick.

Who is the first sentence about? [John]
Who is the second sentence about? [John]
What word in the second sentence tells you that it is about John?" [he]
That's right, 'John' and 'he' refer to the same person. 'He' replaces 'John' in the second sentence. It *stands for* John. You could replace 'he' with 'John' and the sentence would mean the same thing. Try it. [Students read it.]

"Writers often use two different words that mean the same thing. If you are not aware that they are doing this, you can get confused when you are reading. Today we will practice figuring out what words such as 'he,' 'she,' 'they,' and others are replacing."

4.   (P I) Have students find pronoun referents in Mother Goose rhymes or other familiar material. For example:

Dr. Foster went to *Glo'ster*
In a shower of rain.
He stepped in a puddle, up to *his* middle,
And never went *there* again.

* Irwin, 1986.

B.   PRACTICE IN IDENTIFYING ANAPHORIC TERMS

☞   These practice activities are *not* real reading. Use *only* when students have problems in identifying anaphoric terms. Provide opportunities for application to real reading tasks.

1.   Gone But Not Forgotten   J H A

Procedure: 1.   Make a work sheet of paired sentences demonstrating the use of ellipsis as an anaphoric relationship. In ellipsis, the repeated term is omitted. For instance, in the following example *candy* is omitted from the second sentence:

He bought *candy*. He gave some to Susie.

Here are some other examples to use:

I *don't care* about him. Do you?
Three little *pigs* went to the market. Only two came home.
The entire *class* tried out for the football team. Only two made it.

My father is really *mad at me*. My mom, too.

The teacher said he was *sick and tired of all the tardiness*. So was the principal.

2. Have the students write the omitted words above the appropriate line.

3. Show them other examples in their reading materials.

Variation: Have students find these omissions in each other's writing. Stress that these procedures are natural and effective ways to write.

2. Make It Shorter*   PIJHA

Procedure: 1. Prepare a work sheet of pairs of sentences in which anaphoric substitution could be used to shorten *one* of the sentences. For example:

A. Lucy and Linus went to the store.
B. They went to the store to buy some candy.
(They went *there* to buy some candy.)
A. I hate spinach.
B. My brother hates spinach.
(My brother does, too.)
A. My mother always cries over sad movies.
B. My Aunt Wilma always cries over movies like that, too.
(My Aunt Wilma does, too.)

2. Have students complete the work sheet and discuss in class the types of substitution they used.

Variation: Give the students sentences containing anaphora and have them expand each sentence to its original two- or three-sentence form.

* Irwin, 1986.

3. Similar Stories*   IJHA

Procedure: 1. Prepare a work sheet of several pairs of stories. In each pair, one uses anaphora and one does not.

2. Students' task is to identify the words in the nonanaphora story that have referents in the anaphora story. (See Figure 12-2.)

* Baumann and Stevenson, 1986.

4. Question–Answer Sentences*   PIJHA

Procedure: 1. Prepare exercises that require students to answer questions about anaphoric relationships in sentences (see Figure 12-3).

2. Do similar questioning during reading sessions.

* Baumann and Stevenson, 1986.

FIGURE 12-2

Directions: Here are two stories that contain the same information. The story on the left has some underlined words. Look in the story on the right and find the word or words that mean the same as the underlined words. Circle these words and next to them write the number of the words that mean the same in the other story. The first one has been done for you.

Nora and Alice went to the beach.
   1
They both liked to swim and were
        2
very happy to be there. Alice was a
               3
very good swimmer and so was
              4
Nora. They swam for half an hour.
        5
After they finished, Nora said that
 6   7
she was hungry, so they ate a picnic
        8
lunch there.

Nora and Alice went to the beach.
        1
Nora and Alice both liked to swim and were very happy to be at the beach. Alice was a very good swimmer and Nora was a very good swimmer. Nora and Alice swam for half an hour. After Nora and Alice finished swimming, Nora said that Nora was hungry, so Nora and Alice ate a picnic lunch at the beach.

Based on Baumann and Stevenson, 1986, p. 112

5. Question–Answer Paragraphs*   I J H A

Procedure: 1. Prepare short paragraphs followed by questions focusing on their anaphoric relationships (see Figure 12-4).

2. Do similar questioning during reading sessions.

* Baumann and Stevenson, 1986.

FIGURE 12-3

Directions: Read the following sentences and answer the questions.

1. William made a beautiful box and gave *it* to his father.

    What does *it* refer to?
    _____

2. My mother baked chocolate chip cookies and gave me *some*.

    What does *some* refer to?
    _____

3. Did you finish your homework? I *did*.

    What does *did* refer to?
    _____

4. We've got five kittens. Would you like *one*?

    What does *one* refer to?
    _____

Based on Baumann and Stevenson, 1986, p. 114.

FIGURE 12-4

Directions: Read the following short paragraphs and answer the questions about them.

1. The president and her husband came to dinner last night. She wore a black satin suit, and he wore a navy blue one.

   Who wore the black satin suit? _____
   Who wore the blue suit? _____

2. My father has a very old 1960 Ford. It had been his family's car, and my grandfather gave it to him when he graduated from high school. Even then, the car was considered old.

   Who gave the writer's father the car? _____
   Who had first owned the car? _____
   When was the car considered to be "old"? _____

3. The whole class had a Read-In day last Tuesday. Each student chose an interesting book to read. Some chose mysteries and others chose biographies. Most of the students chose adventure stories. Only one student wanted to read science fiction.

   How many students were able to read a favorite book? _____
   What was the most popular type of book? _____
   What was the least popular type of book? _____
   What other types of books were chosen? _____

Based on Baumann and Stevenson, 1986, p. 114.

Variations:
1. Use a story as the basis of questions about anaphoric relationships.

2. Have students *replace* all the anaphoras in stories with their referents to see why authors use this strategy in order to avoid awkward prose.

C. PRACTICE USING ANAPHORIC TERMS AND ANTECEDENTS

☞ These practice activities are *not* real reading. Use *only* when students have problems in this area. Provide opportunities for application to real reading tasks.

1. Anaphora Substitution*   PIJHA

Procedure: Prepare a work sheet of sentences containing underlined words, which are to be replaced by anaphoric words. At the bottom of the work sheet, supply the words to be substituted (see Figure 12-5).

Variations:
1. The activity can be made more difficult by not supplying the anaphoric words.

2. Use a short story, underlining the parts to be replaced by anaphoric

FIGURE 12-5

Directions: "Each of the following sentences contains one or more under-lined words. Read the sentences. Then look at the row of words following the sentences. For each sentence, select a word from the row that means the same as the underlined part and write it on the line next to the sentence. The first one has been done for you." (Baumann and Stevenson, p. 112–113)

1. <u>Maria</u> is going to the movies.   1. she _____

2. I had a horrible dream about a monster. The <u>monster</u> was going to eat me.   2. _____

3. My brother is going to the circus. I am going <u>to the circus</u>, too.   3. _____

4. <u>My brother</u> Jack broke the TV.   4. _____

5. The cat chased the mouse and the dog <u>chased the mouse</u>.   5. _____

6. My mother hates spiders. She is afraid of <u>spiders</u>.   6. _____

she	he	them	there	it	did	too

Based on Baumann and Stevenson, 1986, p. 112–13.

words and supplying blanks above the words for the students to write the answers. For example:

1. _____

Bill and Betty are going on a picnic. <u>Bill and Betty</u> went to the beach. When

2. _____

they got <u>to the beach</u> it was raining.

* Baumann and Stevenson, 1986.

2. Anaphora Bingo*   **P I**

Materials: Anaphora Bingo cards, containing anaphoric words (see Figure 12-6) flash cards containing words in which an antecedent is identified markers to cover Bingo cards

FIGURE 12-6   Anaphora Bingo Card

BINGO

HE	MINE	IT	OUR	HER
THAT	ITS	THEN	DID TOO	BOTH
THEM	MY	FREE	YOU	HERE
WE	I	MY	ALL	YOUR
NONE	SOME	SHE	THEY	THEIR

Based on Baumann and Stevenson, 1986, p. 118.

Procedures: 1.   Caller selects flash card randomly from pack and reads it, saying which word or group of words is the antecedent to be replaced.

2.   Players who have an anaphoric word corresponding to the antecedent cover that word on their Bingo card.

3.   The first person with a straight line of five covered terms wins.

* Baumann and Stevenson, 1986.

BIBLIOGRAPHY

BAUMANN, J. F. AND J. A. STEVENSON. "Teaching students to comprehend anaphoric relations," in *Understanding and Teaching Cohesion Comprehension,* ed. J. W. Irwin. Newark, Del.: International Reading Association, 1986, 95–123.

IRWIN, J. W. *Teaching Reading Comprehension Processes.* Englewood Cliffs, N.J.: Prentice-Hall, 1986.

chapter 13

CONNECTING SENTENCES

Definition: *Understanding the connective concepts that tie sentences and clauses together*

RATIONALE

Understanding how clauses and sentences connect to each other is an essential part of the comprehension process. Authors often use connective words, or conjunctions, to express these connections. For instance, in example 1 the author has used the word *because* to connect the clauses of a sentence in a causal relationship. In example 2 the author has used the word *after* to connect the clauses in a time-sequence relationship.

1. She stopped because she was tired.
2. After she stopped, she decided to go home.

Table 13-1 gives some examples of connective concepts and the words authors use to express these concepts. Study this table.

Authors sometimes expect readers to infer the concepts that connect sentences and clauses. In such cases, the concepts are stated only implicitly. The sentences in example 3 are connected in an implicit causal relationship. The sentences in example 4 are con-

nected in an implicit time-sequence relationship. Many connectives are implied in this manner. In fact, research indicates that there are several implicit connectives in every 500 words in school textbooks, regardless of grade level.

3. It rained for three days. The river flooded.
4. He went to school. He went to the store.

Example 3 shows how prior knowledge can enhance a student's ability to infer an implicit connective concept. If a student understands the relationship between rain and flooding, this inference will be much easier. Numerous such examples can be found in content-area textbooks, whose authors often assume that the students have the prior knowledge required to make such inferences.

This skill also provides a good example of the necessity of reading actively. Students who approach reading tasks passively and students who do not expect the text to make sense will be less likely to make the active inferences necessary to recognize connec-

TABLE 13-1 Some Common Types of Connective Concepts

Types	Cues Used	Example
Conjunction	and in addition to also along with	Jack went to the store. Sally went <u>also</u>.
Disjunction	or <u>either</u> . . . <u>or</u> . . .	<u>Either</u> Jack went to the store, <u>or</u> he went home.
Causality	because so consequently	Jack went home <u>because</u> he was sick.
Purpose	in order to for the purpose of so that	Jack went home <u>in order to</u> get his money.
Concession	but although however yet	Jack left for home, <u>but</u> he hasn't gotten there yet.

Contrast	in contrast
	similarly
	(also comparative and
	    superlative forms of
	    adjectives)
		Jack was very sick. <u>In contrast</u>, I feel better!

Condition	If . . . then . . . unless except	<u>If</u> Jack is sick, <u>then</u> he can't play ball.
Time	before always after while when from now on	<u>Before</u> Jack got sick, he went to the store.
Location	there where	Jack is at home, <u>where</u> he will be able to rest.
Manner	in a similar manner like as	Jack was blue and feverish, <u>as</u> Sally was yesterday.

Source: The list of connectives is derived from a taxonomy presented by A. Turner, and E. Greene, *The Construction and use of a Propositional Text Base,* Technical Report no. 63, Institute for the Study of Intellectual Behavior, University of Colorado Boulder, 1977. The table is reprinted with permission from Irwin, J. W. Irwin, 1986, p. 34.

tive concepts, even though such inferences are clearly intended by the author.

You should probably practice locating explicit and implicit connectives in school materials before extensively teaching this skill. Try your hand at the following passage. Underline the explicit connectives and place a caret (∧) where you detect implicit ones. The answers are provided in Figure 13-1.

> People were building homes and stores. They bought more and more wood. The sawmills were very busy. But soon there was no wood left to cut down. One after another, the sawmills closed. Workers had to find something else to do. They began to plant wheat so they could sell it. Thus, farming became important after all the trees had been cut down. Now, more people were farmers than builders.

Source: E. A. Anderson, *Communities and Their Needs* (Morristown, N.J.: Silver Burdett, 1972), p. 62. Reprinted by permission.

INFORMAL DIAGNOSIS

Of course, you may assess your students' abilities simply by asking comprehension questions about explicit and implicit connectives that you see in the reading assignments. Explicit connectives should be easier for students because understanding them does not require active inference and prior knowledge. If students have difficulty with an implicit connective inference, you should try to assess whether the problem is a lack of prior knowledge or a lack of an active inference strategy. Only then can you remediate appropriately.

GENERAL TEACHING SUGGESTIONS

1. You may find that one type of connective causes more trouble than another. Research indicates,

for instance, that causal connectives are more difficult than time-sequence ones.

2.   Some connective words can express two things. For instance, *so* can express cause or purpose: "He got chilled, so he got sick" versus "He rested so he could play his best."

3.   Using the activities related to building prior knowledge (Chapter 7) will also help students to make connective inferences. These activities might be especially appropriate for any students who find the activities in this chapter too difficult.

4.   Discussions of implicit connectives are best interwoven informally into other lessons when the need arises.

5.   Be sure to model connective inference for students before asking them to perform this skill for you.

6.   If you choose to use the games and isolated work-sheet activities provided in this chapter, remem-

ber that you have not taught *reading* until the strategy of connecting sentences is applied to *real reading tasks*.

FIGURE 13-1   Answers to Sample Passage

People were building homes and stores. ∧ They bought more and more wood. ∧ The sawmills were very busy. But soon there was no wood left to cut down. ∧ One after another, the sawmills closed. ∧ Workers had to find something else to do. ∧ They began to plant wheat so they could sell it. Thus, farming became important after all the trees had been cut down. Now, more people were farmers than builders.

Source: E. A. Anderson, *Communities and Their Needs* (Morristown, N.J.: Silver Burdett, 1972), p. 62. Reprinted by permission.

chapter 13. CONNECTING SENTENCES
Activities

A.   INTERPRETING EXPLICIT AND IMPLICIT CONNECTIVES

1.   Signal Search*   **P I J H A**

Procedure: 1.   Explain to students that there are certain words that are "signals" for showing how two sentences, or parts of a sentence, are related to each other (see Table 13-2).

2.   Use relevant examples to demonstrate the concept, such as "I ate too much pizza, *so* I got sick."

3.   Using sentences from current textbook assignments, demonstrate different types of connective relationships. Have students tell you which relationship is being indicated by a signal.

4.   Have students practice on selected current textbook material. Choose passages for them to work on that contain explicit connectives, and indicate the number of signals they should find. For example, ask them to read page 12, paragraphs 1 and 2, find the four signals there, and be prepared to discuss the relationships these words indicate.

Variations: 1.   If the class is engaged in reading aloud either a story or a textbook, take the opportunity to point out connectives and ask how they function in sentences.

TABLE 13-2 Signal Words

Connective	Pattern
after, then, finally, before, even earlier, initially, preceding, following	Chronological
because, hence, consequently, on that account, therefore, thus	Cause–Effect
furthermore, in addition, also, another, besides, first, second, third, etc.	List
to the north (east, west, etc.), inland, coastal, nearby, close to, beside, next to	Spatial
however, on the contrary, the other, in contrast, a different, nevertheless	Compare/Contrast

2.   Have students bring in newspaper articles with signals underlined. Make a bulletin board display.

* Adapted from Pulver, 1986.

2.   Where Is It?*   P I J H

Procedure: 1.   Explain to students that often connective relationships are not stated directly in prose, and that it is up to the reader to figure out which type of connective relationship is being used (see Figure 13-2).

2.   Give students examples from their daily lives or from current topics and help them find the connectives.

3.   Point out the three rules for finding implicit connectives:

a.   Look at where sentences come together to see how they are related.
b.   Try to use a connective word between sentences and see if the resulting sentence makes sense.
c.   Use the information we already have in our heads in figuring out the relationship.

4.   Give students sample passages and have them find the implicit connectives (see Figure 13-1 for an example).

5.   Have students find implicit connectives in their textbook assignments.

6.   Reinforce the skills often, when students are reading textbook assignments or the newspaper.

* Adapted from Pulver, 1986.

FIGURE 13-2   Discussion of Implicit Connectives

Teacher:	For example, if I were to read, ''The Knicks were a very popular basketball team. All of their games were sold out,'' what would be the connection between the two sentences?
Student:	Everyone wanted to go to their games because they liked them, so you couldn't get tickets.
Teacher:	Right. They were popular, *so* all of their games were sold out. We can see that one sentence is the cause of the other even though it isn't directly stated. *We* have to supply the connection in our heads. If we wanted to insert a connecting word, what would it be?
Student:	Probably ''so.''
Teacher:	Right. (Teacher discusses a few more examples.) Textbooks do that a lot. Let's look at an example and see if we can find out where there *should* have been a connective.

B. SUPPLYING CONNECTIVES

☞ These practice activities are not real reading. Use them sparingly, for students who are having problems.

1. Connective Cloze   P I

Procedure: 1. Cut out the connectives from an old basal story.

2. Have the students supply the connectives.

3. Students compare results with the original story and discuss reasons for choices.

2. Crazy Connections   P I J H A

Procedure: Have students complete sentences by giving whimsical or silly answers after the supplied connective, or provide silly sentences for them to complete. For example:

1. The witch likes to have people come for dinner because . . . they taste good.
2. Hertz Rent-A-Wagon was created because . . . the pioneers were moving their families west.
3. John is five feet three inches tall so . . . he is playing center on a professional basketball team.
4. My aunt didn't go to the party because . . . she is allergic to people.
5. Our school had a holiday because . . . the principal lost the key.

3. Cause–and–Effect Magic Squares*   I J H A

Procedure: 1. Be sure students are familiar with the magic square problem:

a. "In a magic square, the sum of the numbers is the same in any row or column. That sum is the magic number."

b. "The first task is to find the magic number so that you can use it as a basis for filling in the other columns."

2. Students select from column A in Figure 13-3 the *causes* that led to the *effects* in column B. In this example the causes and effects refer to a specific reading assignment.

3. Students put the number of each cause in the corresponding cell of the magic square answer box. Then they determine the magic number.

4. At the bottom of Figure 13-3 are some sample number combinations. Many more can be generated simply by rearranging rows or columns.

* Vacca, 1975.

FIGURE 13-3 Cause–and–Effect Magic Squares

COLUMN A *CAUSES*	COLUMN B *EFFECTS*
____ 1. Jenny took an overdose of pills. (p. 9)	a. The unemployment rate for the Blackfeet is about 50%.
____ 2. The buffalo herds were destroyed and hunger threatened. (p. 10)	b. The first victim of this life is pride.
____ 3. Indians remained untrained for skilled jobs. (p. 10)	c. Blackfeet became dependent on the help of whites for survival.
____ 4. The temperature reaches 50 below zero. (p. 10)	d. Blackfeet turn to liquor.
____ 5. There are terrible living conditions. (p. 10)	e. The Indians are robbed of their self-confidence.
____ 6. Pride and hope vanish from the Blackfeet. (p. 11)	f. They are always down-graded.
____ 7. Because we're Indians. (p. 12)	g. Eighty percent of the Blackfeet must have government help.
____ 8. The old world of the Indians is crumbling and the new world of the white rejects them. (p. 13)	h. Hope is a word that has little meaning.
____ 9. The attitude of the Bureau of Indian Affairs. (p. 13)	i. She killed herself.

The magic number is ____.

a	b	c
d	e	f
g	h	i

MAGIC NUMBER COMBINATIONS

7	3	5
2	4	9
6	8	1

0*   15**

10	8	6
2	9	13
12	7	5

*4   24**

7	11	8
10	12	4
9	3	14

5*   26**

9	2	7
4	6	8
5	10	3

18*   18**

9	7	5
1	8	12
11	6	4

3*   21**

** magic number   * foils needed in answer column

Adapted from Vacca, 1975, p. 589. Reprinted with permission of Richard T. Vacca and the International Reading Association.

Provide a Link*   **P I J**

Procedure: 1. Prepare sentences with missing connectives (see Figure 13-4 for examples).

2. Give students 3-by-5 cards on which connective words have been written.

3. Present sentences one at a time on the overhead projector. Students determine which connective would make the most sense and hold up the appropriate card.

4. Discussion can develop about the reasons for the use of different connectives.

FIGURE 13-4

1. I'm going to the football game on Saturday _____ I hope the weather is good.
2. My mother ran over my brother's bike _____ he left it in the driveway.
3. My dog was panting in the heat _____ I gave her some water.
4. I really love to eat chocolate chip cookies _____ my mother bakes some every week.
5. Jackie gained seven pounds _____ she ate ice cream for lunch every day this month.

Variations:
1. Work sheets in this format can be used.

2. Use sentences from current textbooks in creating the lesson (see Figure 13-5 for examples).

3. Have students create work sheets by finding sentences from their text-book reading assignments.

4. Have students supply connectives for passages of textbook material.

5. Provide sentences for students to combine. Have them randomly draw cards with connectives on them. They must use the connective drawn to combine two of their sentences. Discuss the results.

* Adapted from Pulver, 1986.

5. Connective Rummy   **P I**

Materials: 3 × 5 cards, each with a connective written on it slips of paper with clauses written on them

Procedure:
1. Provide each student with ten clauses, randomly selected. These should be placed face down on the student's desk.

2. Provide each student with five connective cards, also randomly selected and also placed face down on desks.

3. When you give a signal, students turn over their clauses and connectives and create *sensible* sentences. The first person to create five sentences wins.

FIGURE 13-5

1. The settlers wanted to take land from the Indians _____ it was fertile.
2. General Gage closed the port of Boston _____ the colonists had dumped boxes of tea into the harbor.
3. Many farmers lost their farms _____ they were not able to pay back money loaned to them by the banks.
4. Revival meetings made frontier life better _____ the revival ministers preached against fighting, drinking, and swearing.
5. California had good soil, fine seaports, and rich gold fields _____ thousands of Americans went there to live.

Variations:

1. Students work in teams.

2. Students work individually and try to better their own records.

3. Use clauses from a content-area textbook in order to review material.

4. Use this procedure in a noncompetitive situation to reinforce connective use.

6. Match a Clause*   IJ

Procedure:

1. Provide students with sets of clauses written on pieces of paper (see Figure 13-6 for examples). One of each set of clauses should contain an explicit connective.

2. Instruct the students to match the clauses to make complete sentences that make sense.

3. Ask the students to explain the relationships between the clauses.

Variations:

1. Have the students make up clauses and exchange them.

2. Crazy Clauses—present students with silly clause combinations. For example:

My brother is a werewolf	so we have to lock him up when there is a full moon.
My uncle is a cannibal	so we can't have the class party at his house.

* Adapted from Pulver, 1986.

7. Order, Please!   PI

Materials:

ten cards, each with one sentence on it, which combine to form a story (see Figure 13-7) the connectives are deleted; a set of cards is needed for each student or group of students; cards should be shuffled

connective cards, one set for each student or group of students

FIGURE 13-6

1. I can't find my house key	because he was afraid of mice.
2. My sister needs braces	so he has to wear a cast.
3. John broke his leg playing basketball	so I will have to wait outside until my mother comes home.
4. Ramon likes to read about Spanish history	so the manager had to work at the checkout counter.
5. The man screeched when the mouse ran across the room	because there was a traffic jam.
6. The bus was late	so he is going to write a paper about Spain for social studies.
7. The supermarket was busy	because her teeth are crooked.

FIGURE 13-7 A Ten–Sentence Story (Connective Cards Consist of the Words in Parentheses)

---

1. (Once upon a time) There was a little boy who lived with his father in a little house in a field near a forest.
2. In this forest lived a big gray MORGENWURP beast.
3. (So, As a result) The little boy's father made him promise that he would never, ever go into the forest alone.
4. (Then) One day the father had to go into town.
5. (Once again, Therefore, So, And) He reminded his son of his promise never to go into the woods alone.
6. (However, But) As soon as his father left, the little boy went across the field and into the woods.
7. (Although, Even though) He was scared, he wanted to get some flowers for his father.
8. (Before) He finished gathering flowers, the MORGENWURP beast leaped out of the bushes and growled at him.
9. (When, As soon as) The boy saw the MORGENWURP, he ran out of the woods, crossed the field, and got safely back home.
10. (So, Therefore, As a result) The little boy never, ever went into the woods alone again.

Procedure: 1. Each group of students is given a set of sentence cards and a set of connective cards.

2. Groups must assemble the cards into the proper order to make a story. Students must use connective cards to make the story coherent by connecting the sentences.

3. When groups are finished, a recorder from each group reads its story to the class.

4. Lead a discussion on the different ways groups put the sentences together.

BIBLIOGRAPHY

IRWIN, J. W. *Teaching Reading Comprehension Processes.* Englewood Cliffs, N.J.: Prentice-Hall, 1986.

PULVER, C. J. "Teaching Students to Understand Explicit and Implicit Connectives," in *Understanding and Teaching Cohesion Comprehension,* ed. J. W. Irwin. Newark, Del.: International Reading Association, 1986, 69–82.

VACCA, R. T. "Reading reinforcement through Magic Squares," *Journal of Reading,* 18, May (1975), 587–89.

INFERRING ASSUMED INFORMATION

Definition: *Inferring basic facts necessary for a coherent interpretation of the author's message*

RATIONALE

It is impossible for writers to be completely explicit when they write. There are many facts they need to assume that the reader will know and infer in order to make the text hang together. For instance, what fact must be inferred to connect the sentences in example 1?

1. She stirred her coffee.
   The spoon was silver.

Yes, the writer is assuming the reader knows that coffee is stirred with a spoon. Otherwise, there would be no way for the reader to see a connection between the two sentences. Good readers are constantly inferring such information, which is necessary if they are to make a coherent whole out of the text. In fact, if you were to ask them if this information had been stated directly, they would probably assume that it had been.

Of course, most people reading example 1 would know that the coffee was stirred with a spoon. But, it is possible to imagine a child from an alternative culture who would not know. Prior knowledge is critical in making these necessary inferences. So is an active approach toward getting meaning out of the text.

You may wish to distinguish between these necessary text-connecting inferences and those that go completely beyond the text (discussed in Chapters 18–22). The former are required for making sense of the text. They connect one sentence to another. They logically relate events. They are intended by the author. There is often only one appropriate inference, as illustrated in examples 2–4.

2. She dropped the china plate.
   Her mother was afraid of the broken glass.
   (Assumed inference: The plate broke.)
3. The rain turned to ice on the street.
   She decided to wear a coat.
   (Assumed inference: It was cold outside.)
4. The Sioux had little to eat that winter.
   All the buffalo had been killed.
   (Assumed inference: The Sioux usually ate buffalo.)

INFORMAL DIAGNOSIS

You can get much information about your students' ability to make these necessary text-connecting inferences of assumed information just by asking questions. You will need to be careful, however, to distinguish between mistakes that reflect a lack of prior knowledge and mistakes that reflect the lack of an active inferencing strategy. Also, you may wish to assess the extent to which students are refraining from active inference because they think that you *want* them to be very literal and passive. For instance, poor readers tend to be more literal in a testing situation than in an informal one. Try asking them questions in both situations. Make it clear that they are allowed to think for themselves.

GENERAL TEACHING RECOMMENDATIONS

1. Introduce inferring by modeling your own inference process and by explaining the importance of making inferences. Explain that that is what the author intended! An example is provided in Figure 14-1 (activity A.1).

2. Younger children may need more help when the two critical sentences are not adjacent. Show them which sentences you want them to connect.

3. Be sure to activate prior knowledge as the first step in promoting inference of assumed information.

4. Be sure to add inferential questions to your usual questioning menu. Research indicates that texts and teachers usually ask too few of these. This will take a little extra planning at first, but after you have developed such questions your teaching will be more effective forever!

5. You should ask your poor readers as many inferential questions as you ask your good readers. The poor readers may need them even more than the good readers because they need more encouragement to be active meaning seekers.

6. Remember that students who make appropriate inferences in stories may not do so in content-area materials. The types of inferences required vary with the type of material, and separate instruction for or practice with each type of writing would be very useful.

FIGURE 14-1 What a Teacher Might Say to Introduce Inference

"Do you know what it means to *infer* something? [Students respond.] That's right—inferencing is a sort of detective process that readers perform; they find *clues* in their reading material and combine these with information that they have in their heads. When they put these two ingredients together, they figure out what the author has *implied,* but not really said.

Implied information is information that is not really stated directly, but that most people would logically assume. For example, suppose I read, 'The television news commentator was worried that her fondness for hot fudge sundaes and chocolate chip cookies would ruin her career. She could hardly get into her expensive wardrobe. She decided to go on a diet.'

The question I ask myself is 'Why would a fondness for ice cream and cookies ruin a career?'

Well, I know myself from watching TV that news commentators are usually slim and well dressed. I also know that people really like television personalities to be slim, well dressed, and attractive. From my *own* experience I also know that if you eat ice cream and cookies you'll put on weight. When I look in the text, I find that there's information there that tells me she has gained weight—"she could hardly get into her expensive wardrobe." It also says that she decided to go on a diet, which people do to lose weight. Knowing that television personalities rely on their popularity with the public to keep ratings up, and knowing that the public would prefer a slim, attractive news commentator, I decide that she felt her career would be damaged if she got fat, so she went on a diet.

What did I do?

I put together my ideas and experiences with what was written in the text—and I made an inference. In other words, I created a new idea of my own."

chapter 14.   INFERRING ASSUMED INFORMATION
Activities

A.   GENERAL INFERENCE AWARENESS

1.   Inference Awareness*   **P I J H A**

Procedure: 1.   To prepare to teach inferencing skills, think about your own thinking strategies when making inferences.

   2.   Model the steps you use when making inferences (see Figure 14-1).

   3.   Model the process several more times, using different examples from different disciplines. Make two columns on the board—one for text-explicit information, one for required inferences.

   4.   Have students read a selected paragraph and make two columns—one for evidence and information from the text, one for their own knowledge and inferences.

   5.   Ask inferential questions and have students fill in their inference columns.

   6.   Discuss which information in the text was important, and which material "in their heads" was used to make the appropriate inferences.

   7.   Reinforce the skill with selected textbook paragraphs in class assignments.

* Adapted from Gordon, 1985.

2.   Author's Assumptions   **P I J H A**

Procedure: 1.   Discuss with students the fact that authors cannot write down everything their readers need to know in order to understand their prose. They assume that their readers will supply the unstated knowledge, that they will infer certain facts. For example, the author of "After looking outside, I decided to take my umbrella to school" assumes the reader will infer that it is (or is going to) rain. The reader is expected to supply information that the author has not stated in the text. Similarly, "He had little time for lunch. He went to McDonalds" might have little meaning to a reader who didn't know what McDonald's was.

FIGURE 14-2 Practice Sheet for Inferencing

	ASSUMED INFORMATION
1. He fought in Vietnam. The wound continually bothered him.	He was wounded in Vietnam.
2. She dropped the plate. The pieces scattered.	
3. My brother had the measles. We soon had a houseful of patients.	
4. After hearing the weather forecast, I decided to wear my boots.	
5. The line in front of the movie theater was long.	

2. Provide examples of everyday materials, such as advertisements, that require the reader to make assumptions. Have the students supply the assumptions.

3. Have students work on a practice sheet of sentences that require inferencing (see Figure 14-2).

4. Use textbook assignments to practice and reinforce this skill. Remind students that they will have to use their prior knowledge to fully understand what the author is saying.

3. **Inference Partners*** I J

Procedure: 1. Use short articles of four to eight paragraphs containing seven to ten inference questions or statements that can be verified with information found in the article. If you do not have time to create your own materials, you can find commercial materials for this exercise, such as the "Find the Evidence" activities in the Reading–Thinking Skills series put out by Continental Press but it is better to find material on a topic about which students have expressed interest.

2. Conduct prereading activities and have the students read the lesson.

3. Instruct the students to choose partners.

4. Both partners must discuss the answers to the inference questions or statements and must come to an agreement about the answers. Only one set of answers, signed by both students, is required from each team.

5. Each pair decides which of the partners will write the answers. If you wish, the person who writes the answers can put an asterisk beside his or her name and receive bonus points.

6. During the discussion, move around the room, monitoring the teams and giving needed hints where appropriate.

7. Be prepared for classroom noise, because the students will be actively discussing the material.

* Sawkin, 1984.

B. INFERENCE OF CHARACTER, PLOT, AND SETTING IN STORIES

1. Character Clues   PIJHA

Procedure: 1. Students divide a piece of paper in half vertically. In the left-hand column they list ten things that a story character did. On the right-hand side they list *why* the character did each act.

2. At the bottom of the paper, students write what these clues tell them about the character.

3. Class discussion focuses on the reasons the students inferred for the character's actions, and the resulting conclusions about the character.

2. Point of View   PIJHA

Procedure: 1. Hand out to students one of two versions of an unfinished story. Half of the stories should have a male hero, the other half a female hero. Do not advise the students of this.

2. Students read their story and write a conclusion.

3. Lead a discussion of the story and the endings, comparing the different endings on the basis of the sex of the main character.

4. Make a list on the board of the different assumptions made by the readers on the basis of the sex of the main character. List also the different types of endings.

5. Discuss the importance of making inferences in reading.

3. Where Are We?   PI

Procedure: 1. Demonstrate to students the assumptions we often make when reading about where an event took place. For example, "He dribbled the ball along the floor, his back glistening with sweat as he drove towards the basket" causes you to assume that a gym is the location. Similarly, "The smell of medicine filled the air as she walked into the ward" leads the reader to picture a hospital room.

2. Have students work on practice sentences (see Figure 14-3).

FIGURE 14-3   Practice Sentences for Inferring Location

Directions: Fill in the location.

1. She looked up, her breathing apparatus heavy on her back, and watched the shark slowly swim by. _____
2. The desks were in order, the pencils sharpened, the chalkboard ready for another year. _____
3. The fumes of the trains, the stale air of the tunnel, and the rushing crowds gave her a headache. _____
4. As he glanced at the valley below, fear gripped him and he clung more closely to the ledge. _____
5. It was ten o'clock. The stores were closing, so there was a crowd as the people began to walk outside to their parked cars. _____

FIGURE 14-4   What's Next?

Directions: Write down what is going to happen next.

1. After eating breakfast, Joanne picked up her books, grabbed her lunch, and went to wait at the corner. _____
2. John looked out the window, put on his coat, picked up the snow shovel, and went outside. _____
3. After glancing at her watch, Joan picked up her pocketbook and ran out the door. _____
4. My mother baked a cake for us today. She wasn't there when we got home from school. _____
5. We returned home after school, hungry from a long day's work. _____

---

3.   Use textbook and story sentences for further practice.

4.   Have students construct or find sentences that require the reader to make assumptions about location. Make up practice sheets of their sentences.

5.   Make a bulletin board display of these "Where Are We?" sentences.

6.   To reinforce the skill, ask similar inference questions when reading to or with the class.

Variation: Use a similar procedure for "What Time Is It?" "What's the Weather Like?" "When Is It?" (what season, century, etc.), and "What Happened?"

4.   What's Next?   P I J

Procedure: 1.   Provide students with sample sentences and have them supply what is going to happen next (see Figure 14-4).

2.   Have them make up similar items for each other.

☞   This is a demonstration activity. Be sure to provide opportunities for application to meaningful reading tasks.

5.   Comic Strip Connections   P I J

Procedure: 1.   Give students copies of comic strips with the frames numbered.

2.   Have students supply what happened between selected frames.

3.   Discuss answers in class.

☞   This is a demonstration activity. Be sure to provide opportunities for application to meaningful reading tasks.

BIBLIOGRAPHY

GORDON, C. J. "Modeling inference awareness across the curriculum," *Journal of Reading,* 28, February (1985), 444–47.

SAWKIN, E. M. "Inferential reading partners," *Reading Teacher,* 38, December (1984), 359.

FINDING THE MAIN IDEA

Definition: *Finding the general idea that summarizes a paragraph*

RATIONALE

Because it is impossible to remember every detail, good readers are constantly extracting general ideas from the information they are reading. Finding the most important general point of each paragraph is usually called finding the main idea of that paragraph. It can also be called summarizing at the paragraph level.

We often ask teachers why so much emphasis is placed on finding the main idea, and are continually surprised by how many do not know. The real reason is *recall*. There is a limit to how many unrelated details we can remember. If, however, these details are connected to central ideas, we can remember many more of them. That is one of the reasons that students who can find the main idea are also the ones who do well on tests of recall.

Researchers and linguists have defined four processes that help readers find general ideas. These are also the processes readers use to find the main point of a paragraph. Study this list. The processes are actually pretty obvious when you think about them.

superordination: combining specific terms into general ones
deletion: eliminating unimportant information
selection: choosing general statements to retain
invention: creating a general topic statement

Deletion is probably the easiest of these processes, and invention is probably the hardest. Research indicates that even high school and college students have some trouble with invention, and sometimes with the other processes as well. Thus, the activities in this chapter focus on each of these four processes.

Baumann (1982) has suggested that there is hierarchy of skills related to finding the main idea (see Table 15-1). The first skill involves categorizing words (what we called superordination in the list just presented). The first six activities in this chapter deal with this skill. We suggest using these games only if you find that your students are having difficulty in this area.

The next skill is selecting the main idea of a sen-

TABLE 15-1 Content of Main Idea Instruction

Lesson Number and Title	Description
1. Main Ideas in Lists of Words	Students are taught how to analyze a list of related words and determine the main idea. For example, *shirt, pants, dress, hat,* and *shoes = clothing.*
2. Main Ideas in Sentences	Students are taught how to analyze a sentence and determine its topic and what is said about the topic, which collectively describe the main idea. For example, in the sentence ''Susan, the girl who lives down the street in the blue house, goes to Girl Scouts every Wednesday afternoon, the topic is *Susan,* what is said about the topic is *goes to Girl Scouts,* and the main idea is *Susan goes to Girl Scouts.*
3. Topics and Explicit Main Ideas in Paragraphs	Students are taught to generalize the skill of determining topics and what is said about them to paragraphs. After such a main idea is determined students learn to look for a sentence that states the main idea (topic sentence).
4. Explicit Main Ideas and Supporting Details	Students review finding explicit main ideas and are then taught to identify details that support main ideas.
5. Topics and Implicit Main Ideas in Paragraphs	Students are taught to identify implicit main ideas by following the procedure learned in lesson 3—determining the topic and what is said about it. Students are then taught to compose a main idea when they are unable to find a topic sentence in a paragraph.
6. Implicit Main Ideas and Supporting Details	Modeled after lesson 4, this lesson teaches students to associate details with inferred main ideas.
7. Topics and Explicit Main Ideas in Passages	Students are taught to identify the topic of a passage and what is said about the topic (i.e., the content of the paragraphs in the passage), and then identify the main idea (theme statement) for the entire passage.
8. Topics and Implicit Main Ideas in Passages	Students are taught to infer main ideas for passages lacking a theme statement. This lesson is modeled after lesson 5.

Source: Baumann, 1982. Reprinted with permission.

tence. This skill is covered in Chapter 10, so it is not repeated here. Though deletion is not included in Baumann's chart, we suggest that it should also probably be taught early in main-idea instruction. Accordingly, activities B.1 and B.2 deal with deleting unimportant information.

The next process is choosing explicit main ideas—selection—and the activities in section C of this chapter are designed to teach this. The most difficult task covered in this chapter (section D) is invention—finding the main idea when it is not directly stated. (Note that for Baumann the most difficult task is to perform superordination, deletion, invention, and selection on an entire passage. This will be covered in the following chapter on summarizing.)

INFORMAL DIAGNOSIS

You should probably try to diagnose student abilities in terms of the continuum of skills identified by Baumann (Table 15-1), rather than in terms of one process. First, ask the students to identify categories of words. Then ask them to pick the important words from a sentence. Then try to provide tasks involving selecting topic sentences from varying places in a paragraph. Finally, provide tasks in which students must supply their own topic sentences or titles.

Talk to the students while they are working on these tasks in order to find out what processes they are using. First, see if they can delete unimportant information. Then discuss their criteria for superordination, deletion, selection, and invention. Use materials at a variety of levels, with a variety of organizational patterns, and on a variety of topics. Don't generalize from just one paragraph!

GENERAL TEACHING SUGGESTIONS

1. Teach the process of finding the main idea in the context of reading assignments in which this skill would be useful.

2. Show students why finding the main idea is important by giving them fifteen unrelated words to recall. Then give them fifteen words that fall into five categories. Let them see how many more they can recall. Do the same thing with reading material that has been organized around main ideas and reading material that has not.

3. Model the thinking processes you yourself use when you are looking for the main idea of a paragraph.

4. Teach students to look for patterns in the placement of topic sentences.

5. Stress main ideas in your tests and class discussions.

6. At first, you may need to provide the main ideas for students who cannot find them. But after seeing your main ideas for a while, they may get the hang of it!

chapter 15.   FINDING THE MAIN IDEA
Activities

A.	CATEGORIZING WORDS: SUPERORDINATION	
	1. Condense a List	P I
	2. Go Fish a Category	I J
	3. Five Up	P I J
	4. Which List?	P I
	5. Category Game	P I
	6. List, Group, Label	P I J
B.	DELETING UNIMPORTANT INFORMATION	
	1. Trivia Chase	I J H A
	2. Color Me Shorter	P I
C.	SELECTING THE MAIN IDEA	
	1. Topic Sentence Patterns	I J H A
	2. Helping Hands	P I
	3. Rank the Sentences	I J H
	4. Paragraph Sense	J H A
	5. Main-Idea Detection Strategy	J H A
D.	INVENTING THE MAIN IDEA	
	1. Main-Idea Wheel	I J
	2. Main-Idea Pix	I J H A
	3. Picture It	P I

A.   CATEGORIZING WORDS: SUPERORDINATION*

☞   * Categorizing words is not reading. However, many have found that it is a useful introduction to finding the main idea. Thus, we have included it here as an introduction to the more meaningful main-idea activities. Be selective in your use of the activities in this section.

1.   Condense a List   P I

Procedure: 1.   Prepare paragraphs containing lists for students to condense (see Figure 15-1).

FIGURE 15-1   Condensing Lists (Prepared Paragraph)

> *Directions:*   Condense the lists in this paragraph into categories.
> *Hint:*   You should find five categories.
>
>   My big brother likes to eat *Big Macs, french fries, pizzas, cheeseburgers, and Kentucky Fried Chicken.* My sister, who is always on a diet, eats *lettuce, tomatoes, carrots, peppers, celery, and alfalfa sprouts.* My little brother loves to eat *cookies, candy, ice cream, cake,* and anything else that will give him cavities and make him fat. I like to eat *steak, roasts, chops, and hamburger* because I run the *100 and the 220,* do the *high jump,* and am on the *relay squad.*
>
> *Answers:*   fast food, salad vegetables, sweets, meat, track sports

FIGURE 15-2   Condensing Lists (Textbook Selection)

> The South has long been famous for its cooking. *Candied yams, watermelon pickles, shrimp pie, sweet potato pudding, key lime pie, Lady Baltimore cake, Tennessee jam cake, pecan pie, and Louisiana asparagus shortcake* all originated in the South. In addition, other southern cooking often makes generous use of *butter, milk, and cream.* The dairy cow has been important in the South since its first settlers.
>
> *Answers:*   southern recipes, dairy products

2. Have students create their own material that needs to be condensed and switch papers with a partner.

3. Have the students work on relevant material in their texts (see Figure 15-2).

2. Go Fish A Category   I J

Materials: deck of cards, each containing a category, such as colors, names, dogs, cats, fish, fruit, vegetables, and numbers

forty detail cards, four for each category—for example, red, green, blue, and yellow for colors

Object of Game: to accumulate the most complete sets of category and detail cards

Players: three or more

Procedure: See directions for Fish in Appendix B.

3. Five Up   P I J

Procedure: 1. Give students (or have them make) a chart containing five categories. For example:

Countries   *Continents*   *Capitals*   *Rivers*   *Mountains*

2. Each player takes a turn naming a category and a letter.

3. Players write down letters on their charts, and are given five minutes to fill in their columns.

4. The player with the most spaces correctly filled in wins. (See Figure 15-3 for a sample filled-in chart.)

Variations: 1. For content-area review, prepare the chart, with categories and letters indicated, before the game begins.

2. Organize the class into teams, whose members share answers.

3. Divide the class into two teams and play the game on the board. Have players come up two at a time, one from each team, draw a folded piece of paper containing one category and one letter, and fill in that category on the board.

FIGURE 15-3

COUNTRIES	CONTINENTS	CAPITALS	RIVERS	MOUNTAINS
P: Pakistan	*A:* Asia	*P:* Paris	*M:* Meuse	*H:* Himalaya
Peru	Australia	*W:* Washington	Mississippi	*A:* Appalachians
G: Germany	*E:* Europe	Winnipeg	*N:* Nile	Alps
Ghana		*T:* Taipei		*P:* Pyrenees
Goa		*M:* Moscow		
I: Italy		Madrid		
Iran				
India				
Indonesia				

4.   Have teams prepare category charts for each other, using review material.

4. Which List?   P I

Procedure: 1.   Create lists of like items, such as *he, she, they, I; red, blue, yellow, green; big, huge, tall, immense; sea–sea, know–no, slay–sleigh; car, train, plane, dog sled; violin, guitar, cello, viola.*

2.   Students supply the category for each list.

3.   Primary children can work with word cards and create a top card for each pile.

Extension: Students create their own lists and try to puzzle the class.

Variation: Supply students with several lists mixed together. Their task is to find the categories and label them.

5. Category Game   P I

Materials: decks of 3-by-5 cards consisting of four category cards and twenty subordinate-details cards
answer key
duplicate decks if pairs play

Number of Players: one or two

Procedure: Pairs: 1.   Students shuffle cards and time themselves (if working individually) while competing to organize the deck into "suits" of categories, with the category card on top and the details cards beneath.

2.   For pairs, the first one finished with all correct wins.

Individual: Follow step 1 for pairs. Keep records of different students' achievement.

Variation: Use content-area material to review. Have students in teams prepare decks for one another.

6. List, Group, Label*   P I J

Procedure: 1. Provide students with a stimulus word from a lesson.

2. Students must think of at least twenty-five words related to that word.

3. Ask students to construct smaller lists, using words from the large list that have something in common.

4. Record some of the lists on the chalkboard and have the students who created them explain how the words are related.

5. Words that cannot be categorized can be placed in a misfit list.

* Readence and Searfoss, 1980.

B. DELETING UNIMPORTANT INFORMATION

1. Trivia Chase   I J H A

Procedure: 1. Prepare copies of paragraphs containing unnecessary material.

2. The students' task is to underline in red all trivial information.

3. To introduce the skill, use material with which students are very familiar, such as a write-up of a favorite TV show that includes the name of every character and actor or actress, or a paragraph about the class that contains information about each student's sisters and brothers.

4. To develop this skill with relevant material, use textbook paragraphs to which you have added unnecessary information (see Figure 15-4).

5. Have students delete the least important information in something they are reading for pleasure. Show how it isn't important to remember everything.

2. Color Me Shorter   P I

Procedure: 1. Cut up old basal readers to make consumable stories, or cut up old magazines to make individual booklets.

2. Pass these out, one to a student, and tell the class to use their crayons to ''color'' them shorter.

3. Have students use blue to color over sentences that are unimportant. Tell them these would be the ones they could take out without hurting the story or article.

FIGURE 15-4 Material Containing Redundancies (redundancies underlined)

> The father was the head of the Roman family. The mother was not the head of the family. When Rome first developed as a community the father had complete authority over his wife and children, even to the power of life and death. The father had total control over the lives of the family members. Although the father's power later was broken, the Roman family remained a close group for along time.

4. Have them go back and color the most important sentences with yellow. Then they can color the remaining sentences red.

5. Have them read just the yellow and red sentences on each other's selection. They then decide if the passage still makes sense.

☞   This is a demonstration activity. Be sure to provide opportunities for application to meaningful reading tasks.

C. SELECTING THE MAIN IDEA

1. Topic Sentence Patterns*   I J H A

Procedure: 1. There are five ways in which the information in a paragraph is organized around the main idea. The following code represents these structures:

▽ = topic sentence at the beginning of paragraph

△ = topic sentence at end of paragraph

⧖ = topic sentence at beginning and end

◇ = topic sentence within paragraph

◯ = topic sentence not stated

2. Orally introduce and illustrate the use of these organizational patterns.

3. Provide samples of each type and have students work on their own.

4. Use a work sheet or overhead transparency with paragraphs from content-area text and trade books.

5. Use content-area textbooks and trade books themselves.

6. In steps 3–5 discuss the answers, having students give reasons for their choices. This helps develop the skill.

Variation: Pass out to each student a different main-idea sentence. Students write a paragraph containing this sentence, using whichever pattern they choose. Students exchange paragraphs and try to find each other's main-idea sentence. Or the teacher can collect the paragraphs and use several for class practice.

* D'Angelo, 1983. Reprinted with permission of K. D'Angelo and the International Reading Association.

2. Helping Hands*   P I

Procedure: 1. Have student trace their hands, one hand to a piece of paper.

2. Students print MAIN IDEA in the center of the palm; on the fingers they print DETAILS.

3. Read a paragraph to the students and then demonstrate how to select the main idea and print it on the palm, details going on the fingers.

4. Students read a selection, fill in the other hand, and discuss the results.

5. Supervise practice with this process.

6. Students work independently.

* Kostka, 1985.

Variations: 1. Use stories and have students fill in the fingers with the 5 W's (who, what, where, when, why).

2. Have students read on their own, fill in hands, exchange hands, and try to re-create each other's material (orally). Use general words in order to increase the guessing—for example, "Some animals wanted to build a house" rather than "Three little pigs . . . ."

☞   This is a demonstration activity. Be sure to provide opportunities for application to meaningful reading tasks.

3. Rank the Sentences*   I J H

Procedure: 1. List on the board in random order the sentences from a paragraph.

2. Demonstrate reading the sentences, selecting the main-idea and detail sentences, and ranking the sentences according to importance. For example, "Mary is the best runner on the team" supplies the reader with more important information than "Mary began running races when she was five years old."

3. Using copies of sentences randomly arranged, provide students with supervised practice.

4. Have students work independently on textbook or trade book material rewritten in a random fashion. They check their work by consulting the book to see if their choice for the main idea was the actual topic sentence of the paragraph.

5. Show them how knowing what is important can help them with real reading tasks.

* Stewart and Tei, 1983.

4. Paragraph Sense*   J H A

Materials: glue
3-by-5 cards
selection of interesting paragraphs, each having an explicit topic sentence

Procedure: 1. Cut the paragraphs into sentences. Glue each sentence to its own 3-by-5 card. Label all sentences from the same paragraphs with the same letter on the back of the card.

2. Shuffle the cards and distribute them to students.

3. The students get together with their paragraph group.

4. Students assemble the paragraph.

5. One student in each group reads the paragraph aloud to the rest of the group. The group decides which is the topic sentence.

☞   This is a practice activity. Be sure to provide opportunities for application to meaningful reading tasks.

Variations: 1.   After assembling the paragraph and deciding on the topic sentence, students read the paragraph to the class and ask others to decide which is the topic sentence.

2.   Use paragraphs from a section of the text the students are using.

3.   Mystery Paragraphs: Leave out the topic sentence and label one card with a question mark. Students' task is to create the topic sentence. They check their answer with the actual topic-sentence card.

4.   Individual work: Use the procedure or any of the variations that are appropriate for individual work.

* Adapted from Cunningham and Cunningham, 1984.

5.   Main–Idea Detection Strategy*   J H A

Procedure: 1.   Tell students that if the main idea of a paragraph is stated explicitly, it will *probably* be located in either the first or the last sentence.

2.   As main ideas are more frequently found in the first sentence, look for three patterns:

a.   Statement and examples: Is the first sentence a statement, followed by other sentences giving examples supporting that statement? For example:

McDonald's is having a sales promotion this month. Double cheeseburgers are half price and free cokes are given with every order over five dollars. Besides that, french fries are being sold two orders for the price of one.

b.   Statement and reasons: Is the statement in the first sentence followed by reasons that support it? For example:

Turkey vultures are useful animals. Although they are awkward birds on the ground, moving with a shuffling gait, they are most graceful in the air, where they soar for hours looking for food. Turkey vultures eat all kinds of carrion. Their prompt removal of dead animals makes them much appreciated by humankind, especially in tropical countries.

c.   Statement and details: Is the statement in the first sentence followed by details that support it? For example:

The panda is a popular animal. Stories about the panda in the Washington zoo are always front-page news and important features on television newscasts. Stuffed pandas are among the most popular toys for children, and panda postcards are always in demand in zoo gift shops.

3.   If these three patterns don't contain the solution to the main-idea puzzle, consider the possibility that the main idea is contained in the last sentence and try out these patterns:

d.   Examples and statement: Do the other sentences in the paragraph supply examples that support the statement made in the last sentence?

e.   Details and statement: Do the other sentences in the paragraph contain details that support the statement in the last sentence?

f.   Reasons and statement: Do the other sentences in the paragraph supply reasons that support the statement made in the last sentence?

4.   If the paragraph doesn't conform to any of these patterns, there's a good

chance that the main idea is not stated explicitly. Sometimes, however, the main-idea sentence is in the middle of the paragraph. Once students have mastered the two strategies explained here, they can use them to help find this third type of placement of the main idea.

5.   Show students how to use this technique when they are reading content-area assignments, newspapers, magazines, and trade books.

* Duffelmeyer, 1985.

D. INVENTING THE MAIN IDEA

1.   Main–Idea Wheel*   I J

Procedure: 1.   Review how to find explicit topic sentences. Then explain the What, Why, How, and When of the new skill.

WHAT   2.   Explain the purpose of the skill—finding the main idea of a paragraph
WHY   that lacks a topic sentence. This skill is important because many paragraphs have unstated main ideas, and to understand and remember them you need to figure out what the main idea is.

HOW   3.   Demonstrate the three steps in finding unstated main ideas:

a.   Decide what the *topic* of the paragraph is. The topic is similar to a short title telling what the paragraph is about.

b.   Read the paragraph and decide what is said about the topic—what the other sentences tell you about it. Write a sentence that includes both the topic and what is said about it. This sentence will be your main idea.

c.   Check yourself by rereading each sentence and asking if it supports the

FIGURE 15-5   Main-Idea Wheel

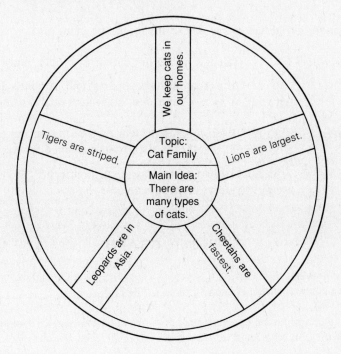

main idea. If it does, it is a *detail* that supports your main idea. If you find several sentences that do not support your main idea, go back to step a and begin again.

4. Fill in the wheel illustrated in Figure 15-5 while demonstrating the three steps with a paragraph, noting that the details (spokes) support the main idea (hub).

5. Provide supervised practice for the students, using read classroom assignments.

WHEN   6. Be sure to discuss *when* this strategy is appropriate—when students are reading informational writing, reading about facts, reading in textbooks, and so on. This strategy is not needed for reading stories, as writers don't convey their information in the same way they do in informational writing.

* Adapted from Baumann and Schmitt, 1986.

2. Main–Idea Pix*   I J H A

Materials: copies of magazines with good pictures (*National Geographic* is a good source)

Procedure: 1. Divide class into groups of six or less.

2. Distribute copies of the same magazines to each group and direct them to selected photographs.

3. Groups must develop a main idea and inference statement for each photograph.

4. Discuss the results, reinforcing the idea that the main-idea choice was literal thinking, the inference statement inferential thinking.

* Luvaas-Briggs, 1984. This activity was used in a community college reading class.

3. Picture It   P I

Purpose: to develop the skill of inventing the main idea

Procedure: 1. Select a paragraph with a main idea that can be visualized.

2. After reading a short paragraph, students draw a picture of its main idea. Artistic ability is not needed; stick figures are acceptable.

Variations: 1. (P I) Students draw a cartoon frame for each sentence read. Cartoons are then put together in a cartoon sequence for the paragraph.

2. (P I) Students draw a cartoon frame for each paragraph read. Cartoons are put together in a sequence for the selection.

BIBLIOGRAPHY

BAUMANN, J. "The effectiveness of a direct instruction paradigm for teaching main idea comprehension." *Reading Research Quarterly,* 20, Fall (1984), 93–115.

BAUMANN, J. "Teaching children to comprehend main ideas," paper presented at the annual meeting of the National Reading Conference, Clearwater, Fla., December 1982.

BAUMANN, J. F. AND M. C. SCHMITT. "The what, why, how, and when of comprehension instruction," *Reading Teacher,* 39, March (1986), 640–46.

CUNNINGHAM, P. M. AND J. W. CUNNINGHAM. "The hidden agenda of sequencing," *Clearing House,* 56, April (1984), 362–63.

D'ANGELO, K. "Precise writing: Promoting vocabulary development and comprehension," *Journal of Reading,* 26, March (1983), 534–39.

DUFFELMEYER, F. A. "Main ideas in paragraphs," *Reading Teacher,* 38, January (1985), 484–86.

DURR, W. K. Lecture at the Benchmark School, Media, Pa., October 24, 1980.

KOSTKA, B. "Helping hands improve reading comprehension," *Reading Teacher,* 39, October (1985), 121.

LUVAAS-BRIGGS, L. "Some 'whole brain' activities for the community college reading class," *Journal of Reading,* 27, April (1984), 644–47.

READENCE, J. E. AND L. W. SEARFOSS. "Teaching strategies for vocabulary development," *English Journal,* 69, October (1980), 43–46.

STEWART, O. AND E. TEI. "Some implications of metacognition for reading instruction," *Journal of Reading,* 27, October (1983), 36–43.

SUMMARIZING

Definition *Extracting the general ideas from a passage longer than one paragraph*

RATIONALE

As stated in Chapter 15, good readers are constantly summarizing the information they are reading. Summaries help them to remember the content because they provide an informational scaffold on which details can be hung. Poor readers often do not summarize and, as a result, have poorer recall of what they read.

Procedures for teaching the summarizing of individual paragraphs (a skill often called finding the main idea) were given in Chapter 15. This chapter is concerned with teaching students to summarize longer passages. It may be useful for students to be able to find the main idea of individual paragraphs before being asked to summarize longer passages, because summarizing a long passage often involves finding the main ideas of several paragraphs and then combining those main ideas into a summary of the whole.

A set of rules for summarizing is provided in Figure 16-3 (activity B.3). Begin summarizing instruction with these or similar guidelines. Carefully explain and model each step. Only after guided practice should students be asked to write their own summaries. Several of the activities in Chapter 15 can also be used to teach summarizing of longer passages. See especially activities 15.C.5 and 15.D.1.

INFORMAL DIAGNOSIS

You can get a general idea of students' concepts of what makes a good summary by giving them summaries of varying quality and asking them to select the best (see activity 16.2). You can also provide diagnostic tasks in which you ask students to select the summary statement(s) or create their own summary. You may also wish to do this with different types of materials. A student who can summarize a story may not be able to summarize a science passage, for instance.

GENERAL TEACHING SUGGESTIONS

1. Ask students to summarize whenever possible. You can do this with oral activities as well as with written assignments.

2. Avoid asking trivial questions about information that should be deleted during normal summarizing. Otherwise, although you may find the one person who can remember everything, you will be creating readers who are afraid to summarize as they read and therefore remember nothing.

3. Use very easy materials when you first teach summarizing.

4. Use different kinds of materials when you teach summarizing.

5. Be sure that students can find the main idea of individual paragraphs before you ask them to summarize whole passages.

chapter 16.   SUMMARIZING
Activities

A.	RECOGNIZING A SUMMARY	
	1. Select the Best	I J H A
	2. Which One?	P I J H A
B.	WRITING A SUMMARY	
	1. Pyramiding	P I J H A
	2. Summary Maps	I J H A
	3. Summary Instructions	I J H A
	4. Headlines	I J H A
	5. One-Minute Report	P I J
	6. Content-Area Summaries	J H A

A.   RECOGNIZING A SUMMARY

1.   Select the Best*   I J H A

Procedure: 1.   Create several summaries of the same passage. Include one summary at an easy level that contains unimportant information and one that contains all the important information. (See Figure 16-1.)

2.   After reviewing the rules for making a summary (Figure 16-3), have the students choose the best summary and give reasons for their choice.

3.   Follow up with activities in which they write their own summaries of classroom materials.

* Irwin, 1986.

2.   Which One?*   P I J H A

Procedure: 1.   Provide students with copies of several short selections of interest to them.

2.   Supply a list of questions (more than the number of selections) and have the students choose the question each selection answers.

3.   This question and its answer are the summary of the selection.

Variations: 1.   After reading self-selected magazine articles, students select the best title from a list.

2.   Students "make books" by matching pictures with the paragraphs they illustrate.

* Adapted from Greene, 1985.

B.   WRITING A SUMMARY

1.   Pyramiding*   P I J H A

Procedure: 1.   After students read an interesting selection, have them try to identify the main ideas and details.

FIGURE 16-1

ORIGINAL PASSAGE:

Once there was a very tall girl named Alice. Alice was the tallest girl in her class. All of her classmates made fun of her. This made her feel very bad. She even tried walking with her knees bent so that she would appear to be shorter. That just made her look funny. Looking funny made her feel even worse.

One day Alice's teacher said that they were going to have a guest speaker, and in walked the tallest woman Alice had ever seen. She was the star of the local women's basketball team. She talked to the students about the new league, the games that had been played, and what it was like to be a professional athlete. Everyone admired her.

Alice was very excited. She asked the speaker if she could be a player someday. The woman replied that since she was so tall, she probably would have a better chance than many other girls. For the first time, Alice was proud of being tall. (Irwin, p. 47)

SUMMARY A

Alice looked funny because she walked with her knees bent. When a member of a women's basketball team came to her class, everyone admired her. She told Alice that she had a good chance of being a player.

SUMMARY B

Alice felt bad because she was the tallest girl in her class. One day a very tall woman, a professional basketball player, came to her class and told the students what it was like to be a professional athlete, and everyone admired her. After the woman athlete told Alice that she might have a better chance than most girls of becoming a basketball player, Alice felt proud of being tall.

---

2. Students write down phrases and terms they think are important.

3. Conduct a class discussion, using the chalkboard to create a pyramid of these facts and phrases, grouped into logical categories (see Figure 16-2).

4. Encourage the class to either find or create a summary sentence that answers the question "What is the author saying about these ideas?" This sentence becomes the base of the pyramid.

5. Provide supervised practice of the strategy, using relevant content-area material and other outside readings.

* Maring and Furman, 1985; Clewell and Haidemos, 1983.

2. Summary Maps*   I J H A

Materials: large pieces of drawing paper

wide felt-tip markers

Procedure: 1. Divide students into small groups.

2. The members of each group read passage or article, underlining the main ideas and supporting details.

FIGURE 16-2   Example of a Pyramid

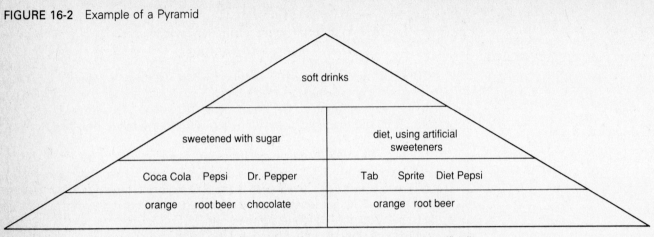

Beverage companies make a variety of both natural and artificially
sweetened soft drinks.

Source: Adapted from Maring and Furman 1985, p. 696.

3.   Each group constructs a ''map'' of the material read, using the markers and drawing paper (see Chapter 17, activity B.2)

4.   Hang the maps on the wall.

5.   If everyone has read the same thing, lead a discussion comparing the maps.

6.   If the groups have read different articles, have each group ''summarize'' the content by explaining their maps to the rest of the class.

* Luvaas-Briggs, 1984.

3. Summary Instructions*   I J H A

Procedure: 1.   Distribute copies of textbook or trade book paragraphs.

2.   Model on an overhead projector the five rules for writing a summary (see Figure 16-3).

3.   Work with students on remaining paragraphs, sharing results and discussing the five steps. Using colored pens (for example, red for lists, blue for unnecessary detail, and so on) will make the steps more visible for the students.

4.   Provide additional practice with selected interesting paragraphs throughout the year.

* Hare and Borchardt, 1984.

4. Headlines   I J H A

Procedure: 1.   Collect interesting newspaper articles of different lengths about various subjects.

2.   Mount the articles on plain paper, numbering each article and cutting off the headlines.

3.   Number the headlines to correspond to the articles and keep them as a separate list.

FIGURE 16-3 Five Rules for Writing a Summary

1. *Collapse lists.* If there is a list of things, supply a word or phrase for the whole list. For example, if you saw *swimming, sailing, fishing, and surfing,* you could substitute *water sports.*
2. *Use topic sentences.* Sometimes authors write a sentence that summarizes the whole paragraph. If so, use that sentence in your summary. If not, you'll have to make up your own.
3. *Get rid of unnecessary detail.* Sometimes information is repeated or is stated in several different ways. Some information may be trivial and unnecessary. Get rid of repetitive or trivial information. Summaries should be short.
4. *Collapse paragraphs.* Often paragraphs are related to each other. For example, some paragraphs simply explain or expand on other paragraphs in a selection. Some paragraphs are more important than others. Join together the paragraphs that are related. Keep important paragraphs.
5. *Finally, polish the summary.* When you collapse a lot of information from many paragraphs into one or two paragraphs, the resulting summary sometimes sounds awkward and unnatural. There are several ways you can remedy this: you can add connecting words such as *like* or *because,* or you can write introductory or closing statements. Another method is to paraphrase the material; this will improve your ability to remember what you read and enable you to avoid plagiarism—using the exact words of the author.

Source: Hare, V. and Borchordt, K., 1984, p. 66.

4.   Pass out the articles. (Start with one-paragraph articles and increase the length as students progress.) Be sure to use materials they are interested in. Instruct students to write appropriate headlines. You may specify the length of the headline if you want.

5.   After students have written their headlines, they can compare their answers to the actual headlines. Which is better? Why?

☞   This is a demonstration activity. Be sure to provide opportunities for application to meaningful reading tasks.

5.   One–Minute Report   P I J

Procedure: 1.   Let each student select a story to read. For students who prefer nonfiction, suggest articles from newspapers or magazines.

2.   Tell students that their task will be to tell the class the main points of the story or article in one minute. Give them time to read and prepare.

3.   Go around the group and have each person deliver his or her one-minute report.

6.   Content–Area Summaries   J H A

Procedure: 1.   Have students complete their content reading in short segments, one per night or session.

2. The students' task is to summarize the assignment into a paragraph of three to five sentences.

3. Demonstrate by summarizing a passage with the group or class. Explain to students that summarizing is a very useful study strategy that can help them remember what they read. Tell them that good readers continually summarize when they read.

4. Give students the first reading assignment along with several summaries to pick from. The next session, discuss which one they picked and why.

5. When students can select the appropriate summary, assign them to write one themselves.

6. Have students compare summaries. Perhaps they can select the best one in the group. Make sure they can say why that one is the best.

BIBLIOGRAPHY

CLEWELL, S. F. AND J. HAIDEMOS. "Organizational strategies to increase comprehension," *Reading World,* 22, March (1983), 314–21.

GREENE, B. N. "Developing comprehension: Finding the main idea," *Reading Teacher,* 39, October (1985), 116.

HARE, V. AND K. M. BORCHARDT. "Direct instruction of summarization skills," *Reading Research Quarterly,* 20, Fall (1984), 62–78.

IRWIN, J. W. *Teaching Reading Comprehension Processes.* Englewood Cliffs, N.J.: Prentice-Hall, 1986.

LUVAAS-BRIGGS, L. "Some 'whole brain' activities for the community college reading class," *Journal of Reading,* 27, April (1984), 644–47.

MARING, G. H. AND G. FURMAN. "Seven 'Whole Class' Strategies to help mainstreamed young people read and listen better in content area classes." *Journal of Reading,* 28, May (1985), 694–700.

chapter 17

UNDERSTANDING THE ORGANIZATION

Definition: *Organizing one's memory according to the organizational pattern used by the author*

RATIONALE

Research has shown that organizing one's memory of a passage according to the author's organization facilitates recall. For narrative materials, this entails understanding typical story patterns, called *story grammars*. For expository materials, it entails understanding different kinds of patterns, such as time-sequence, description, and definition–example. It also includes being aware of the main idea–detail structure of the passage (see Chapter 15). An awareness of expository patterns seems to develop later than an awareness of narrative ones. Even high school students reading at grade level may need help in understanding the organization of content-area materials.

STORY GRAMMARS

For younger children, an awareness of a typical story pattern facilitates comprehension. Stein (1979) and Stein and Glenn (1977) have included six elements in their description of a typical story pattern (see Table 17-1, which also contains an example of a well-formed story). Note that the last five categories form one "episode" and that there may be several episodes in one story. You may wish to practice identifying these categories in simple stories before beginning to teach students about narrative organization. However, it is *not* necessary to teach students the names of these categories. Instead, use activities such as the ones included in this chapter to sensitize students to story organization.

ORGANIZATIONAL PATTERNS IN EXPOSITORY PROSE

Once students have begun to read content-area materials, they need to understand new kinds of organizational patterns. Table 17-2 describes some typical examples. Table 17-3 provides some paragraphs for you to practice classifying. Check your answers with the key on page 149. Study these tables. Practice identifying organizational patterns in the materials you use

TABLE 17-1   Organizational Elements of a Simple Story

1. Setting	Introduction of the protagonist; can contain information about physical, social, or temporal context in which the remainder of the story occurs.
2. Initiating event	An action, an internal event, or a natural occurrence which serves to initiate or to cause a response in the protagonist.
3. Internal response	An emotion, cognition, or goal of the protagonist.
4. Attempt	An overt attempt to obtain the protagonist's goal.
5. Consequence	An event, action, or end state which marks the attainment or nonattainment of the protagonist's goal.
6. Reaction	An emotion, a cognition, an action, or an end state expressing the protagonist's feelings about his or her goal attainment or relating the broader consequential realm of the protagonist's goal attainment.

A Well-Formed Story

1. Setting	a. Once there was a big gray fish named Albert.
	b. He lived in a big icy pond near the edge of the forest.
2. Initiating event	c. One day, Albert was swimming around the pond.
	d. Then he spotted a big juicy worm on top of the water.
3. Internal response	e. Albert knew how delicious worms tasted.
	f. He wanted to eat that one for his dinner.
4. Attempt	g. So he swam very close to the worm.
	h. Then he bit into him.
5. Consequence	i. Suddenly, Albert was pulled through the water into a boat.
	j. He had been caught by a fisherman.
6. Reaction	k. Albert felt sad.
	l. He wished he had been more careful.

Source: Stein, "How Children Understand Stories: A Developmental Analysis," in L. Katz, *Current Topics in Early Childhood Education,* Vol. 2 (Norwood, N.J.: Ablex, 1979), p. 265.

before teaching comprehension. Then you will be ready to use the activities in this chapter.

One set of clues sometimes used for identifying organizational patterns consists of structure words in the text. Table 17-4 lists some of these words. You may wish to share this list with your students when you are teaching organizational patterns.

Many of the activities for teaching awareness of organizational patterns in expository texts involve various diagrams and charts. Activities B.1–B.4 provide examples. Another procedure sometimes used is out-

TABLE 17-2   Types of Organizational Patterns

Type	Description
description	describes the subject; often includes a list of characteristics
temporal sequence	describes or lists events in their order of occurrence
explanation	explains such things as causes, effects, and enabling circumstances
comparison/contrast	compares or contrasts two events or concepts
definition/example	defines or gives examples
problem/solution	explains the development of a problem and/or suggests solutions
process description	describes the parts of a process
classification	explains how concepts are classified

TABLE 17-3   Sample Paragraphs for Classification

Simple Paragraph	Pattern Used?
The two groups used very different approaches. One group tried to solve the problem alone, while the other group immediately began to look for someone to ask. One group divided the tasks among the individuals, while the other group did everything as a whole.	
There were many reasons for the move from country to city. There were more jobs in the city. There were also more cultural events, more shops, and more educational opportunities.	
A chemical change is a process by which new substances are created. Burning and rusting are examples of chemical changes.	
There were so many people moving into the cities that many had trouble finding places to live. New homes were built at an amazing rate.	

lining. Activities using outlining are included in Chapter 24, on study skills, because outlining is usually used as a study skill. When you are choosing between outlining and diagraming as an instructional technique, remember that students differ in their responses to them. Some students will learn best from charts; others will learn from outlining.

TABLE 17-4 Common Structure Words

Organizational Pattern	Structure Words
spatial description	across, over, at, from, into, between, beyond, outside, near, down, far, up, within
temporal sequence	next, first, second, then, originally, finally, before, earlier, later, after, following, then, while, meanwhile, soon, until, since, beginning, during, still, eventually
explanation	because, so, thus, consequently, therefore, for this reason, as a result
comparison/contrast	by comparison, similarly, but, yet, although, as well as, unlike, on the other hand, in spite of, on the contrary, nevertheless, whereas
definition/example	for example, such as, that is, namely, to illustrate, for instance

INFORMAL DIAGNOSIS

For younger children, you may wish to assess story-grammar awareness. Ask them to tell you a story. Ask them to finish a story, or during a story ask them to predict what is coming next. Listen for an awareness of typical story structure. Do not ask them to identify parts.

For older students working with content-area material, ask them to recall what they have read. Listen to see if the recall is organized like the passage. Another idea is to give students a set of three paragraphs, two of which are organized the same. Ask them to find the two that are the same. Do this with different kinds of patterns and materials.

GENERAL TEACHING SUGGESTIONS

1. Teaching the identification of the main idea and outlining are other ways to teach organizational

Key to Table 17-3: A Simple Exercise in Identifying Organizational Patterns

Simple Paragraph	Pattern Used?
The two groups used very different approaches. One group tried to solve the problem alone, while the other group immediately began to look for someone to ask. One group divided the tasks among the individuals, while the other group did everything as a whole	Comparison/contrast
There were many reasons for the move from country to city. There were more jobs in the city. There were also more cultural events, more shops, and more educational opportunities.	Explanation
A chemical change is a process by which new substances are created. Burning and rusting are examples of chemical changes.	Definition/examples
There were so many people moving into the cities that many had trouble finding places to live. New homes were built at an amazing rate.	Problem/solution

Source: Irwin, 1986. Table 17.3, p. 52; Answer Key, p. 65–66.

awareness. If this approach is more appropriate than teaching the patterns in Table 17-2, you can refer to Chapters 15 and 24.

2. Games and other practice activities are of limited use in teaching students organizational awareness. It is best for them to learn this skill through real classroom tasks that require it.

3. Use pattern guides to focus student attention on the organization of their content-area texts (see activity B.1).

4. Writing activities are useful for teaching both story grammar and content-area organizational pattern (see activity B.4).

5. Movie viewing also provides opportunities to identify organizational patterns. You may wish to begin by providing a pattern guide (see activity B.1).

6. You can read to students to develop story-grammar awareness. Stop and ask students to predict and summarize. Make sure they include the important parts.

7. Make sure your class presentations are organized whenever possible. Present material on the board in the form of charts or outlines.

chapter 17. UNDERSTANDING THE ORGANIZATION
Activities

A. NARRATIVE
1. Pattern Stories   P
2. Circle Stories   P I
3. Story Pictures   P
4. Story Recipe   P I
5. Prediction Task   P I J
6. Choose Your Own Ending   P I J
7. Fill in the Middle   P I J
8. Scrambled Stories   P I J
9. Story Maker   P I J
B. EXPOSITION
1. How to Make a Pattern Guide   I J H A
2. Mapping   I J H A
3. Chart-It   I J H A
4. Pattern Writing   I J H A
5. Picture It   P I J

A. NARRATIVE

1. Pattern Stories*   P

Materials: a very short picture book with a patterned story, such as *The Wonderful Feast* (Slobodkina, 1967)

Procedure: 1.   Read the story aloud to the students once or twice, so that they become familiar with it. You might want to sketch the series of events on an overhead projection or on the board as a four- or five-frame comic strip of stick figures.

2.   Suggest to the students that you might create a story together based on the same pattern.

3.   Encourage the students to suggest other people and animals to substitute in the story. Draw the new comic strip.

4.   Following the pattern, have the students dictate the new story.

5.   To encourage individual work, give each student a piece of paper folded into four parts. On each part should be drawn a part of a story based on a similar sequence. These stories may be teacher-based, initiated by a story starter, or individually created.

* Smith and Bean, 1983.

2. Circle Stories*   P I

Materials: large piece of butcher paper, on which a circle is drawn
patterned storybook wherein the main character starts at one location and returns there after a series of adventures; suitable stories: *Journey Cake, Ho* (Sawyer, 1953) *Millions of Cats* (Gag, 1953) *The Runaway Bunny* (Brown, 1942)

Procedure: 1.   Divide circle into as many pie-shaped sections as there are adventures in the story chosen.

2.   Draw a house at the top of the circle to represent both the beginning and end of the character's journey in the story. The house represents "home," whether that home is a house, a cabin, or the lap of Mother Rabbit.

3.   Read the story aloud to the class.

4.   Lead a discussion to recall the events of the story and to decide what sequence of events should be drawn on the circle diagram.

5.   Draw these events in the sections of the circle diagram.

Variations: 1.   Give small groups one story each to diagram on large papers. Each child in a group illustrates one portion of the circle. The groups share their work when finished.

2.   Individuals complete circle-story boards for favorite stories.

3.   Use circle-story boards as a book review format.

4.   Students create a circle-story board and then write the story from the board.

5.   Students create story boards from well-known tales and see if other students can identify them.

6.   Students create original circle-story boards and pass them on to a neighbor, who then writes the story.

7.   (IJH) As many novels and classics are based on this form, the circle strategy could be used to review the plot of the *Odyssey, Tom Jones,* and other famous books. Similarly, the circle story could be used as either a study guide or a prereading aid for such novels.

* Jett-Simpson, 1981.

3. Story Pictures*   P

Materials: large butcher paper divided into six squares containing pictures representing the major elements of story grammars (see Figure 17-1):

1–3.   Setting—who, where, what

4–5.   Initiating events

6.   Consequence or outcome (Mandler and Johnson, 1977)

simple nursery rhyme, such as "Little Miss Muffet"

Procedure: 1.   Read the rhyme to the children twice.

2.   Lead a discussion about each of the first three pictures. With your help, the children should be able to decide that the pictures represent *who* the story is about, *where* the story is taking place, and *what* Miss Muffet is doing as the story starts. These three pictures represent the *setting* of the story.

3.   Lead a discussion about what happens that changes Miss Muffet's normal behavior. What occurs that makes this not an everyday experience? Have the children identify pictures 4 and 5 as the events that start the story.

FIGURE 17-1

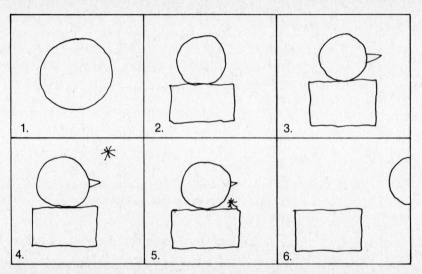

Smith and Bean, 1983, p. 298. Reprinted with permission of Marilyn Smith and the International Reading Association.

4. Discuss Miss Muffet's reaction to the spider and the result of her reaction. The children should identify the sixth square as the story *outcome*.

5. Once the children have mastered the use of this diagram for identifying parts of a story, have them use the diagram with stories in their basal readers.

6. Repeat these terms regularly to reinforce identification of story-grammar components.

* Smith and Bean, 1983.

4. Story Recipe P I

Procedure: 1. Demonstrate how to fill in a story recipe, brainstorming the words needed for an unwritten story and then beginning the story (see Figure 17-2).

2. Have students fill in the story recipe for a story for Halloween, Christmas, or some other occasion, or for a story of a specific type (fable, fantasy, fairy tale, etc.).

3. Students write the stories as homework or classwork.

4. Students read stories to class.

5. Students create a "cookbook" of story recipes and stories, either as an individual record or as a class project.

5. Prediction Task* P I J

Procedure: 1. Provide students with a copy of an unfinished story.

2. Have students discuss what will come next. Use a variety of choices and discuss how the same sort of event tends to come at this point in the story.

3. Gradually call attention to various components of story structure. Fairy tales and folk tales are good examples to use for this activity.

* Whaley, 1981.

FIGURE 17-2   Recipe for a Story

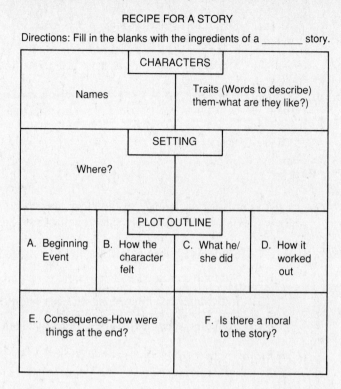

RECIPE FOR A STORY

Directions: Fill in the blanks with the ingredients of a _____ story.

CHARACTERS	
Names	Traits (Words to describe) them-what are they like?)

SETTING	
Where?	

PLOT OUTLINE			
A. Beginning Event	B. How the character felt	C. What he/ she did	D. How it worked out

E. Consequence-How were things at the end?	F. Is there a moral to the story?

6. Choose Your Own Ending   P I J

Procedure: 1.   Brainstorm with students the beginning of a story. Select characters, setting, and initiating event.

2.   Students individually complete the story.

3.   Students create a title indicating the focus of their version of the ending—for example, "If you want to see how the wolf outwits the three little pigs, read on. . . ."

4.   Publish the alternate endings created by the students as a *Choose Your Own Ending* book.

7. Fill in the Middle*   P I J

Procedure: 1.   Give students a copy of a story with the middle section deleted. Students, individually or in groups, fill in the information that they think will logically fit in that section.

2.   Discuss students' contributions. Focus on why one kind of information is usually supplied in the story structure.

Variation: Have different groups complete this task for different portions of the story. A new story can be created by putting all the new portions together.

* Whaley, 1981.

8. Scrambled Stories*   **P I J**

      Procedure: 1.   Separate a story into its components. Scramble the order of the components.

                     2.   Students decide on the best order for the story.

      Variation: Students separate stories of their own choosing and have partners reassemble them.

      * Whaley, 1981.

9. Story Maker*   **P I J**

      Materials: sets of cards for each stage of the story grammar: each card contains a different choice for story development; each choice leads to another set of choices

      Procedure: 1.   Students choose a card for the first stage of their story.

                     2.   Students continue making choices and create stories of their own.

                     3.   Individually or in groups, students hang their choices on a pegboard.

                     4.   Students write new stories using each other's cards.

      * Rubin and Gentner, 1979.

B. EXPOSITION

1. How to Make a Pattern Guide*   **I J H A**

      Procedure: 1.   Identify the essential concepts to be taught in the material. It is more effective to present fewer concepts thoroughly than many sketchily.

                     2.   Determine which organizational patterns are used for the paragraphs.

                     3.   Make a chart or diagram for the students to complete that reflects the organizational patterns and the essential concepts (see Figures 17-3 to 17-7).

                     4.   Decide how much help to give the students.

                     5.   Be sure to make your directions clear—one direction to a sentence. Do not overcrowd the guide.

                     6.   Demonstrate how to use the guide.

      * Niles, 1965; Olson and Longnion, 1982.

FIGURE 17-3   Pattern Guide For History; Chronological Order*   (I J H A)

Using a time line is a good way to see a sequence of events. As you read this chapter, fill in the events on the following time line. Write what happened above the date. Page numbers are given to help you.

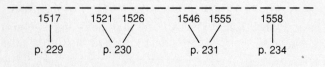

      * Based on Olson and Longnion, 1982.

FIGURE 17-4   Pattern Guide For Science;* Compare–Contrast Organization (H A)

Compare the Body Systems of the Frog and the Grasshopper.

	FROG	GRASSHOPPER
Digestive System		
Respiratory System		
Nervous System		

1.   Fill in this chart with brief descriptions.

2.   a.   In terms of which system are the frog and the grasshopper most nearly alike? _____

b.   Tell how they are the same. _____

3.   a.   In terms of which system are the frog and the grasshopper most different? _____

b.   Tell how they are different. _____

Source: Irwin, 1986, p. 53

FIGURE 17-5   Pattern Guide For History; Cause and Effect (J H A)

In this chapter, look for the cause–effect relationships listed in the following chart. Add the missing causes and effects to the proper column in the chart.

CAUSE		EFFECT
1. Moses Austin wants to bring American settlers into Texas, a Spanish territory.	⇒	Spanish agree and promise to give land to colonists.
2. Mexico revolts against Spain.	⇒	_____
3. _____	⇒	Mexican government lets Americans settle.
4. 20,000 Americans settle in Texas.	⇒	_____
5. Mexico forbids slavery in Texas.	⇒	_____
6. _____	⇒	Texas declares independence.
7. Santa Ana attacks the Alamo.	⇒	_____
8. _____	⇒	Mexicans defeated at San Jacinto.

FIGURE 17-6 Pattern Guide For History; Chronological Order (I H A)

During the fifteenth and sixteenth centuries, the nations of Europe began to explore the world looking for new markets. Listed below are some events from that period. Rewrite the events in the order in which they occurred and place the date of each event in front of it.

1. Balboa discovers the Pacific.   Date ____   1. _____
2. Columbus discovers America.   ____   2. _____
3. Silver discovered in Peru.   ____   3. _____
4. Jews expelled from Spain.   ____   4. _____
5. Cortez lands in Mexico.   ____   5. _____
6. Magellan circumnavigates the world.   ____   6. _____
7. Da Gama sails to India.   ____   7. _____

FIGURE 17-7   Pattern Guide for Science;* Tree Chart (I)

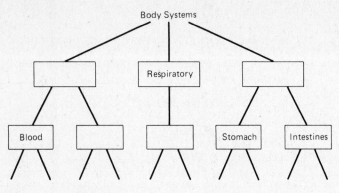

Source: Irwin, 1986, p. 53

1.   Fill in the four empty boxes in the chart.

2.   Add two specific parts for each of the organs.

2.   Mapping*   I J H A

Procedure: 1.   Demonstrate to students how to "map" the relationships of the ideas found in the text. As most students may be familiar with the main idea/supporting detail format, go through the text section to be mapped, selecting the main idea (the largest heading) and the supporting details (smaller headings). Rather than using a heading/subheading format, construct a diagram like the one in Figure 17-8. Place the main idea in the center of the map and draw enough lines out from it to include all the subheadings in the text. Explain to students that this is another way of looking at the material that may help them understand and remember it better.

2.   Have students help you fill in the map, supplying supporting details for the subheadings.

3.   Provide supervised practice constructing a similar diagram for the next text selection. Be sure to use regular classroom materials.

4.   Encourage students to create and share their own kinds of maps. For instance, another student might create something like the one in Figure 17-9.

5.   After sufficient practice, move on to creating charts and tables for com-

FIGURE 17-8   Map of Main Idea and Details in Chapter on
Puritan Values

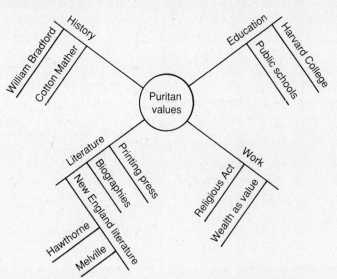

Source: Irwin, 1986, p. 55.

parison–contrast organization, cause–effect organization, time lines, flow charts,
and so on. In demonstrating these patterns, focus on the connective words (see
Figure 17-4) that alert you to the pattern.

* Irwin, 1986.

FIGURE 17-9   Alternative Map of Chapter on Puritan Values

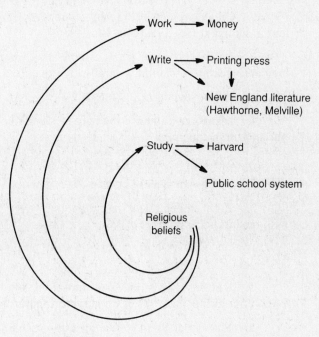

Source: Irwin, 1986, p. 55.

FIGURE 17-10   Chart-It

Listed below the chart are the items to be used in completing it. As you use them, cross them off. Check your answers with the answer sheet.

THE INDUSTRIAL REVOLUTION IN ENGLAND

A.
1. mobile, plentiful labor supply

2.

3. coal and iron resources

4.

5.

B.
1. Early steam engines inefficient

2.

3. ends dependence on animal, wind, and water power

4.

5.

C. Factories
1.

2. employed women and children

3.

4.

D.
1.

2. transported rural workers to cities

3.

4. lowered costs and expanded markets

Fluid capital for financing
Watt improves Newcomen's engine
First factories in textile industry
Origins of the Industrial Revolution
Development of Steam Power
Stephenson's *Rocket* the first locomotive
Managerial talent available
Harnessed heat energy to drive machines
Changed outlook and values of population
Stable government fostered growth

Used in iron and cotton industries
Railroads
Larger workshops needed for new inventions
16 hour workdays

---

3. Chart–It   IJHA

Procedure: 1.   Create a chart of the main concepts and important details in a selected text assignment (see Figure 17-10).

2.   Below the map, list the items that should fill in the spaces. Do not indicate which are main ideas and which details.

3.   Fill in several of the blanks.

4.   Distribute copies of the map to students. Their task is to read the material and fill in the map.

5.   Students check their answers against a prepared answer sheet.

6.   Discuss answers in class.

7.   Have students—either individually or in groups—create "chart-its" for assignments. Use them in class.

4. Pattern Writing   IJHA

Procedure: 1.   Review with students a chosen organizational pattern, such as compare–contrast, using a selection about a familiar subject.

2.   Show a diagram of the selection that focuses on the structure of compare–contrast.

3. Develop a compare–contrast chart for a relevant topic—for example, a comparison of fourth grade and sixth grade:

	4th Grade	6th Grade
subjects		
classrooms		
schedules		
after-school activities		

4. Elicit from students material to complete the chart.

5. Demonstrate writing a short selection in the compare–contrast format using this information. Focus on the topic sentence, pointing out the subject of the paragraph and the connective (transition) words needed to indicate the compare–contrast pattern, such as *but, on the other hand,* and *in contrast.*

6. Have students create compare–contrast charts for topics of their own choice.

7. Students write compare–contrast paragraphs and share these in class or publish them.

8. As a follow-up, have students read selected parts of their textbook assignments and locate paragraphs written in the compare–contrast pattern. Have them fill in a compare–contrast chart and indicate the *clues*—the connective words—that alerted them to the pattern.

Variations: 1. Students write paragraphs from charts they have constructed and exchange the paragraphs with a partner. Each student then fills in a chart for the other's paragraph and checks with the writer to see if it is correct.

2. Students create charts for different types of organizational patterns and write paragraphs based on them. Students exchange paragraphs and try to figure out the organization of their partner's paragraph and create an appropriate chart. Students check with their partner to see if they were right.

5. Picture It   P I J

Materials: pairs of pictures of items or actions that are similar or dissimilar
(or pairs of pictures of events that are causes and effects)

Procedure: 1. Demonstrate how to list the similarities and dissimilarities of two pictures. Explain that you are comparing and contrasting the two.

2. Distribute one pair of pictures to each student. Each student makes a list of similarities and differences, then switches pictures with another student and repeats the procedure.

3. Students compare results.

4. If cause–effect pictures are used, mix up the pictures and have students select those that portray a cause–effect relationship.

☞ This is a demonstration activity. Be sure to provide opportunities for application to meaningful reading tasks.

BIBLIOGRAPHY

IRWIN, J. W. *Teaching Reading Comprehension Processes.* Englewood Cliffs, N.J.: Prentice-Hall, 1986

JETT-SIMPSON, M. "Writing stories using model structures: The circle story," *Language Arts,* 58, March (1981), 293–300.

LUVAAS-BRIGGS, L. "Some 'whole brain' activities for the community college reading class," *Journal of Reading,* 27, April (1984), 644–47.

MCLAUGHLIN, E. M. "QuIP: A writing strategy to improve comprehension of expository structure," *Reading Teacher,* 40, March (1987), 650–54.

MANDLER, J. M. AND N. S. JOHNSON. "Remembrance of things parsed: Story structure and recall," *Cognitive Psychology,* 9, June (1977), 111–51.

NILES, O. "Organization perceived," in *Developing Study Skills in Secondary Schools,* ed. H. Herber. Newark, Del.: International Reading Association, (1965), 57–77.

OLSON, M. W. AND B. LONGNION. "Pattern guides: A workable alternative for content teachers," *Journal of Reading,* 25, May (1982), 736–41.

RUBIN, A. AND D. GENTNER. "An educational technique to encourage practice with high level aspects of text." Paper presented at the annual meeting of the National Reading Conference, San Antonio, Tex., December 1979.

SLOBODKINA, E. *The Wonderful Feast.* Eau Claire, Wisc.: E. M. Hale, 1967.

SMITH, M. AND T. W. BEAN. "Four strategies that develop children's story comprehension and writing," *Reading Teacher,* 37, December (1983), 295–301.

STEIN, N. L. "How children understand stories: A developmental analysis," in L. Katz (ed.), *Current Topics in Early Childhood Education,* Vol. 2. Norwood, N.J.: Ablex Publishing Co. 1979.

STEIN, N. AND C. G. GLENN. "An analysis of story comprehension in elementary school children," in R. Freedle, ed., *Multidisciplinary Approaches to Discourse Comprehension.* Norwood, N.J.: Ablex Publishing Co., 1977.

WHALEY, J. F. "Readers' expectations for story structures," *Reading Research Quarterly,* 17, Fall (1981), 90–114.

PREDICTING

Definition: *Forming hypotheses about the content likely to come next*

RATIONALE

Good readers are constantly forming hypotheses about what is to come next in the passage they are reading. This may involve predicting the next word, the next event, or the content of the entire section to follow. Like so many other comprehension skills, this requires prior knowledge about the content and about the structure of what is being read. It also requires that the reader be actively involved in making meaning out of the words.

The traditional skill of using the context can be placed within the category of prediction. Good readers rely on the context in identifying words. The first group of exercises in this chapter deal with predicting words, because this is an essential part of fluent comprehension.

Tables 18-1 and 18-2 list the content and structure clues that good readers use (see Collins and Smith, 1980) to predict events or whole sections. Sample questions that you might ask to encourage the use of such clues are included in these tables. Note how such questions are more useful to students than the simple "What do you think will come next?" which gives them little information about how to get the answer. Also note that one table is for stories and one is for content-area or nonfiction materials. This is because prediction is very different for these two types of texts. Students who can predict in one type of text may not be able to do so in another.

TABLE 18-1 Clues for Prediction in Stories

Type	Possible Question
Character	What do you know about this character that helps you to guess what she or he will do next?
Situation	Given this situation, what do you think will happen next?
Text Signals	Look at the picture. Look at the title. [Etc.] What does this tell you about the events to follow?
Genre	Given that this is a fable, what do you think will come at the end?
Story Grammar	What kind of information usually comes next in a story? [See Chapter 17.]

TABLE 18-2 Clues for Prediction in Nonfiction

Type	Possible Question
Topic	What do you already know about X that can help you to guess what will be covered next?
Causality	What type of thing does this usually lead to?
Organization	Given the way this is organized, what do you think will come next?
Text Signals	Look at the subheading. Look at the table. Look at the pictures. [Etc.] On the basis of this [these], what do you predict the author will cover in this chapter?
Author's Purpose	Why did the author write this? What does this tell you about what probably comes next?

Encouraging prediction is closely connected to encouraging the use of prior knowledge. Indeed, predicting is really just one of the ways students can use their prior knowledge to make sense of what they are reading. The following chapter describes more general ways to encourage students to use their prior knowledge to understand their reading assignments.

Finally, it is important that encouragement of predicting *not* be limited to specific, planned lessons. Students should be encouraged to make predictions in incidental, informal situations as well. Students can be asked to predict the content of a variety of reading materials in a variety of content areas (see the general teaching suggestions that follow).

INFORMAL DIAGNOSIS

You can informally diagnose students' abilities any time you introduce a piece of reading material, by asking the students to make predictions. Also, you can interrupt a reading assignment and ask the students to make predictions about the end. Be sure to check prior knowledge before assuming students are bad predictors. No one can make a content or structure prediction without previous knowledge about the content or structure of what is being read!

GENERAL TEACHING SUGGESTIONS

1. Whenever possible, ask a variety of prediction questions (see Tables 18-1 and 18-2).

2. Teaching organizational patterns can be tied to making predictions (see Chapter 17). Simply ask students to use what they know about the organization to predict what is coming next.

3. You can teach prediction in the younger grades when you read to the students. Simply read part of a story and pause to let the students predict!

4. Be sure to tell students about the importance of making predictions. Model your own prediction process.

5. Let the students do some predicting each time you make a reading assignment. This will help them develop the habit of predicting.

6. Avoid the "one-right-answer" approach when teaching prediction. Let the students know that many different predictions can be equally good even if only one turns out to be "right."

chapter 18.   PREDICTING
Activities

A.   PREDICTING WORDS

1.   Predict–A–Word*   P I

Procedure: 1.   Introduce to the students the idea that they don't have to use *all* the information on a printed page in order to read the words (see Figure 18-1).

2.   After the students have had several opportunities to practice the process described in Figure 18-1, distribute sheet of sentences with the vowels eliminated and have the students complete them independently. Discuss results.

3.   In the next lesson, after reviewing the use of consonant cues to predict words, introduce to the students the idea that the initial letter of a word, in a sentence in context, can also help them predict the word. Use predictable sentences such as these:

On my birthday I am going to have a p____. We will eat i__ c____ and c___ and play g____.

4.   Provide supervised and individual practice.

Variations: 1.   Students make up their own sentences without vowels or sentences with only the initial letter of a word. They then switch papers and work on each other's Predict-A-Word.

2.   Use students' sentences to make up Predict-A-Word work sheets.

3.   Use the Predict-A-Word format to create study guides for content-area material.

FIGURE 18-1   Introducing Word Prediction (Primary Grades)

Teacher: You've all been reading words and sentences for some time now, and you're getting very good at it. In fact, you're doing so well that I'd like to show you that you can read words *without* seeing all of the letters in the words. [Writes on chalkboard "m_th_r _nd f_th_r."] Who can tell me what these words are?

Students: "Mother" and "father"; that's easy.

Teacher: How did you know?

Students: They just *look* like them, that's all. There aren't any other words that *look* like that.

Teacher: Good thinking. What clues helped you to figure it out?

Students: The letters.

Teacher: And the type of letter that was given was . . . do you know?

Students: Umm . . . not vowels. Consonants.

Teacher: Right. And our language has so many consonants, and so few vowels, that if the vowels are left out we can still figure out the word. In fact, we don't *need* all the information we get in our reading material. We can really sort of predict as we go along, not using all the information given us. Let's try some more of these words. [Th_ b_g d_g ch_s_d th_ l_ttl_ c_t. Th_ l_ttl_ c_t ch_s_d th_ m__s_. Etc.]

    This is a demonstration activity. Be sure to provide opportunities for application to meaningful reading tasks.

* Feldman, 1978.

2. Selective Deletion*   **P I J H A**

Procedure: 1. Choose a selection that is easy to read and blank out a few predictable words that have many synonyms. Keep the first and last sentences intact.

2. Prepare this selection in a cloze format (see Figure 18-2).

3. Divide students into small groups. Give each group copies of the selection.

4. Have students discuss which words they could put in the blanks and still have the selection make sense. Students list these words on their selections.

5. When the class reassembles, write down the words on an overhead projection sheet or the chalkboard.

6. Emphasize that no one answer is correct; many answers would be appropriate. Show the actual words deleted, and discuss how the words suggested were very similar in meaning, so that substituting made little difference in the meaning of the passage.

7. Lead the discussion to the conclusion that reading involves prediction

FIGURE 18-2

On the morning of April 18, 1906, San Francisco was just beginning to wake up when suddenly the earth under the city began to lift and buckle, as if some giant animal had burrowed underneath it and was heaving it up. Frightened people ____1____ into the streets; they saw familiar buildings crumble and fall, ____2____ holes appear suddenly in the streets, and gas and water mains ____3____ open and ____4____ their contents in all directions. The earthquake struck San Francisco in two separate shocks. The first, which lasted about forty seconds, ____5____ at 5:12 A.M. The second shock struck the ____6____ city ten seconds later. Although this shock lasted only fifteen seconds, it did more ____7____ than the first. Fires broke out immediately and burned almost ____8____ for three days. Five hundred city blocks containing 28,000 ____9____ were ____10____, leaving many people homeless. Four hundred fifty-two people were killed in the earthquake and fire.

Words deleted: 1. dashed
                          2. great
                          3. crack
                          4. shoot
                          5. hit
                          6. frightened
                          7. damage
                          8. uncontrolled
                          9. buildings
                          10. destroyed

and guessing. Ask which clues might have made their guesses coincide better— initial-letter clues, median-letter clues, or final-letter clues.

☞ This is a demonstration activity. Be sure to provide opportunities for application to meaningful reading tasks.

* Rigg and Kazemek, 1985.

3. **They Did** *What?*   **PIJ**

> *Procedure:*   1. Have students take familiar stories and replace important words with errors.
>
> 2. Students exchange stories, find the errors, and correct them.

4. **TV Bloopers**   **PIJ**

> *Procedure:*   1. Have each student create a dialogue with intentional errors.
>
> 2. Students read or act out their dialogues. The class tries to find and correct the errors.

5. **Predingo**   **PI**

> *Procedure:*   1. Take predictable stories and delete predictable words.
>
> 2. Create Bingo cards with different selections of predictable words.

3. Read the story and have students follow Bingo procedure in supplying the eliminated words.

6. Clozewords*   P I

Procedure:

1. Select a 200-word passage that students can easily read. You may want to vary the length according to the grade level.

2. Leave the first two to three sentences intact. Then replace every fifth word with a blank. Do not omit proper nouns.

3. Number all the blanks.

4. Put passage on an overhead projection sheet. Have students number their papers to correspond with the number of blanks in the passage.

5. Read the first two or three sentences to the students. Tell them that their task is to predict the story's meaning from the words available, and to write down a word for each blank.

6. Set a time limit. It is not necessary for all students to complete the material for this exercise to be successful.

7. When time is up, encourage students to tell the class their word choices, justifying their selections. Write the words for each blank on the board. Discuss the choices.

8. The class votes on the best word choices. Point out that the early selections will limit the later choices because of the context.

9. Create a class version of the story by filling in the blanks with the class's word choices.

10. Compare the class version with the original and note and discuss changes.

* Brazell, 1985.

7. I Guess*   P I J H A

Procedure:

1. Students look at chapter titles and headings of material to be read.

2. They predict words that will be found in the selection. Words are written on the board.

3. After reading the selection, students report how many of the words they found in the reading.

* Kaplan and Tuchman, 1980.

B. PREDICTING WHAT COMES NEXT

1. Find the Error*   P I J

Procedure:

1. Select a highly predictable passage of eight to ten sentences.

2. Replace some of the predictable words with anomalous words (see Figure 18-3).

FIGURE 18-3 Find the Error

Directions: There are 8 errors in this paragraph. Find the errors and correct them.

Last week the president of the United States drove to the airport in her favorite horse. When she arrived at the airport, she climbed the rope ladder and sat down in *US 1,* the presidential train. After the cook contacted the control tower, the plane took off into the woods. Two hours later it landed, the jet engines making a big squeak as the plane pulled in to the airport of Chicago, Illinois. The president smiled as she said, "I am really miserable to be here in Chicago." Then she climbed into a big tricycle and drove off.

---

3.   Tell students that they are going to practice finding errors in written material, a very useful strategy to use when reading. Provide relevant examples of material that could be checked for errors (movie timetables, directions for tests, and so forth) and have them suggest other examples.

4.   Demonstrate how to find errors in the passage, explaining the clues you used (syntax, prior knowledge) to do so.

5.   Provide supervised practice for the students, having them share results and being sure they explain *how* they decided where there was an error. Be sure to specify how many errors there are in each selection.

6.   Provide copies of a selection for students to work on individually. Have students share their results with the class and specify how they found the errors.

Variation: Content-area review: Select a summary from a content-area text and replace predictable and important words with errors. Have students correct the selection.

* Goodman and Burke, 1972.

2. Directed Reading/Thinking Activity (DR/TA)*   I J H A

Procedure: 1.   Divide material to be read into segments appropriate for students' reading level.

2.   Tell students the purpose of the strategy they are about to learn—to help them comprehend when reading by previewing, predicting, and using their prior knowledge.

3.   Have students preview the material, reading titles, headings, graphic aids, and so forth.

4.   Based on their previewing and prior knowledge, students predict the content of the material.

5.   Write the predictions on the chalkboard.

6.   Students read the first segment of the material.

7.   To encourage students to use context, do not introduce vocabulary before they read. Explain this to the students.

8.   After the segment is completed, discuss how the content did or did not match the predictions.

9.   Repeat steps 6–8 for the remaining sections.

* Stauffer, 1969.

3.   Directed–Inquiry Activity (DIA)*   I J H A

Procedure: 1.   Use the same procedure as for the Directed Reading/Thinking Activity. Ask six key questions to focus students' predictions: Who? What? Where? When? Why? How?

2.   Students fill in a six-column study guide with their predictions.

Variations: 1.   Content-area review: Students fill in all but one or two of the columns for different historical events they have chosen. They then try to complete each other's papers. Groups may use a charades approach.

2.   Content-area review: Use a partially filled in work sheet for a study guide or a test.

* Stauffer, 1969.

4.   I Predict   P I J

Procedure: 1.   Tell the students that they will have the opportunity to create their own sentence and story endings, and that to do so they will have to predict what they think will happen. To make good predictions, they will have to draw on their own knowledge and on their knowledge about the words in the sentences.

2.   Have them generate possible endings to sentences such as "One day the teacher decided to _____. He knew that this would make the class happy because _____.

3.   After several suggestions have been made, change "teacher" to "king" and "class" to "his subjects" and have the students develop these sentences.

4.   Encourage students to explain why the endings changed when the words changed, and why they would have different expectations for a teacher and class than for a king and his subjects.

5.   Provide the students with a group of sentences that constitute the skeleton of a story. Have them complete the sentences individually or in groups. Share the different stories with the class.

5.   Comic Strip Prediction   P I

Materials: comic strips with the final frame(s) cut off
construction paper
manila folders

Procedure: 1.   Mount each comic strip on a piece of construction paper. Number or letter the paper for identification.

2.   Mount each final frame on a manila folder. Number or letter the folder on the back to correspond with the strip it completes.

3.   Tell the students that they are going to have the opportunity to help a writer of comic strips finish a story. For younger children, you might dress this up by saying the endings have been lost.

4.   Show an overhead transparency of an uncompleted comic strip with a predictable ending, and demonstrate how to use clues in the story to predict the ending.

5.   Draw a stick-figure representation of a possible story ending.

6.   Show the students the actual ending of the story, and compare it with the one you have just completed. Demonstrate how to find the ending of the comic strip by matching the number of the strip with the number of the final frame.

7.   Repeat this process with another comic strip, using suggestions from students to complete the strip.

8.   Once again, compare this ending with the actual ending. Be sure to make clear reasons for any discrepancies, focusing on where the information for the prediction was found (in the strip or in past experiences). Indicate that there could be several possible endings all of which can be good.

9.   Give the students a copy of a mounted, unfinished comic strip.

10.   Tell them that their task is to read the strip and decide what the ending is to be. They must then draw the final frame of the strip in stick figures.

11.   Students can then go to the box or file where you have stored the actual final frames of the strips, look for the corresponding ending, and compare their endings with the actual one. If desired, they can enter their results on a Comic Strip Record Sheet, indicating the number of the comic strip they used.

12.   Students may then choose another comic strip to predict.

Variation: Have students cut out their own favorite comic strips and make additional comic strip cards for use in this activity.

6.   Open–Ended Story with a Slant*   I J H A

Procedure: 1.   Create a story that is brief, filled with action, and headed quickly for a climax.

2.   Type up two versions of the story (see Figure 18-4), the only difference being the sex of the protagonist. Do not explain this to the students.

3.   Distribute one version of the story to half the class, the other version to the other half.

4.   Students are to read the story and write the ending.

5.   Insist that there be no discussion or sharing during the completion of the exercise.

6.   When the students have completed their stories have volunteers read their endings.

7.   Lead a discussion about how the sex of the protagonist led to different endings. Focus on the different details used for each protagonist.

* Shuman, 1978.

FIGURE 18-4 Sample Open-Ended Story (in the alternate version *Joanna* is replaced by *Juan*)

> It was a cold and windy night in December. Joanna had not wanted to go out to get a pizza by herself, but no one else in the dorm would volunteer. She ordered the pizza at Joe's, paid her money, and began the long walk home to the campus. Her heart pounded as she passed the old Gatling mansion, its shutters slapping in the wind, its empty windows staring blindly at her. She had never liked the vacant homestead of a once famous family; it looked as if it contained memories of the notorious Prohibition mobsters who once lived and worked there. As she walked briskly past the property, she noted a light flickering in one of the windows. A cold feeling gripped her, and she began to walk even faster. Suddenly, as she passed the stone gateposts of the mansion, a tall man dressed in strange, old-fashioned clothes stepped in front of her, blocking her way. In an instant _____

7. What's Next? P I J

Procedure: 1. Cut up old books and insert prediction questions at appropriate points.

2. Letter and number the sections of each book.

3. Place the book sections in independent learning packets. Students read a section, make predictions, and check the predictions by reading the next section.

☞ This is a demonstration activity. Be sure to provide opportunities for application to meaningful reading tasks.

8. Then What? P I J

Procedure: 1. Students write stories and cut them up into sections.

2. Students write prediction questions at the end of each section—for example, "Then what?"

3. Students letter and number their story sections, exchange them, and make predictions for each other.

Variations: 1. Stories can be taken to lower-grade classrooms for reading material. The lower-grade students make predictions, which are returned with the stories to the authors.

2. Students give their stories a twist. For example, they write the beginning of a story about Mary, ask for predictions, and then reveal in the next section that Mary is a horse and her school is a riding school.

9. What Will Happen Now? I J H A

Procedure: 1. Establish a routine whereby students, upon finishing one chapter of a text, write down a prediction of the content of the next chapter. They must give reasons for their predictions. For example, if Chapter 1 was "Portugal Becomes Rich," a possible prediction might be that other countries would also begin to colonize the New World because they too wanted to get rich. Another prediction might be that other countries would also begin to look for a shorter route to Asia.

2. Students keep a record of their predictions and their accuracy. As the course develops, their predictions should improve.

10. What's in a Chapter?   I J H A

Procedure: 1.   Write the title of Chapter 1 of an assigned text on the board—for example, "Europe Discovers the Riches of the East."

2.   Ask "What East?" "What riches?" "What part of Europe?"

3.   Students provide answers. Write them on the board.

4.   Ask students what graphic aids they think will be in the chapter. Write answers on the board.

5.   Tell students to *skim* the chapter to confirm their predictions about the meaning of the title and about the graphic aids.

11. What's in a Course?   I J H A

Procedure: 1.   Before students have had a chance to look at their content-area textbooks, tell them to leave the books closed on their desks.

2.   Ask what they think will be contained in the text, based on the title and what they already know about the course.

3.   Write the predictions on the board.

4.   Encourage use of prior knowledge of the subject and prior knowledge of school procedures, such as exams and the curriculum.

5.   Have students help you categorize the topics of the course, and put these in time order if appropriate.

6.   Encourage elaborations about topics—for example, "What *about* the Civil War will be included?"

7.   Ask students if anything else should be contained in the book. Write down the answers—maps, glossary, index, and so on.

8.   Students open books. Check off on the board all correct predictions. Write in any omissions.

9.   Discuss reasons for omissions—lack of prior knowledge, lack of interest, the feeling that *everyone* knows that, and so forth.

10.   At this point there are several alternatives:

a.   Have students predict times and content of exams.

b.   Have them make a graphic overview of the book's contents.

c.   Have them use similar procedure to predict the first chapter.

d.   Ask students if they can see the value of this procedure—namely, that it helps them organize what they already know, predict what they are about to learn, and see the organization of the course.

12. True or False*   P I J

Procedure: 1.   Create a list of statements about the material to be read.

2.   Read the statements to the students *before* they read the material. Have students number their papers to correspond with the statements. Ask them to hypothesize whether each statement is true or false and to mark their papers accordingly.

3. Divide students into small groups. Groups read the text to verify their hypotheses.

4. Students share results with the class, discussing the reasons for correct and incorrect hypotheses.

* Gaskins, 1981.

13. Directed Prediction* PIJHA

Procedure:

1. Choose one or two major turning points in a story to be read.

2. Stop the reading at these chosen points and ask "What do you think will happen?" Encourage differences of opinion.

3. Encourage students to give arguments for their predictions by asking "Why do you think so?" Students must supply the reasons for their predictions, using prior experience and/or the material in the story.

4. After students have read more of the story, have them evaluate their original predictions in light of the material they have just read: "Do you *still* think that X will happen, or have you changed your mind?" Have students give reasons for retaining or changing their original predictions: "Why do you want to change [retain] your original prediction? What did you read that helped you make this decision?"

5. Create follow-up activities, such as writing and drawing, that facilitate reflection on the story's content and language.

6. Directed prediction is a modification of the prereading procedure of asking "Have you ever . . . ?" and then "What do you think X will do now?" The difference is the focus of the questions. Directed prediction encourages students to focus on the text and to support their predictions with reasoning.

* Nissel, 1987.

BIBLIOGRAPHY

BRAZELL, W. "Group instruction with the cloze procedure," *Reading Teacher,* 39, October (1985), 121–22.

COLLINS, A. AND E. E. SMITH. *Teaching the Process of Reading Instruction.* Technical Report no. 182, Center for the Study of Reading, University of Illinois. Urbana-Champaign, 1980.

DEVLIN, N. "Essays on Education," *Princeton Packet,* June 18, 1985.

FELDMAN, J. M. "Who needs vowels?" in L. C. Ehris, R. W. Barron, and J. M. Feldman (eds.), *The Recognition of Words.* Newark, Del.: International Reading Association, 1978, 57-71.

GASKINS, I. W. "Reading for learning: Going beyond basals in the elementary grades," *Reading Teacher,* 35, December (1981), 323–28.

GOODMAN, Y. AND C. BURKE. *Reading Miscue Inventory Manual.* New York: Macmillan, 1972.

KAPLAN, E. M. AND A. TUCHMAN. Vocabulary strategies belong in the hands of learners. *Journal of Reading,* 24, October (1980), 32–35.

NISSEL, D. "A new face of comprehension instruction: A closer look at questions," *Reading Teacher,* 40, March (1987), 604–6.

RIGG, P. AND F. E. KAZEMEK. "For adults only: Reading materials for adult literacy students," *Journal of Reading,* 28, May (1985), 726–31.

SHUMAN, R. B. "Writing workshops and the teaching of reading." Paper presented at the annual meeting of the International Reading Association, Miami Beach, Fla, May 2–6, 1978.

STAUFFER, R. G. *Directing Reading Maturity as a Cognitive Process.* New York: Harper & Row, Pub., 1969.

USING PRIOR KNOWLEDGE

Definition: *Making inferences that link the information in the reading passage to information previously known*

RATIONALE

In some ways, all comprehension consists of tying new information in a passage to information already known. In this chapter, we will look at ways to encourage students to do this during and after reading. We include this chapter in Part VI, which deals with elaborating on the text, because the inferences that students make to tie new information to old are often unique to the individual and often go beyond the intended meaning of the author.

It is important to realize, however, that such inferences are not just luxuries for the better students to use after they get the information in the text. These inferences are essential for understanding and recalling the text. Every reader must use them to learn and recall new information. Thus, the tying of new information to old must become a habit for all readers.

Teaching elaboration of prior knowledge requires a classroom in which students are encouraged to express divergent opinions, in which many answers are accepted as correct, and in which the students' cultures and backgrounds are valued. Indeed, the sup-

pression of culturally specific prior-knowledge inferences may account for some of the difficulty of culturally different students.

There are many steps involved in tying new knowledge to old. First, students must have some prior knowledge in the first place. Second, they need to know which information to apply, and they need to have it "in the front of their minds." If students do not have the necessary prior knowledge or do not know which knowledge to apply, then they or you will have to do some prereading preparation. Some suggestions for building prior knowledge and activating it are included in Chapter 7.

Finally, students need to keep the pertinent prior knowledge in mind while they are reading, and they need to actively make those individual inferences that link the new to the known. Activities specifically designed to encourage this are included in this chapter. We have divided them into activities that include direct instruction (section A) and practice activities that use guided reading (section B).

Guided reading refers to any activity that students complete while they are reading. This could include responding to questions inserted in the text, completing a reading guide at selected intervals, or pausing to discuss the text with you. These activities are useful because they affect the students' "on-line" thinking.

You will find that many of the activities elsewhere in this book include steps that build, activate, or refer to prior knowledge during or after reading. This is because prior knowledge is used for many comprehension strategies and cannot be separated from any act of comprehension (see Chapter 2). Always keep this in mind, regardless of the strategy you are trying to teach.

INFORMAL DIAGNOSIS

It is important for you to diagnose the various steps of prior-knowledge integration separately. First, determine if the students have enough necessary prior knowledge. Ask general questions about the topic, or, if you have the time, read a passage and note the knowledge that is assumed. Question the students about some of this. If they are able to answer most of your prior-knowledge questions, then see if they make inferences that link the new information to the knowledge they already possess. Have them read the passage and recall it for you. Ask questions that will elicit prior-knowledge inferences. Questions such as "What does this remind you of?" or "What picture did you get in your mind?"—questions that require students to go beyond the information in the text—will do this.

GENERAL TEACHING SUGGESTIONS

1.   Be sure to let students know that it is okay to use their prior knowledge in interpreting incoming information. Model this process for them. "Using your own life" is a phrase coined by children to describe this (Hansen and Pearson, 1983).

2.   Be sure students know that their inferences may be unique and still appropriate. Encourage the feeling that all answers are somewhat correct.

3.   Make sure students know that their prior experiences and their individual interpretations will be valued. Tell students that because everyone has different experiences, everyone's opinion is important.

4.   Encourage students to actively interact with the material by asking them to complete study guides that require them to tie new information with information they learned previously (see the activities in section B).

5.   Be sure to build or review prior knowledge at the beginning of each reading assignment (see Chapter 7).

6.   Cut up books and insert questions in the text that ask the students to use their prior knowledge to interpret what they are reading. The students can then answer these questions during reading. This will help them to keep the appropriate prior knowledge activated.

7.   Conduct a guided reading session in which you question the students after a portion of the text is read. Design questions that encourage the ongoing use of the appropriate prior knowledge.

8.   Ask students to write down the parts of their text that remind them of something they have experienced. They should do this while they are reading.

9.   Use one passage as prior knowledge for another.

10.   If a student can't answer a question because he or she forgets to use prior knowledge, explain to the student how the question could have been answered. Don't just say that he or she is wrong!

11.   Be sure to use postreading questions that build on the same prior knowledge you activated before having the students read.

chapter 19.   USING PRIOR KNOWLEDGE WHILE READING
Activities

    A.   DIRECT INSTRUCTION
        1.   X Marks the Spot   P I J H A
        2.   Only Elaborations   P I
        3.   Reading Interaction   I J H A
    B.   GUIDED READING
        1.   Anticipation Guide   J H A
        2.   Statement-Based Reading Guides   I J H A
        3.   K–W–L (What We Know, Want to Learn, and Have
             Learned)   I J H A
        4.   To Be Continued   P I J H A

A.   DIRECT INSTRUCTION

1.   X Marks The Spot*   P I J H A

Procedure: 1.   Read aloud to the students, stopping at appropriate places and sharing your use of prior knowledge to elaborate upon the text. For example, if reading *Heart of Darkness* by Joseph Conrad, you might pause and say: "I like how the Director of the Companies is described as looking 'nautical.' It reminds me of an old sea captain I knew when I was a kid. Like this character, he liked to look out to sea. I can just see him with a cap, beard, and pipe. I think this also indicates that he is hardened and used to being alone, a quiet person always dreaming about the old days."

    2.   Explain that this is an appropriate use of prior knowledge, as it helps you see the character being described and is relevant to the story's progress.

    3.   To clarify your meaning, you might want to give an example of an inappropriate use of prior knowledge: "If I had said 'This description reminds me of my Uncle John, who used to be a sailor and who ran off and left my Aunt Molly,' this would not really help me with the story. This knowledge is too *personal,* and could not help me understand the story any better."

    4.   After demonstrating your use of prior knowledge, pause at various places in the narrative and encourage students to provide examples of their own elaborations. Discuss whether these are appropriate or inappropriate.

    5.   As a final step, give the students material to read in which you have marked possible places for integration with prior knowledge.

    6.   Reinforce this skill whenever possible with natural reading tasks.

Variations: 1.   Have students mark the places in reading material where integration with prior knowledge is appropriate.

    2.   Teacher and students read the same material, mark where integrations were made, and share the elaborations they used. Comparing and contrasting both the places where the procedure was used and the elaborations made would illustrate not only how prior knowledge is important in reading, but how different prior knowledge can create different interpretations of a book.

3.   Young students can take home marked copies of books and have their parents share their elaborations with them at appropriate places.

4.   Young readers can read familiar animal tales and then suggest what elaborations animals hearing the stories might make.

* Irwin, 1986.

2.   Only Elaborations*   P I

Procedure: 1.   *Purpose discussion:* Lead a discussion designed to make students aware of *how* they are learning. Encourage them to realize that they use old knowledge to understand new knowledge—that they are *elaborating*.

2.   *Strategy discussion:* Have the students compare something from their own lives with something that might happen in a story they are about to read. Select two or three concepts to be developed and lead a discussion on the connections students will have to make when elaborating. For example, if the story is about an adult who has a certain fear, ask the students what they think an adult could be afraid of. Help students formulate hypotheses to answer your questions. When the discussion is finished, instruct students to read the story to see if their hypotheses were correct. Students should always read the story directly after the Purpose and Strategy discussions.

3.   *Postreading discussion:* This discussion is composed of ten questions, all of which encourage prior-knowledge elaboration. Because students cannot formulate their answers simply by reading statements from the text, interaction will result as they present evidence from both the text and their own experiences to support their answers. From this and the previous two discussions students come to realize that the meaning of the text does not lie only within the words on the page. There may be as many meanings as there are readers. Students will also have demonstrated that there can be more than one answer to a question.

Variations: 1.   Model prior-knowledge elaboration using a content-area text. When students finish their text reading assignment ask only elaboration questions.

2.   Use familiar folk stories and fairy tales as the basis of strategies for prior-knowledge elaboration.

3.   Have students make up questions about prior-knowledge elaboration from familiar stories.

* Hansen and Hubbard, 1984.

B.   GUIDED READING

1.   Anticipation Guide*   J H A

Procedure: 1.   Read the passage to be studied and identify the major concepts. Decide which concepts to stress in the guide.

2.   Determine which concepts will challenge the students' beliefs and which will support their beliefs.

3.   Create three to five statements that challenge or support any ideas the students probably have about the major concepts. Refer to generally accepted

FIGURE 19-1   Anticipation Guide

Directions: Before reading the selection about big lunches and skipped breakfasts, read each of the following statements and decide whether you agree or disagree with it. If you agree, put a check beside it. Be prepared to discuss your reasons for your decisions in class.

___ 1. If you have to skip breakfast, a big lunch will serve as a good pick-me-up and give you needed energy.

___ 2. Students who eat breakfast do better in school.

___ 3. If you don't have time to eat breakfast, a glass of juice is better than nothing at all.

___ 4. Onion soup with cheese, meatloaf, and a tuna sandwich are all good choices for breakfast.

Based on Readence, Bean, & Baldwin, 1981, p. 132.

common knowledge and cliches. Students are stimulated most by concepts about which many people have opinions but few facts.

4.   On an overhead transparency, a ditto sheet, or the chalkboard write the statements you have created, leaving spaces to the left of each for student responses (see Figure 19-1).

5.   Discuss each statement and have the students respond by defending their opinions, not simply by answering yes or no. (Or have students respond first individually and then meet in groups, come to a consensus, and report to the whole class.)

6.   Instruct the students to alter their answers while reading, if appropriate.

7.   After students have read the text, use the Anticipation Guide in a discussion about changes or modifications that had to be made because of new textual information.

* Readence, Bean, and Baldwin, 1981.

2.   Statement–Based Reading Guides*   I J H A

Procedure: 1.   Create three groups of statements—one each on the literal, interpretive, and applied levels—that focus on concepts you want to develop in the new reading material (see Figure 19-2).

2.   Have the students read the material and respond to the statements while they are reading. A good strategy is to have them work in groups.

3.   Lead a discussion about the material and the responses. Students must justify their responses by referring to the text or to prior knowledge.

FIGURE 19-2   Shakespeare's Sonnet 29: Text and Reading Guide

When in disgrace with fortune and men's eyes
I all alone beweep my outcast state,
And trouble deaf Heaven with my bootless cries,
And look upon myself and curse my fate,
Wishing me like to one more rich in hope,

Featured like him, like him with friends possessed,
Desiring this man's art and that man's scope,
With what I most enjoy contented least—
Yet in these thoughts myself almost despising,
Haply I think on thee, and then my state,
Like to the lark at break of day arising
From sullen earth, sings hymns at Heaven's gate.
　　　For thy sweet love remembered such wealth brings
　　　That then I scorn to change my state with kings.

Literal Level
　Directions: Here are several statements related to the sonnet. Check those that contain information included in the sonnet. Refer to the sonnet to verify your answers.

____　1. The poet cursed fate for his loneliness and disgrace.
____　2. In his unhappiness, even the things he enjoyed displeased him.
____　3. The poet prayed to God to change his state.

Interpretive level
　Directions: Here are statements that contain some possible hidden meanings. Check those you think contain hidden meanings that might be in the sonnet. You may refer to the sonnet to find these items.

____　4. Remembrance of happiness in the past can bring strength to one who is unhappy.
____　5. It is useless to pray to get help for unhappiness.
____　6. When you hate your fate, you may come to hate yourself.

Applied level
　Directions: Here are statements that, according to your beliefs and according to the sonnet, may or may not be true. Check those statements with which you think you can agree.

____　7. Love makes all things bearable.
____　8. The grass is always greener on the other side of the fence.
____　9. An optimist sees a glass half full; a pessimist sees it half empty.
____ 10. Time heals all wounds.
____ 11. One person's hero is another person's villain.
____ 12. To be without love is real poverty.

---

* Riley, 1980.

3.   K–W–L (What We *Know, Want* to Learn, and Have *Learned*)*   I J H A

Procedure:　　1.   STEP K: WHAT WE KNOW

　　　a.   Students brainstorm information they know about the topic assigned for reading—for example, seagulls.

　　　b.   Write all information on the chalkboard or overhead projector.

c.   Provide students with a form on which they can record information. Use three columns labeled, K-What we know, W-What we want to learn, and L-What we have learned and still need to learn respectively.

d.   Help students think of more general topics of information for the brainstormed material. For example, if you look at all the information, you will probably note that much of it is about what seagulls look like. Suggest that an easy way to organize this information would be to mark *L* for *looks* next to these similar facts.

e.   Continue modeling and encouraging student comments. Make a chart with a topic heading for each category that you and the class have found.

f.   Have students fill in column K of their work sheets—What We Know—with these categories.

2.   STEP W: WHAT DO WE WANT TO LEARN?

a.   Before beginning to read, students write down on their work sheets the questions they are most interested in having answered.

b.   Have the students read and answer their questions. Depending on the length of what is to be read, use one or more sessions for this.

3.   STEP L: WHAT WE LEARNED

a.   While reading, students fill in column L of their work sheets.

4.   After reading, students share the information they have learned, which reinforces the content, and share the questions that still need to be answered, which reinforces the concept that each reader brings different interests and background knowledge to reading. They can then add these questions to the L column.

Variations: 1.   Provide a library of materials on the reading topic to facilitate further research. Encourage students to write up their findings and add them to the library.

2.   Have the students who have researched additional material make a tape: "What You Always Wanted to Know about _____ but Couldn't Find Out." Add this tape to the materials library and the classroom library.

3.   Make a bulletin board display of student questions and answers.

* Ogle, 1986.

4.   To Be Continued   PIJHA

Procedure: 1.   Establish a routine for reading new material whereby students review the material already studied. Suggest that the procedure is just like following a TV soap opera: you have to have a summary of what has gone before to be able to understand what is going to happen next.

2.   Students may review prior material by reading chapter summaries, reviewing the table of contents, or reading their own previously completed study guides.

3.   To facilitate this process, provide students with a map, graphic outline, or summary sheet, which they add to as they go along. By using different colors

for each section of the map or outline, students can highlight areas where different material was added.

4. Reinforce this routine if reading books aloud to the students. Have several students summarize the previous events in the story before reading on.

BIBLIOGRAPHY

HANSEN, J. AND R. HUBBARD. "Poor readers can draw inferences," *Reading Teacher,* 37, March (1984), 586–89.

HANSEN, J. AND P. D. PEARSON. "An instructional study improving inferential comprehension of good and poor fourth grade readers," *Journal of Educational Psychology,* 75, December (1983) 821–29.

IRWIN, J. W. *Teaching Reading Comprehension Processes.* Englewood Cliffs, N.J.: Prentice-Hall, 1986.

OGLE, D. M. "K–W–L: A teaching model that develops active reading of expository text," *Reading Teacher,* 39, February (1986), 564–70.

READENCE, J. E., T. W. BEAN, AND R. S. BALDWIN. *Content Reading: An Integrated Approach.* Dubuque, Iowa: Kendall/Hunt, 1981.

RILEY, J. D. "Statement-based reading guides and quality of teacher responses," *Journal of Reading,* 23, May (1980) 715–18.

chapter 20

IMAGING

Definition: *Forming mental images of sensory experiences; includes visual, aural, tactile, olfactory, and kinesthetic imagery*

RATIONALE

Good readers often form mental images while they read. Such images seem to increase recall, at least for some readers. Research has indicated that for high-picture learners (students who learn more easily from pictures than from words), instructions to image while reading have improved comprehension. Teachers also report that imagery instructions often increase enjoyment and elaboration.

Remember that though some students may often form images when they are reading stories and novels, they may be less likely to image when reading content-area materials, even though imaging may be even more crucial there. Thus, instruction should involve all types of materials.

Also remember that different students will need different types of images, and that some students are more picture-oriented than others. This is largely because people have their own learning styles. Many believe that children learn best when encouraged to take advantage of their own preferred style, which may or may not include imaging.

You can use direct instruction to encourage students to image (see section A), or you can integrate direct instruction with drawing and writing activities (section B). Finally, reading a picture is the reverse of forming one's own mental image and can be very important in some situations. Thus, activities for teaching picture reading have also been included in this chapter.

INFORMAL DIAGNOSIS

You will probably learn most about your students' ability to form different types of mental images by asking them to describe their images after reading. This description may take many forms: discussing orally, writing an essay, drawing a picture, selecting from predrawn pictures, role playing, and so forth. Be careful to use a form with which the students are comfortable.

GENERAL TEACHING SUGGESTIONS

1. Be sure to grade students on the accuracy of their reported images, rather than on the quality of their picture, essay, or whatever.

2. Set the stage for imaging by modeling: describe your own mental images to the students.

3. Be sure to encourage imaging with all the senses: kinesthetic, visual, auditory, olfactory, and tactile!

4. Use writing activities to show students how authors try to express their sensory experiences.

5. To stimulate during-reading imaging, show pictures before students read.

6. Be sure to teach imaging with many different types of materials, including trade books and content-area texts.

7. Use filmstrips, films, artifacts, experiments, or pictures when introducing new material.

8. Draw diagrams of rooms or other pertinent settings on the board when discussing reading materials.

9. Have students illustrate material they are reading or writing.

chapter 20. IMAGING
Activities

A.	DIRECT INSTRUCTION	
	1. Mental Images	P I J H A
	2. Picture It	P I J H A
	3. Program-Music Imagery	P I J
B.	DRAWING AND WRITING	
	1. Describe It	P I
	2. Stick Pix	P I
	3. Sense-Write-Read	P I J H A
	4. Scene of the Crime	P I J H A
	5. Prediction Pix	P I
C.	PICTURE READING	
	1. Which Pix?	P I J H A
	2. Picture Bingo	P I

A. DIRECT INSTRUCTION

1. Mental Images*   P I J H A

Procedure: 1.   By presenting many examples of imaging, introduce the idea of using mental images to determine word meaning.

2.   Have students close their eyes and listen as you read to them a descriptive passage with one unknown word. Instruct students to imagine the person, place, or thing as you read.

3.   Students describe their images to the group and brainstorm key words from their descriptions. Write these words on the board. Often these key words will be good synonyms for the unknown word.

* Luvaas-Briggs, 1984.

2. Picture It*   P I J H A

Procedure: 1.   Choose short passages or selections that contain vivid descriptions.

2.   Read the students one of the passages. Then have them listen to another selection after instructing them to try to visualize the scene (or person) being described.

3.   Ask the students to describe the scene or person in each passage. "Which one do you remember better? Why?" The one best remembered will most likely be the one they were instructed to visualize.

4.   Explain that many people comprehend and recall information better when they try to picture what they are reading. This skill of making a mental image of material read will not only help them remember what they have been reading; it will also make the material more interesting to read.

5.   Suggest that they try a "picture it" technique. Have them relax, close their eyes, and listen to you describe a situation. For example, you might describe a local eating spot, including not only visual details but descriptions of sounds and tastes.

6. Ask them if they can "see" what you just described. Have students share their own perceptions of the scene.

7. Have the students once again relax and close their eyes. This time read to them one of the passages you have chosen.

8. Have students create a mental image of the passage and verbally summarize their images.

9. Practice this technique with other types of writing, including directions.

10. When assigning material, encourage students to use this skill as they read.

Variation: Select for imaging practice certain parts of material to be read.

* Luvaas-Briggs, 1984.

3. Program—Music Imagery   P I J

Procedure: 1. Choose program music that has a definite and easily identifiable theme. Holst's *The Planets* and Tchaikovsky's *1812 Overture* and *Peter and the Wolf* are examples.

2. Give students a general overview of the story content of the music. The record jacket or tape-container insert will provide much of this information.

3. Have students close their eyes and listen to the music, trying to imagine the story being portrayed.

4. Discuss with students the mental pictures they saw as they listened to the music. Identify the passages in the music that provided clues about the story. If you use *The Planets,* which is particularly appropriate if the class is studying Greek and Roman gods, you can ask the students to guess which planets are being represented by the various passages in the piece.

B. DRAWING AND WRITING

1. Describe It   P I

Procedure: 1. Ask students to choose an event in their past that is very vivid and memorable to them.

2. So that they can explain to others what this event was like, have them create a chart with five columns:

SIGHTS   SOUNDS   SMELLS   TASTES   FEELINGS

3. Their task is to re-create the event by filling in the columns with as many details as they can remember.

4. Once the chart is filled in, have them write a description of the event, using as many of the details as possible.

5. Once the descriptions have been written, have the students exchange papers and draw a picture of their partner's description.

Variation: Use people or animals as subjects.

2. Stick Pix   P I

Procedure: 1.   Give students sentences describing an action—for example, "Mary is eating an ice cream cone." "The alligator is eating my brother."

2.   Have the students draw stick pictures illustrating the sentences.

3.   After students have practiced this skill, have them draw stick figures for groups of sentences.

Variation: Mix up the pictures and the sentences and have students try to match them up.

3. Sense–Write–Read   P I J H A

Procedure: 1.   Review with students the importance of being able to see images when reading. Read a vivid description passage to illustrate the use of sensory imagery. Have students tell you the senses appealed to in the selection.

2.   Write on the board under the headings *sight, sound, smell, taste,* and *touch* the images they supply. Discuss the effect of such imagery in making the passage vivid, memorable, and easy to comprehend.

3.   Provide students with a Senses Work Sheet (see Figure 20-1) and have them think of a personal experience to write about. Students fill in columns with the sensory details they recall about the event. They note which detail was most vivid in their memory of the event.

4.   Students write a short paragraph describing the experience, using the sensory details they have recorded.

5.   Students exchange paragraphs. Using another work sheet, partners read each other's paragraph and record the details included. They list the details they found most vivid and appealing. They can also write any questions about the paragraph they might like answered, such as "How much did the cat weigh? How thick was its fur?"

6.   Students compare original notes with partners' record sheets. They may then rewrite their paragraph if they have omitted details or want to add more details.

FIGURE 20-1   Senses Work Sheet

Directions: List below each sense the details you want to include in your paragraph. Try to include at least ____ in each column. Use this work sheet when writing your paragraph.

SIGHT	SOUND	SMELL	TASTE	TOUCH

Which detail is most vivid to you? _____

7. Students read each other's paragraphs to the group. The other students close their eyes and try to envision the scene.

8. Class discussion focuses on the sensory images used and their effect in clarifying the description.

4. Scene Of The Crime   P I J H A

Procedure: 1. Show students on the overhead or board a typical room layout found in a mystery novel. Agatha Christie novels are a good source.

2. Discuss how mystery authors frequently supply such diagrams to help the reader solve the mystery; the plan of the room is often essential to the solution. The game of Clue is another good example of this. Explain that these diagrams are not often given in other books, because authors rely on giving descriptions and assume that their readers will create a picture in their head.

3. Provide students with a written description of a room and demonstrate how to create a diagram of it.

4. Have students use another description to create a diagram. Share results.

5. Extend this activity to relevant content-area material.

Variations: 1. Have students write descriptions of a room, exchange papers, and diagram each other's descriptions.

2. Have students write descriptions (or draw diagrams) of familiar rooms. Make copies of their descriptions and have the class try to identify the rooms.

5. Prediction Pix   P I

Procedure: 1. Choose a storybook with vivid descriptions and good illustrations. Tell the students that you are going to try an experiment to see what kind of illustrations they can create in their heads for a good story. Read the book aloud to the students. Do not show them the illustrations. Cover the book in brown paper if the cover is well illustrated. You may want to read the story more than once.

2. Students create one or more illustrations for the book. Read aloud descriptions if students need reminders.

3. Students can compare their illustrations with those in the book.

4. Discuss how their illustrations were similar to and different from those in the book.

C. PICTURE READING

1. Which Pix?   P I J H A

Procedure: 1. Collect groups of pictures, each group about one subject, such as old men, football games, or television stars.

2. Model giving a description of a picture. For example, ask the students to picture "a man with a tired, kindly face, who looks as if he's had a difficult life. He's not well dressed; his clothes are rumpled and his hands are gnarled. Perhaps

he has worked outdoors all his life—his skin is ruddy and coarse.'' Give as many physical details as possible.

3. Hold up three pictures of old men and have the students vote for the one they think you described—the one they pictured as you talked. Discuss which is the right choice, and why.

4. Divide students into pairs and give each pair a set of pictures. One student describes one of the pictures for his or her partner, who then has to choose the correct picture from the set.

5. Students reverse roles and repeat step 4 with a new set of pictures.

Variation: Students collect pictures and bring them in for the exercise.

2. Picture Bingo   P I

Materials: bingo cards with sentences written in each box

pictures illustrating these sentences, with the sentence written on the back

markers for the cards

Procedure:
1. Give each student a card.
2. Hold up a picture and ask if anyone has the sentence describing it.
3. Students having the sentence illustrated cover up the box on their card.
4. The first person with a row of covered boxes wins.

Variations:
1. Use pictures of animals, and give descriptions without naming the animal.
2. Use pictures of people.

BIBLIOGRAPHY

LEVIN, J. R. AND P. DEVINE-HAWKINS. ''Visual imagery as a prose learning process.'' *Journal of Reading Behavior,* 6 (1984), 23–30.

LUVASS-BRIGGS, L. ''Some whole brain activities for the community college reading class.'' Journal of Reading, 27, April (1984), 644–47.

PRESSLEY, M. ''Imaging and children's learning: Putting the picture in development perspective.'' *Review of Educational Research,* 47 (1977), 585–622.

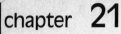

CRITICAL READING

Definition: *Analyzing and evaluating the ideas expressed in the text; includes but is not limited to the following:*

making judgments about the credibility of the author

distinguishing fact from opinion

distinguishing reality from fiction

detecting propaganda techniques

detecting fallacies of reasoning

detecting emotionally laden words

detecting the author's mood, purpose, or point of view

establishing evaluation criteria and then making judgments about good and bad, right and wrong, and so forth

RATIONALE

Though many regard the process of critical reading as a luxury, it could be argued that it is the very heart of reading comprehension. It is here that readers truly think for themselves. It is here that readers become truly active and literate. Clearly, the quality of a democratic society rests on the ability of its citizens to resist propaganda and similar verbal manipulation, to make judgments, to define standards, and so on. Moreover, when students read material critically, they are more motivated and more likely to use the other active processes that lead to effective comprehension. Thus, the importance of encouraging students to interact critically with the material cannot be overemphasized, and discussions that encourage this should be woven into the entire curriculum.

The following list of strategies has been gathered from a variety of sources and is not meant to be exhaustive. Activities for teaching each of these are provided in this chapter. The one exception is the process of detecting fallacies of reasoning. This is too large a topic for a book of this size.

Making judgments about source credibility. Good readers are always aware of the author's credibility. For instance, a veterinarian would be less credible than a doctor on the subject of human health. A farmer would be less credible than a teacher if the subject were education.

Distinguishing fact from opinion. Good readers are also able to distinguish facts from opinions. Facts are verifiably true. "It is forty today" is an example. Opinions are relative statements, such as "It is cold today." Some might find forty cold and others not. Opinions are often, but not always, identified with qualifying words such as *I believe, usually,* and *probably,* and are more likely to contain emotionally laden words: "It was miserably cold today." Students are constantly reading opinions and must be encouraged to see them as such.

Distinguishing reality from fiction. Some students, especially younger ones, sometimes confuse fiction with reality. In some texts, such as tall tales, these are woven together. Teach students to be aware of this.

Detecting propaganda techniques. Propaganda is

a method of persuading people without their being aware of it. Students should be made aware of how propaganda is used. A table of common propaganda techniques is provided in Table 21-1. Study this table before teaching this.

Detecting fallacies of reasoning. This is a fairly sophisticated strategy, and a thorough discussion of common fallacies is beyond the scope of this book. For an excellent discussion of eight common fallacies, see Burmeister (1978) or other texts on logic and reasoning.

Detecting emotionally laden words. This is perhaps the easiest type of biased writing for students to detect. They can practice using such words in their own writing. Or they can rewrite biased articles, removing the emotionally laden words. Other activities are suggested herein.

Detecting the author's mood, purpose, or point of view. This is a traditional comprehension skill that still gets measured on some standardized tests. Again, students who are actively communicating with the author will have less trouble with this than students who are just passively taking in information. Try to set up the comprehension act so that the students are aware of the author as another fallible human being.

Establishing evaluation criteria before making judgments. This is one of the most important yet most ignored comprehension process. Although research on teaching questioning shows that evaluation questions are often asked, it also shows that students are almost never asked to set up or define their criteria. A question is really not an evaluation question unless criteria are included. Consider a teacher who asks students if a story was good. The students answer yes. Now consider a teacher who asks students what would make a good story. The students list the following criteria: easy to understand, exciting, realistic, colorful, full of description, characters who are like people. The teacher then asks if the recent story was a good one. With which teacher are the students learning to think critically?

Judgments should be made only after criteria have been defined. Make sure students can explain the basis for their judgments. Doing so will help them become more aware of their values, standards for quality, and so forth.

INFORMAL DIAGNOSIS

Very few students are truly skillful at critical reading, so you may not need to do much diagnosis in this area. Of course, you will learn a lot about students' abilities during discussions in which you ask critical-reading questions. One research finding is worthy of note: Students who are classified as good readers according to standardized tests of basic skills are not necessarily good critical readers.

GENERAL SUGGESTIONS FOR TEACHING

1. To teach critical reading, you must be a good critical reader yourself. Read each assignment with an eye to the author's credibility, mood, purpose, persuasion techniques, and so on. Many textbooks reflect the biases of their authors. Be aware of these and share them with your students.

2. Be on the alert for good materials for teaching critical reading. Folktales, humorous stories,

TABLE 21-1 Typical Propaganda Techniques

Name	Definition	Example
Name calling	Calling people or things by names with pleasant or unpleasant connotations designed to evoke emotional response	1. Calling local politician a "communist" 2. Calling one politician "skinny" and another "slim"
Implication by association	Using testimonies of trusted people or associating a person or thing with pleasant or unpleasant concepts	1. A distinguished actor tells about how he uses a given product every day. 2. Calling a product something like "The All-American Pen"
Half-truths	Omitting qualifying details or using one truth to imply an opinion	Quoting a noted authority but leaving off the qualification: "If the world were different, this would be great" becomes "This would be great."
Overgeneralizations	Stating sweeping generalizations as if they were facts; failing to give critical details	1. "This vacuum cleaner is the best that has ever been made." 2. "If I am elected, I will work toward ending war and poverty."
Bandwagon	Appealing to the reader's desire to belong: the "everyone does it" approach	"Over two million people have already bought our product."

Source: J. W. Irwin, *Teaching Reading Comprehension Processes* (Englewood Cliffs, N.J.: Prentice-Hall, 1986), p. 81.

newspapers, and even some textbooks provide excellent examples.

3. You may wish to have students read for the facts before you stress critical reading. Then have them do a second reading, this time with critical questions in mind.

4. Be sure to respect the reasoning and values of all students. Critical reading requires thinking for oneself, and students will not do this unless they believe that their opinions will be respected.

5. Avoid the "one right answer" and "guess what I'm thinking" approaches when you ask critical-reading questions.

6. Try to create a critical-reading atmosphere in your class. Encourage the students to ask critical questions. Share your own critical thoughts.

chapter 21.   CRITICAL READING
Activities

A.   MAKING JUDGMENTS ABOUT THE CREDIBILITY OF THE AUTHOR

1.   Who Said?   P I J H A

Procedure: 1.   Tell students that you heard Christmas was no longer going to be a school holiday.

2.   After their response (''Who said so?'') ask why it matters who told you.

3.   Following discussion, suggest four possible sources and have them decide which would be the most reliable. Possible sources might include a student, the school principal, a friend who heard the news on the bus, and a television comic.

4.   After a discussion of the importance of knowing the source of information in evaluating it, students work on a Who Said? work sheet (see Figure 21-1).

5.   Students share results, giving reasons why the sources they chose are credible.

FIGURE 21-1 Who Said?

Directions: Check the best source for the given information. For item 10, supply your own statement and possible sources. We'll discuss these in class.

1. A diet consisting only of fast-food hamburgers and Coke is nutritious.
___ a. Regina Brown, 5'3", 182 pound high school sophomore
___ b. John Wood, manager of McDonald's
___ c. Joseph Lee, high school home economics teacher

2. The Boston Celtics have the best chance of winning the NBA championship.
___ a. Wilhelmina Jones, high school basketball coach
___ b. Reggie Wilson, Cub Scout
___ c. Maximilian Grouch, local drama critic

3. It's going to rain tomorrow.
___ a. your Aunt Martha, who has an arthritic knee
___ b. TV weather forecaster
___ c. manager of the local shopping mall

4. The American colonies acted illegally in declaring independence from England in 1776.
___ a. *The Colonies Revolt,* a textbook published in London
___ b. *The American Revolution,* a textbook published in New York
___ c. *Pravda,* a newspaper published in the USSR

[Teacher supplies five more items.]
10. Make up your own statement and sources.

---

6. Students read relevant material, such as newspaper and magazine articles and current textbooks, and check the sources of information.

2. Best Source   I J H A

Procedure: 1.   After students have been introduced to reference aids such as the atlas, dictionary, encyclopedia, and thesaurus, reinforce their reference skills. Divide the class into pairs or small groups and give each a list of questions to answer, such as ''Where is Zimbabwe?'' ''What are the main exports of Italy?'' ''What does *maxillary* mean?''

2.   Groups decide on the best source for each topic and find the information. You may want to set a time limit.

3.   After discussing the sources and information, show students other reference tools that would be the best sources for other types of information. Have a selection of newspapers, road maps, telephone books, magazines, timetables, and so forth, for them to use.

4.   Ask the groups to find information such as recent sports scores, batting averages, weather forecasts, routes to the next town, phone numbers, and TV schedules.

5.   Share results. Discuss the different sources used for different information.

6.   Reinforce this skill at opportune moments during lessons.

Extension: Students create their own best-source tasks for each other.

3.   Whose Point Of View?   **I J H A**

Procedure: 1.   Students read an unbiased, factual announcement about a subject of interest to them—for example, an explanation of a new school dress code.

2.   Elicit from the students the facts in the announcement. Write them on the board.

3.   Discuss the announcement, asking for their points of view and inquiring if there might be other points of view.

4.   After discussing different viewpoints about the same facts, have each student write an article from one of several points of view, using the facts given but trying to convince the readers of that point of view. You may want to have them draw their point of view from a box. Possible sources of viewpoints might include a student, a teacher, a parent, a school administrator, and an owner of a shop specializing in teenage apparel. Students do not state the identity of the source in their articles.

5.   Students read their articles aloud (or publish them), and the class decides whose point of view is being represented, listing the clues that led to its decision.

Variation: Students exchange articles.

B.   DISTINGUISHING FACT FROM OPINION

1.   Fact Or Opinion   **I J H A**

Procedure: 1.   Read or make some statements, such as ''All Americans are interested in baseball'' or ''Sixteen percent of those surveyed prefer pickles to ice cream.'' Ask students if they are facts or opinions. Remind them that the difference between facts and opinions is that facts can be proved and opinions cannot.

2.   Lead a discussion, using examples, about the clues that can alert a reader to whether it is an opinion or a fact that is being expressed:

    a.   Adjectives about qualities (*nicer, finer,* etc.), qualifying expressions (*I believe, in my opinion, usually, probably*), and words that indicate a future action or obligation (*should, must, ought*) are often contained in opinions.

    b.   The more general a statement, the more likely it is to be an opinion. (All teenagers like potato chips.)

    c.   The more specific a statement, the more likely it is to be a fact (Sixty-six percent of all teenagers eat a bag of potato chips a week.)

    d.   Emotional language is found more often in opinions.

    e.   Opinions can't be verified.

3. Discuss the importance of being able to distinguish fact from opinion.

4. Distribute a work sheet (see Figure 21-2) containing statements that the students are to evaluate as fact or opinion.

5. Ask students to indicate next to the factual statements *where* they could find information to verify the facts. Encyclopedias, dictionaries, experiments, and newspapers would be examples.

6. Students circle the clues in the statements on the sheet and share results in a class discussion.

7. Students work independently or in small groups on copies of paragraphs from their current textbook assignments, underlining the facts, circling the opinions, and indicating where they could verify the facts.

FIGURE 21-2 Fact Or Opinion: What Do *You* Think?

Directions: For each of the following statements, tell whether you think it is a fact or an opinion by placing F or O in the blank. If it is a fact, indicate where or how you could prove it. Circle the clues that helped you make your decision.

STATEMENT		PROOF
____	1. Cervantes was a Spanish writer.	
____	2. Spanish writers are better than American ones.	
____	3. Water freezes at thirty degrees Fahrenheit.	
____	4. Sixty degrees Fahrenheit is too cold for swimming.	
____	5. El Salvador is a country in Central America.	
____	6. El Salvador is the most important country in Central America.	
____	7. There are fifty states in the United States of America.	
____	8. There are too many states in the United States.	
____	9. Understanding long division is very easy.	
____	10. There are four calculations in every long division problem.	
____	11. The Tigers massacred the Rangers yesterday.	
____	12. The Tigers beat the Rangers yesterday.	
____	13. John spends 75 percent of his leisure time with Mary.	
____	14. John loves Mary.	
____	15. Midwesterners have funny accents.	
____	16. Midwesterners pronounce *Mary, merry,* and *marry* identically.	

Source: Adapted from Irwin, 1986, p. 80.

2. Find The Best   IJHA

Procedure: 1.   Give students copies of an article or advertisement—for instance, an article about buying a used car or an advertisement for a new car.

2.   Students read the material from the perspective of someone who wants to buy a car.

3.   Students list the five (or whatever number is appropriate) most useful facts or ideas they found in the material based on this perspective.

3. Hyper Headlines   IJHA

Procedure: 1.   Bring in examples of newspapers that use sensational headlines to attract readers.

2.   Lead a discussion about the clues that can alert a reader to whether statements are facts or opinions (see activity B.1).

3.   Read a headline and have the students help you predict what the content of the article should be if the headline is factual. An example: "In 13 Years You May Be Living on Mars!"

4.   Read the article and compare the content with the predictions based on the headline.

5.   Ask why the headlines was written the way it was.

6.   Ask students what clues in the headline should have suggested to them that it expressed an opinion, not a fact.

7.   Have students read similar articles, making predictions, underlining facts, and circling opinions. They share with the group the difference between their predictions based on the headline and the actual content of the article.

8.   Students bring in examples of hyper headlines and stories.

9.   Students create hyper headlines for daily events.

Variation: Students create hyper headlines for historical events or familiar stories.

4. Less Hype   JHA

Procedure: 1.   Review the difference between fact and opinion, use of emotive language and propaganda techniques.

2.   Read a record album cover or insert and have students dictate to you the facts in the blurb. Make one column for these facts, and then another column for the hype—the persuasive words used to make people want to buy the record. You may also wish to do this with paperback book jackets.

3.   Demonstrate rewriting the blurb using only facts.

4.   Distribute copies of record jacket blurbs. Have students find the facts and the hype and rewrite the blurbs so that they contain only facts.

5.   Share results in class.

6.   Use a similar procedure for write-ups on book jackets, movie advertisements, and other materials that use hype.

5. 3–Phase Fact/Opinion (3PFO)*   I J H A

Procedure: PHASE I

A.   Present to students a great variety of statements and tell them their task is to decide whether each is:

1.   an opinion

2.   a fact

3.   an undetermined statement of fact

4.   an incorrect statement of fact

Model the procedure, using the checklist illustrated in Figure 21-3.

B.   Provide students with blank copies of the work sheet. Students work in pairs to complete task.

C.   Students share results in a class discussion.

PHASE II

A.   Model reading a longer piece of writing, such as a newspaper article or editorial, using the Critical Reading Model (see Figure 21-4). Then model writing a response to the article.

B.   Students read a longer piece of prose, using the Critical Reading Model to guide their thinking, and write a response on a piece of their own paper.

C.   Students share results in a class discussion.

PHASE III

A.   Select two articles that present different points of view on a relevant topic.

B.   Give a copy of one article to every other student, a copy of the other article to the others.

FIGURE 21-3   3PFO Work Sheet Critical–Reading Information Categories

1. Opinion
2. Fact
3. Undetermined Statement of Fact
4. Incorrect Statement of Fact

STATEMENT AND REASON	CATEGORY
1. Lyons is the capital of France. Reason: *I know that Paris is the capital.*	4
2. The Jets are the best football team. Reason: *There is no way to prove this.*	1
3. Lake Ontario is the largest of the Great Lakes. Reason: *I couldn't find this information.*	3
4. Libya is in North Africa. Reason: *I checked it with the world atlas.*	2
5. . . .	

Source: Dwyer and Summy, 1986, p. 765. Reprinted with permission of Edward Dwyer and the International Reading Association.

FIGURE 21-4 Critical Reading Model

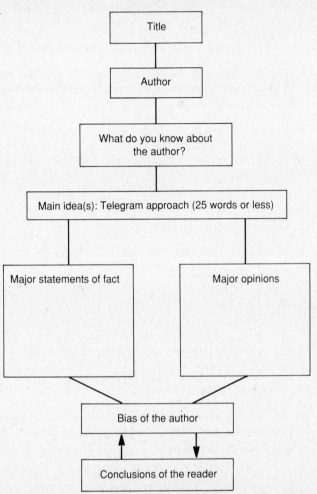

Source: Dwyer and Summy, 1986, p. 766. Reprinted with permission of Edward Dwyer and the International Reading Association.

    C.   Students complete the Critical Reading Model for their article.

    D.   Give students the other article and have them repeat the activity.

    5.   Students compare the articles and draw conclusions.

    6.   Discuss both articles with the students, using the Critical Reading Model to guide the discussion.

* Dwyer and Summy, 1986.

C. DISTINGUISHING REALITY FROM FICTION

1. Funny Folk Songs*   P I

Procedure: 1.   Distribute copies of a folk song such as ''The Ballad of Davy Crockett,'' ''John Henry,'' or ''The Big Rock Candy Mountain.'' Lead a group sing-along of the song.

2. Have students read the lyrics carefully. Ask if there are any statements that might be doubtful, such as "born on a mountaintop" or "killed a bear when he was only three."

3. Discuss the reasons for questioning the truth of these statements.

4. Ask why the author exaggerated when writing the lyrics. Discuss how the fanciful exaggeration makes the song colorful and interesting. Ask for examples of similar songs.

5. Students can use the lyrics as a model and write similar songs to the same tune.

* Zintz, 1984.

D. DETECTING PROPAGANDA TECHNIQUES

1. 5Q Propaganda Detection   I J H A

Procedure: 1. Distribute copies of advertisements that illustrate propaganda techniques and advertisements that are truthful.

2. Elicit from students the reasons they have to learn to read advertisements carefully.

3. Read an advertisement, noting the propaganda techniques used. Explain that *propaganda* used to mean "trying to promote one's cause," but has come to mean using deception or distortion in promoting a cause.

4. Explain that this distortion can be either positive or negative. For example, in describing their own products manufacturers tend to use pleasant words (*marvelous, healthful, nutritious*), whereas in describing competing products they use words with negative connotations (*itchy, harsh, cheap*).

5. Suggest five questions readers should ask when reading material critically:

    a. *Who* are the writers?

    b. *Where* are they coming from? (For whom do they work?)

    c. *Why* are they writing about this subject in this way?

    d. To *what* human emotions and desires are they appealing?

    e. *How* are they writing? (What techniques do they use?)

6. Demonstrate filling in a 5Q (who, where, why, what, how) chart for an advertisement.

7. Students work in groups or independently on copies of advertisements, filling in a 5Q chart for each. Share results in class.

8. Students create advertisements using propaganda techniques. They may exchange their advertisements and fill in 5Q charts.

9. After adequate practice at the advertisement level, move on to editorials and other textual material.

2. Conflicting Reports*   IJHA   🏠

Procedure: 1.   Find two reading selections that present conflicting accounts of the same subject. Nontextbook sources are useful—for example, cigarette ads explaining that nothing proves conclusively that smoking causes disease, versus newspaper reports on the results of scientific studies about smoking; or conflicting reviews of pop music performers or movies. Another example is given in Figure 21-5.

2.   Duplicate the accounts and present them to students, using one of two methods:

   a.   Give one half of the group account A, the other half B. Your questions to get the relevant facts will elicit conflicting responses, which in turn will arouse student interest and involvement.

   b.   Give both accounts to the students, telling them that the purpose for reading is to reach a tentative decision as to which account is closer to the truth.

3.   Students read the material.

4.   Elicit from students all the facts in both accounts and list these on the board under A and B. Do the same for the inferences in each article.

5.   Model the critical-reading skills used in evaluating the source of information by discussing each author's bias, purpose, and competence. Point out propaganda techniques and appeals to emotions in each selection.

6.   Direct students' attention to specific points in the material and encourage them to analyze any generalizations drawn from them, such as "Because Americans are overly concerned about their health, they tend to believe any unproved claims about smoking."

7.   Conceal your own preference and lead the students to think of ways they could resolve the conflict between the two accounts. Help them locate additional reading material for more information on the subject.

FIGURE 21-5   An Example Of Conflicting Reports

Students first read an article from the *World Book Encyclopedia* (1982 edition) about the Japanese people. They then read a 1941 *Time* article called "How to Tell Your Friends from the Japs," which describes Japanese in biased terms reflecting the anti-Japanese sentiment during World War II.

Students help the teacher make a list of the words in each article used to describe the characteristics of Japanese.

Point out obvious contradictions: "e.g. arrogant *vs.* friendly." Focus on the use of emotionally laden words in the list.

After discussion, model critical reading skills by noting that:

1. the accounts were written at different times;
2. both accounts lump together members of a group and associate them with certain traits (that is, they stereotype them);
3. the authors had different purposes and opinions;
4. one account is clearly biased and inaccurate.

Use these points to focus a discussion. Have students examine the descriptions closely.

Adapted from Frager and Thompson, 1985, p. 681–82.

8.   To evaluate student learning, present a third point of view in a different article and have students discuss it, using the new information to resolve the conflict between the two previous articles.

9.   Reinforce this skill by having students read different textbook accounts of the same subject. Another relevant means of reinforcement would be reading different newspaper articles and/or editorials on a subject.

* Frager and Thompson, 1985.

E.   DETECTING EMOTIONALLY LADEN WORDS

1.   Find The Real Message   I J H A

Procedure: 1.   Find examples of synonyms, such as *crowd* and *mob, residence* and *home, slender* and *skinny,* whose different connotations can be elicited from students. Explain that being aware of the use of such language is important in understanding and evaluating what we read.

2.   Use an overhead projection or copies of an article that uses highly emotional words. With the students, find these words and discuss how they slant the message of the article. Supply synonyms for the emotive words. List the facts in the article.

3.   Discuss the reasons for the author's writing a biased account.

4.   Distribute copies of articles to the students and have them circle the emotive words, supply synonyms, and list the basic facts.

5.   Share the results of this exercise.

6.   Students work independently on copies of textbook passages from their current reading assignments.

7.   Have students bring to school articles, advertisements, and pamphlets containing emotive words.

2.   Whose Words?   I J H A

Procedure: 1.   Distribute to the students three accounts of the same event whose language indicates they were written from different points of view (see Figure 21-6).

2.   Explain the difference between *connotation* and *denotation,* eliciting examples from the students.

3.   After students read the material, question them and list on the board in three columns the words they used to describe the denotative terms (see Figure 21-7).

4.   Discuss which report was the most objective, based upon the words used. Similarly, decide the biases of the other writers, based on their word choice.

5.   Students read assigned material, using the column format, and share results in class.

6.   Students work independently on text material.

Variation: Students think of an event, brainstorm synonyms they could use that have different connotations, and create two versions of a story.

FIGURE 21-6

> Writer A
>
> At 4:30 A.M. five courageous officers of our often honored police department braved the cold and dark hours of the night to apprehend a notorious criminal who was lurking in the garage of John Mayberry, a popular local citizen.
>
> Writer B
>
> At 4:30 this morning five policemen took into custody a suspect hiding in John Mayberry's garage.
>
> Writer C
>
> At 4:30 A.M. five husky, powerful cops burst into John Mayberry's garage, where an unfortunate unemployed man was hiding from the cold. With unnecessary force the burly policemen dragged the frail man from the warmth of the garage into the cold night air, forcing him into a police car and driving at top speed to the police station.

FIGURE 21-7

DENOTED WORD	WRITER A	WRITER B	WRITER C
policemen	courageous officers often honored police department	policemen	husky, powerful cops burly policemen
captured	apprehend	took into custody	dragged, forced, drove at top speed with unnecessary force
man	notorious criminal	suspect	unfortunate, unemployed, frail
hiding	lurking	hiding	hiding from the cold
John Mayberry	popular local citizen	John Mayberry	John Mayberry

3. **Word Association***   **P I J**

Procedure: 1. Tell students that you want to play a word association game: you want to find out which words come to their minds when you mention specific words. Have them make a four-column chart on a notebook page.

2. Have them write *black/dark* at the top of the first column. Under this they write for three minutes all the words *black/dark* makes them think of.

3. They write *white/fair* at the top of the second column and follow the same procedure.

4. Students write *fat* at the top of the third column and *thin* at the top of the fourth, and follow the same procedure.

5. Students share their words. Write them on the board.

6. Lead a discussion about the number of favorable or unfavorable words they generated for each column. Ask them why they thought they got the ideas that made these associations. Elicit familiar characters that they associated with the words (*black/dark:* the witch in *Sleeping Beauty* and in *Snow White,* the ugly sisters in *Cinderella,* and the wolf in *Red Riding Hood; white/fair:* the princess in *Sleeping Beauty; fat:* Tweedledee; *thin:* the Pied Piper; among other examples).

7. Discuss stereotypes and how they are used in comics and storybooks. Emphasize that they can be harmful if they constitute the only way we view people. To demonstrate this, have students generate positive examples from their own lives of *black/dark* and *fat,* negative examples of *white/fair* and *thin.*

8. Reinforce this discussion by alerting students to look for stereotypes and word associations in the books they read for assigned work and for pleasure.

Extension: Have students compile a list of stereotypes they observe in television and the movies.

* Zimet, 1983.

F. DETECTING THE AUTHOR'S MOOD, PURPOSE, OR POINT OF VIEW

1. Active Reading*   I J H A

Procedure: 1. Model the use of five basic questions to read expository text actively. Explain the benefit of each step. Sample explanations are given in quotations.

a. What is the selection about as a whole? "You can answer this question by previewing the selection."

b. What is the author's message? "Find the main ideas and details in the selection, deciding what ideas the author is trying to explain, analyze, or convey."

c. How does the author say it? "Analyze the author's background, bias, use of sources, and argument."

d. Do I agree? "Decide if you have enough experience and knowledge of the subject to determine whether the author is being logical and reasonable."

e. How important is this material to me? "Three things must be answered here:

(1) how the material relates to the reader's local, national, and world community;

(2) what ideas can be created to carry this message in other situations;

(3) how much of this material should be remembered—and how that can be done."

2. These questions can be adapted to most text material (see Figure 21-8).

* Sandberg, 1981.

FIGURE 21-8   Questions Adapted to History Text

A. What is the selection about as a whole?	1. What is the historical problem?
B. What is the author's message?	2. What is the chronology of events?
	3. What is the author's hypothesis?
C. How does the author say it?	4. What are the author's sources?
	5. Test the hypothesis.
D. Do I agree?	6. Evaluate.
E. How important is this material to me?	7. How important is this material to me?

Source: Sandberg, 1981, p. 160. Reprinted with permission of Kate Sandberg and the International Reading Association.

2.   Yes, and I Saw The Movie*   **I J H A**

Procedure: 1.   Choose an appropriate book for which a movie videotape is available— for instance, *Sounder, The Outsiders, The Miracle Worker,* or *Raiders of the Lost Ark.*

2.   Preview the movie, looking for breaks in the story line that parallel chapters of the book. Divide the movie into twenty-minute segments. If segments in the movie differ from those of the book, use the book chapters to determine the movie segments.

3.   Explain to the students the purpose of the procedure.

4.   Before showing a segment of the movie, have the students read and/or discuss the chapter about to be viewed.

5.   Students discuss the chapter viewed, comparing and contrasting the book and the movie and presenting their own views on the issues raised. Compare the author's purpose and the director's purpose. Develop the analysis of the director's purpose in terms of altering characters, setting, story line, and action. Discuss the reasons for these alterations and how they change the message of the author.

6.   Precede and/or follow each viewing and reading section with questions that require students to make predictions, draw conclusions, make inferences, analyze and evaluate characters and incidents, and determine relationships. Have students refer to the movie or book to justify their answers.

Variations: 1.   Focus on specific reading skills, such as identifying structural patterns, to answer questions, in step 6.

2.   Have students write movie reviews.

3.   Have students find the original book reviews and movie reviews and discuss them.

4.   (P I) Use videotapes of fairy tales or children's classics.

* Barr, 1986.

FIGURE 21-9 Pickles Will Kill You

Pickles will kill you! Every pickle you eat brings you nearer to death. . . . Pickles are associated with all major diseases of the body . . . they can be related to most airline tragedies. There exists a positive relationship between crime waves and consumption of this fruit of the cucurbit family. For example:

—Nearly all sick people have eaten pickles. The effects are obviously cumulative. . . .

—99.7% of the people involved in air and auto accidents ate pickles within 14 days preceding the accident.

—93.1% of juvenile delinquents come from homes where pickles are served frequently.

Evidence points to the long-term effects of pickle-eating:

—Of the people born in 1869 who later dined on pickles, there has been a 100% mortality.

—All pickle eaters born between 1869 and 1879 have wrinkled skin, have lost most of their teeth, have brittle bones and failing eyesight, if the ills of eating pickles have not already caused their deaths.

—Even more convincing is the report of a noted team of medical specialists: Rats force-fed with 2 pounds of pickles per day for 30 days developed bulging abdomens. Their appetites for wholesome food were destroyed.

Source: Anonymous, in Whitmer, 1986, p. 530.

3. Pickles Are Fatal*   I J H A

Procedure: 1.   Distribute copies of "Pickles Will Kill You" (Figure 21-9).

2.   Ask students to read the selection and find out the author's mood and purpose. Explain that this is an important skill for them to develop in order to understand what they read. Indicate that they will have to use their prior knowledge (common sense) as they read.

3.   Lead a discussion about the author's *purpose and mood*. Have the students refer to the sentences and phrases, such as the title and first sentence, that indicate the author's purpose is humorous.

4.   Question the students about the *validity of the statements*. For instance, "Is there any truth to the statement 'Every pickle you eat brings you nearer to death'?"

5.   Focus on *faulty reasoning* in cause–effect relationships. For example, "Has pickle eating caused wrinkled skin, brittle bones, and failing eyesight among people born between 1869 and 1879? Could there be any other reason?"

6.   Encourage students to question the *use of statistics* and to use prior knowledge to *evaluate the conclusion* of the experiment cited at the end of the selection.

7.   Highlight the difference between *fact and opinion*, referring, for example, to the statement "Pickles are deadly and should be banned!"

8. Summarize on the board the critical-reading skills that students have used in reading the article, explaining that they will find these skills useful in reading any factual material.

Extension: Have students change the subject but use the same format to write other parodies.

* Whitmer, 1986.

G. ESTABLISHING EVALUATION CRITERIA BEFORE MAKING JUDGMENTS

1. Good or Bad?   P I J H A

Procedure: 1. Before students begin reading an assigned story, lead a discussion about books or stories that they have really liked, listing on the board examples of really "good" stories.

2. Ask what *good* means. Ask students to supply characteristics (they will probably mention such things as believable characters, vivid descriptions, real-life dialogue), and write these on the board. Emphasize that they have now given the criteria that they use when evaluating a story; they have given a specific meaning to the word *good*.

3. Once the students have agreed on the criteria, they read the story.

4. Lead a discussion focusing on evaluating the story according to the given criteria. Criteria may be amended as needed.

5. As a follow-up, have students use these criteria when evaluating their assigned reading; make a checklist for them to refer to.

Extension: Use the same procedure when discussing why a television program or movie was good. Point out to students the differences in criteria that they use in these situations. Similarly, employ this method when deciding who was the *best* character in a story, which was the most *useful* idea in a selection, and so on.

2. Picture–Book Values*   I J H

Procedure: 1. Assemble a group of picture books for young children that express values.

2. Tell students they are going to choose books that they can use to read to children when baby-sitting. Referring to a well-known book, ask them "If you read this book to young children, what might they learn from it?" Write on the board:

Questions to Consider

a. What are the values or life principles contained in this book?

Lead a discussion about the values in the book.

3. Tell the students that after identifying each value in the book they must consider the two questions:

b. How important is it that a child be exposed to this value or principle?

    c. What application could be made to the child's daily life? How much assistance would a child need to grasp and apply the principle?

    4. Divide the students into small groups. Each group considers a different group of books, using the three questions as a guide.

    5. The groups compile a "Baby-Sitter's Bibliography of Best Books."

    6. Each group (or student) brings to class two other picture storybooks that could be used for a discussion of values with a child. These books should also be evaluated by means of the three questions.

* Alfonso, 1987.

H. PUTTING IT ALL TOGETHER

1. Four–Step Critical Analysis*   J H A

Procedure: STEP I

    A. Choose an article or editorial about a controversial topic in the school or local paper.

    B. Ask students for their opinions on the issue, listing all responses on the board or overhead.

    C. Categorize the responses with the students. They will tend to fall into the following categories:

    1. experiences

    2. agreement

    3. disagreement

    4. feelings, attitudes

    5. importance of the topic

    D. Students read the editorial or article once for the general ideas; they then read it to find the main viewpoint. The class decides what should be marked as the main idea.

    E. Lead the class in writing a summary statement for the editorial or article.

    F. Lead a class discussion about the issue. List reactions and basic pro and con viewpoints on the board or overhead, along with the reasons for the opinions.

    G. As a class, create a composite group reaction. Begin with a position statement ("I think Classic Coke was (was not) a good idea) and follow with several reasons for this opinion.

    STEP II

    A. Give students a choice of editorials to select for reading.

    B. Students select an editorial and *skim* it. They then complete the prewriting Critical Analysis Chart (see Figure 21-10) before reading.

    C. Students read selection, fill in major concepts and write a summary statement.

FIGURE 21-10   Critical Analysis Chart

A. Name of article _____
B. Before reading the article, complete the following chart to the best of your ability.

PREWRITING

Experiences

Pro

Con

Feelings/attitudes

Importance of issue

C. Read the article. Go back over the article and mark important information.

D. In your own words, write a sentence that tells the main point of the article.

E. Reflect/discuss sections B and D.

F. Choose your best area from part B and write your reaction. Begin your work with a general topic sentence that will introduce your viewpoint. Remember to support your viewpoints.

Source: Brueggeman, 1986, p. 236. Reprinted with permission of Martha A. Brueggeman and the International Reading Association.

D.   Students reading same editorial form a group and create a group summary statement.

E.   Students individually write their reactions, using the format of a position statement followed by supports.

STEP III

A.   Students complete all sections of the Critical Analysis Chart—choosing a topic, prewriting, reading, summarizing, selecting, and writing a reaction with supporting statements.

B.   Have students form topic groups and share reactions. Instruct students to identify opposing points of view and see how they are supported.

C.   Students add to their reactions a paragraph describing an alternate point of view and its supports.

STEP IV

A.   Students choose another editorial or article for independent work.

B.   Students use Author's Voice and Critical Analysis Summary forms (Figures 21-11 and 21-12) as outlines for paragraphs they write about the author and the selection.

* Brueggeman, 1986.

FIGURE 21-11 Author's Voice

Credentials
    Who wrote it? _____
    Occupation? _____
    Age? _____
    Attachment to topic? _____
    Other? _____
Who is the audience? _____

BIAS/POINT OF VIEW/POSITION

Pro issue _____
Con issue _____
Author's side of issue _____
Side not addressed _____

DESIRED OUTCOME

Inform reader _____
Convince reader to agree _____
Take action _____

Source: Brueggeman, 1986, p. 238. Reprinted with permission of Martha A. Brueggeman and the International Reading Association.

FIGURE 21-12 Critical Analysis Summary

Review and mark the selection for the following information:

1. Facts:

2. Opinions:

3. Style/tone:

____ serious	____ inspirational	____ textbookish
____ humorous	____ pleading	____ sad
____ sarcastic	____ threatening	____ other
____ ironic	____ joyous/happy	

4. Emotional words, phrases, slanted words:

5. Technique of appeal:

Example:

____ bandwagoning
____ image builder
____ testimonial
____ name calling
____ scientific evidence

Source: Brueggeman, 1986, p. 239. Reprinted with permission of Martha A. Brueggeman and the International Reading Association.

BIBLIOGRAPHY

ALFONSO, R. "Module for teaching about young people's literature—Module 3: Values children can learn from picture books," *Journal of Reading,* 30, January (1987), 299–301.

BARR, H. R. "I saw the movie, but I couldn't read the book," *Journal of Reading,* 29, March (1986), 511–15.

BRUEGGEMAN, M. A. "React first, analyze second: Using editorials to teach the writing process," *Journal of Reading,* 30, December (1986), 234–39.

BURMEISTER, L. *Reading Strategies for Middle and Secondary Teachers.* Reading, MA: Addison Wesley, 1978.

DWYER, E. J. AND M. K. SUMMY. "Fact and opinion: A new look at an often oversimplified comprehension skill," *Journal of Reading,* 29, May (1986), 764–66.

FRAGER, A. M. AND L. C. THOMPSON. "Conflict: The key to critical reading instruction," *Journal of Reading,* 28, May (1985), 676–83.

IRWIN, J. W. *Teaching Reading Comprehension Processes.* Englewood Cliffs, N.J.: Prentice-Hall, 1986.

SANDBERG, K. "Learning to read history actively," *Journal of Reading,* 25, November (1981), 158–60.

WHITMER, J. E. "Pickles will kill you: Using humorous literature to teach critical reading," *Reading Teacher,* 39, February (1986), 530–34.

ZIMET, S. G. "Teaching children to detect social bias in books," *Reading Teacher,* 36, January (1983), 418–21.

ZINTZ, M. *The Reading Process.* Dubuque, Iowa: Wm. C. Brown, 1984.

CREATIVE READING

Definition: *Combining information in new ways that result in a creative product or an affective response*

RATIONALE

Creative reading is creative thinking about the content. One can think about how information can be applied in new situations while one is reading, or, after reading, one can use the information to create a product such as a story about a society with a cultural difference, a political campaign, a diary of a historical character, and so on.

Often such creative products also require affective responses, and vice versa, so we have put these two things together for purposes of instruction. Affective responses include such things as emotional responses to plot or theme and identification with characters. Obviously, such responses facilitate creative involvement. In many cases, such as literature, these responses are intended by the author and should be seen as a critical part of the comprehension process.

Encouraging creative reading requires the encouragement of diversity and independence. The thought processes of every student should be valued. The product, though difficult to "grade," should probably be evaluated not on the quality of the grammar, the quality of the drawing, and so forth, but rather on the creativity evidenced. These judgments are difficult, but this should not keep you from using activities that encourage creative writing.

One way to add objectivity to the evaluation process is to use a checklist of what is to be evaluated and give it to the students before they begin working on their creative product. You can encourage evaluative thinking by having the students make up the checklist with you (see Chapter 21). Stick to those standards when evaluating the product.

Because creativity can be easily stifled, teachers must be careful to make suggestions for improvement in nonthreatening ways. One of the better ways is to have the students suggest what they would like to improve. Another nonthreatening approach is to have the group respond to a creative work by focusing first on the points they liked and giving reasons for their approval. For instance, "I really liked the way Jane made Columbus's diary look old and waterlogged. That made it more interesting to read." Then ask for suggestions and model phrasing them in a way that doesn't criticize: "It would have been nice to learn more about Columbus's life at home."

In our experience, teaching creative reading and affective response is already a part of many classroom and remedial situations. Thus, we have limited the activities suggested to some that we felt were new and unusual. In this way we hope to stimulate your thinking about other activities you might use. We have also included several activities that encourage creative reading in the content areas (section B). This is one use that is sometimes ignored.

INFORMAL DIAGNOSIS

Ask questions that require creative and/or affective responses. You will need to have established a good rapport before you are likely to get an accurate assessment of the latter. Moreover, these responses are very difficult to assess quickly, so we would warn against coming to any conclusions that label one student as "creative" and another student as not so.

GENERAL CONSIDERATIONS FOR TEACHING

1. Whenever possible, ask questions that require creative thinking.
2. Encourage divergent thinking: Avoid the one-right-answer approach.

3. Wait for answers. Most teachers wait less than a minute before going to another question. This encourages students to think that speed is essential and that thinking in depth is to be discouraged. This will effectively stifle creative thinking!
4. To encourage creative thinking use follow-up activities, such as retelling, dramatizing, and writing the next episode, that encourage the synthesis of an entire story or topic.
5. To encourage affective responses to plots, themes, and so on, ask students to think of similar events that they have experienced.
6. Role playing also encourages affective responses.
7. As a postreading activity, have students write or speak as if they were one of the characters. They can write a letter, diary, and so forth.
8. Dramatic settings that help introduce new reading material, such as turning lights off, lighting candles, and playing spooky music before an Edgar Allan Poe story or playing Tchaikovsky's 1812 Overture before a chapter on Napoleon's invasion of Russia, encourage affective responses in the reader.
9. "What if" questions encourage divergent thinking.
10. Tasks that encourage creative reading and affective responses usually result in the creation of something—a mural, diorama, soap or clay model, tape recording, poster, play, map, game, book jacket, diary, movie, slide show, book, newspaper article, play, song, dance, and more!

chapter 22. CREATIVE READING
Activities

A. GENERAL EXERCISES
    1. Brainstorming   P I J
    2. Conclusion First   I J H A
    3. Class Yearbook   P I J
    4. What's Going On Here? P I J
    5. Now You Tell It   P I J
B. THE CONTENT AREA
    1. Learning Log   P I J H A
    2. Another Way   P I J
    3. Commercial Break   I J H A

A. GENERAL EXERCISES

1. Brainstorming   P I J

Procedure: 1. Collect a group of objects for which students are to brainstorm other possible uses. Coat hangers, chopsticks, discarded parts of engines, and odd-shaped boxes are appropriate.

2. Divide class into groups of six or less.

3. Each group chooses a recorder, who writes down the group's suggestions and reports them to the class.

4. Explain that the object of the exercise is to think creatively. Each group will try to think of as many ways as possible that a specific object can be used. Stress that in brainstorming people write down *all* suggestions; the object is to come up with as many ideas as possible.

5. Set a time limit for brainstorming (three minutes works well).

6. Demonstrate what brainstorming is. Use a coat hanger and have students give ideas for its use. The initial ideas will be obvious ones; encourage more divergent ideas, such as using the hanger as a ruler, trace for making a triangle, a form for a mobile, a back scratcher, or a bracelet for a giant.

7. Hold up a new object; give groups three minutes to brainstorm.

8. Each group tallies up its suggestions.

9. Ask each group how many it has. Write the numbers on the board.

10. Recorders read groups' suggestions. If you have a competition going, the group with the most suggestions can win, the group with the most original suggestion can win, and so forth.

☞   This is a demonstration activity. Be sure to provide opportunities for application to meaningful reading tasks.

2. Conclusion First*   I J H A

Procedure: 1. Put on the board or overhead some thought-provoking statements, such as these

In Michigan, it is against the law to put a skunk in your boss's desk.

In York, Pennsylvania, it is against the law to sit down when you water your lawn.

In Macomb, Illinois, it is illegal for an automobile to impersonate a wolf.

(These and other strange laws are collected in Hyman, 1976.)

2.   Choose one statement and ask the students how this law could possibly have come about. Explain that you are not asking them for the right answer, because you yourself don't know it. You just want them to imagine a situation that could make citizens demand this legislation.

3.   As students offer suggestions, question them in order to establish characters and details of the situation. Write key words on the board—for example, details about the car in the Illinois law.

4.   Ask questions that will help students build the narrative, but be careful not to control the content.

5.   Students then write a story explaining the event. The only requirement is that the story end with the statement "That is why in _____ it is illegal to _____."

6.   Students share completed stories, which can be given to the library with a title such as *Loony Laws*.

7.   Students write Conclusion First stories on their own or in groups and publish them.

* Nessel, 1985.

3. Class Yearbook   P I J

Procedure: 1.   Explain to the students that they are each going to write a class yearbook as a project for the next _____ weeks. The yearbook will have class information as well as contributions by the student.

2.   Have students fill in a questionnaire of biographical information. Collect these and type them together on master sheets to be run off. A possible format is illustrated in Figure 22-1.

3.   Hold a competition for the design of the title page.

FIGURE 22-1   Biographical Questionnaire

Name: _____   Birthplace: _____   Birth date: _____
After-school activities: _____
Hobbies: _____
Favorite sport: _____
Favorite food: _____
Favorite book: _____
Favorite TV show: _____
Favorite movie: _____
I really hate to eat _____
What I will remember most about this year is _____
In ten years I will _____

4.   Include a prophecy page. Print the names of all the students on a hand-out. Each student fills in a prophecy of what he or she will be doing in _____ years.

5.   Distribute decorative pages and have students paste in pictures of friends, family, and other important people in their lives.

6.   Use other decorative pages for students' favorite pieces among their own writing. You may want to assign a specific writing topic for the yearbook.

7.   Each student composes one anagram poem about himself or herself and one about another student, using the letters of their names as the first letters of the lines. For example:

> *F*irst in line for lunch
> *R*uns fastest in the class
> *E*ats everything
> *D*rums are his favorite instrument.

Type up, run off, and distribute these poems.

8.   Students fill in "5&10" pages. Categories might include the following:

> 10 people in history I'd like to meet
> 10 people alive today I'd like to meet
> 5 favorite books
> 5 favorite movies
> 10 things that make me happy
> 10 things that bug me
> 5 historical events I'd like to change
> 10 items for a space capsule that would tell a future civilization about our society
> 10 people to be stranded with on a desert island
> 5 things I look forward to next year
> 10 precious possessions (not alive) to be saved if there were a fire in my house
> 5 wishes I'd like granted
> 10 things to say to a Martian

Sharing these lists in class is a high-interest activity. Material from them can be made into class lists.

9.   Students assemble their own books, including the class and personal pages. Manila folders can be decorated for covers. Blank pages for autographs can be included. Be sure to give the students plenty of time to read their own and each other's books.

4.   What's Going On Here?   P I J

Procedure: 1.   Assemble a file of pictures or drawings from children's books or magazines of situations that could be good story starters—for example, a drawing of a bearded man sitting in bed, holding over him an open umbrella with a cat seated on it.

2.   Choose a picture and underneath it write "What's going on here? Write a story, poem, play, or newspaper article that explains what is happening." Distribute copies to the students.

3.   Model for the students how to begin a story, focusing on who, what, where, when, why, and how.

4.   Students write individually or in small groups.

5.   Students share stories with the class.

6.   Publish the stories in a book with the picture as the cover.

5.   Now You Tell It*   P I J

Procedure: 1.   Explain to students that you will read or tell them a story that many of them may already know. They must listen to this story in a different way this time, because when it is over it will be their turn to tell it by writing a brief account of it on a sheet of paper.

2.   Tell or read them a well-known story, such as a fairy tale.

3.   Give each student a special paper you have created by photocopying a picture from the story on the top of a sheet of blank or lined paper. The picture will help the students remember the story.

4.   Students write the story in their own words.

5.   Students read the story at home to family members.

Variations: 1.   For older students you may want to use other types of stories, such as mysteries or science fiction.

2.   Students write the story but change one component, such as the setting or one of the characters.

* Gold, 1987.

B.   THE CONTENT AREA

1.   Learning Log   P I J H A

Procedure: 1.   Establish a routine whereby students make entries in a Learning Log. The questions to which they will respond in the Learning Log will require them to think creatively about their reading and learning. "What if" and "suppose" questions will require them to synthesize and apply what they have learned, as will compare and contrast questions. (See Figure 22-2.) Stress that there are no right or wrong answers to these questions; you are simply asking them to apply what they already know.

2.   Ask the Learning Log questions in class. Give the students five to ten minutes to answer a question.

3.   Use Learning Log questions to have students predict what will happen next, based on what they have learned so far (see the second question in Figure 22-2).

4.   Use Learning Log responses to diagnose misunderstandings of content, needs for reinforcement, and other areas where help may be needed.

FIGURE 22-2   Sample Learning Log (responses are from a sixth grade class)

Question: "Imagine you are a peasant in the Middle Ages who has an opportunity to move into the city. Describe your reaction."

Student responses: "I'm worried about the filth in the cities and about contracting the Black Death." "It would be good for trade because a lot of people go there and also things you buy are probably cheaper. The thing that would worry me is the garbage and plague that went around." "It gets boring around here, so I'm going to move to the city and become an apprentice for a goldsmith. And wouldn't it be grand to go to the cathedral and listen instead of our small church on the manor."

Question: As we begin our study of the Middle Ages, what problems do you think might develop in the feudal system?

Student responses: "I think that some knights may become unhappy with the system and rebel." "The feudal system may develop some big problems. The common people might think they don't need the lord's help." "Knights might betray people." "I think some problems might be that lots of people will want to become higher rulers and will want to rule lots of land and be greedy."

Question: What is the difference between surface area and volume?

Student responses: "If you need to wrap something you use surface area. If you want to know how many sandwiches fit in a picnic basket you use volume." "Surface area is hard. Volume is easy."

Task: Write a prologue to *Julius Caesar*.

Student responses: "In the year 44 B.C. in the city of Rome, Julius Caesar, a dictator, is trying to keep Rome from going down the drain." "The year is 44 B.C. The scene is outside the Senate. Will they kill Caesar? That's a heck of a story." "In this play Caesar is going through a tough stage of life."

---

2.   Another Way   PIJ

Procedure: 1.   Tell students that you want to evaluate how much they have learned about a subject but you don't want to give them a test. Ask them to help you brainstorm ways they could demonstrate their learning without taking a test.

2.   Write their suggestions on the board or overhead. You may get suggestions such as the following:

Write another chapter.
Tell what happens next.

Write a movie/play script and perform it.

Make a diorama/mural/painting/sculpture.

Write a letter to/from a famous person/book character.

Create illustrations for. . . .

Make a poster/map of. . . .

Make a game (e.g., Communopoly).

Write a children's book explaining. . . .

Make a book jacket.

Tape-record an interview with. . . .

Rewrite the (e.g., history) chapter as it would have been without (a certain character).

Write a guidebook to. . . .

Write a guidebook to our school for a person coming from the . . . period. . . .

Design a. . . .

3. Make an Another Way menu for the class, indicating time limits and other requirements.

4. Students choose and complete tasks. If convenient, hold a display of Another Way tests for the school and/or students' families.

3. Commercial Break   I J H A

Procedure: 1. Choose a film or video about a content-area subject the class has been studying.

2. After introducing the film, explain to students that they will be watching it as if they were living in the area and time of the film. They will watch it as if it were a television show. Discuss the types of breaks that television shows normally have for commercials, focusing on the types of products advertised. Show the film.

3. Brainstorm advertised products and organize them into categories in a chart on the overhead or board. Possible categories might include foods, clothing, travel, drinks, services (banks, travel agencies, credit cards), transportation, and personal products (perfumes, toothpaste).

4. Tell students that their assignment (either individually or in small groups) is to create one (or more) commercials that would be appropriate for the time. Model for them the use of the chart to brainstorm possible products for a specific time. For example, if the video is about Elizabethan England, you might have commercials for the Globe Drama School run by W. Shakespeare, for a medicine to cure the plague, for wigs, or for a travel agency specializing in trips to the New World.

5. After students have created their commercials, share them in a class discussion. This would be a good time to teach the class about anachronisms. You could suggest, for example, a commercial of Julius Caesar looking at his Timex watch.

Variation: Students create news breaks, such as "Spanish Armada Repelled! England Safe!"

BIBLIOGRAPHY

GOLD, J. "Listening and writing," *Reading Teacher,* 40, March (1987), 707.

HYMAN, D. *The Trenton Pickle Ordinance.* Brattleboro, Vt.: Stephen Greene Press, 1976.

NESSEL, D. D. "Let's start with the conclusion," *Journal of Reading,* 8, May (1985), 744–45.

chapter 23

MONITORING COMPREHENSION

Definition: *Knowing when one does and does not comprehend and taking appropriate remedial steps when comprehension breaks down*

RATIONALE

Good readers are more aware than poor readers of when their comprehension falters. This is best demonstrated by their superior ability to detect inconsistencies within passages. This may be because good readers *expect* the text to make sense whereas poor readers may not. It may also be because good readers are active comprehenders who seek meaning whereas poor readers often take a more passive approach.

Students should be taught first to take note when their comprehension breaks down and then to determine the source of the breakdown. Is it the vocabulary? Long, confusing sentences? Inconsistent information? A lack of background knowledge? Poor organization? These and other common types of comprehension failures are listed in Figure 23-1.

Once students have identified the source of the breakdown, they can begin to do something about it. Collins and Smith (1980) have provided a taxonomy of responses (Figure 23-2). Notice that these proceed from the least to the most disruptive. Thus, a reader would use the first whenever possible, proceeding to the second only when the first was unsatisfactory, and so on.

Note that determining the source of the breakdown and deciding what to do about it are really two distinct skills. You may wish to teach them separately.

INFORMAL DIAGNOSIS

You have at least three options for diagnosing students' comprehension-monitoring skills:

1. Give students paragraphs in which some inconsistent information is inserted. Here is an example:

> There were only a few physicians in this country at the time of the American Revolution. They were trained in Europe, where they studied Latin or Greek. There was little science taught in universities in those days, and no medical science. Most physicians learned to practice medicine by being an apprentice to another physician. The scientific training they had been receiving in the European schools was of great help to them at that time. (adapted from Casazza, 1988)

FIGURE 23-1 Taxonomy of Comprehension Failures

1. Failure to understand a word
   a. Novel word
   b. Known word that doesn't make sense in the context
2. Failure to understand a sentence
   a. Can find no interpretation
   b. Can find only vague, abstract interpretation
   c. Can find several possible interpretations (ambiguous sentence)
   d. Interpretation conflicts with prior knowledge
3. Failure to understand how one sentence relates to another
   a. Interpretation of one sentence conflicts with another
   b. Can find no connection between the sentences
   c. Can find several possible connections between the sentences
4. Failure to understand how the whole text fits together
   a. Can find no point to whole or part of the text
   b. Cannot understand why certain episodes or sections occurred
   c. Cannot understand the motivations of certain characters

Source: Collins and Smith, 1980, p. 8. Reprinted with permission.

FIGURE 23-2 Possible Remedies for Comprehension Failures

1. *Ignore and read on,* because this information is relatively unimportant.
2. *Suspend judgment,* because it is likely to be cleared up later.
3. *Form a tentative hypothesis* to be tested as reading continues.
4. *Reread the current sentence(s)* or look for a tentative hypothesis.
5. *Reread the previous context* to resolve the contradiction.
6. *Go to an expert source,* because it simply doesn't make sense.

Source: Collins and Smith, 1980. Reprinted with permission.

Ask them to identify any trouble spots, or ask them to recall the passage and see if they identify the trouble spots on their own.

2. Give students a traditional comprehension test with recall questions. For each question, have them mark how sure they are of their answer: 1 = very sure, 2 = sure, 3 = not sure. Then see if their assessment was accurate. (This is an excellent exercise for introducing comprehension monitoring as well.)

3. When students have trouble comprehending, ask them to identify the source of the problem. Then ask what they might do about it. Can they answer such questions?

GENERAL TEACHING SUGGESTIONS

1. For content-area assignments, let students know the extent to which they should monitor their comprehension. Must it all make sense right away? Should they just try to get the flavor and wait for class to get their questions answered?

2. Always focus on meaning when teaching reading. Use activities that make sense to the students. Use materials that they can understand.

3. Encourage an active approach toward learning by encouraging students to ask questions whenever they do not understand something in class or in their assignments.

4. Try to overcome the students' learned helplessness. Provide situations in which additional effort can make a difference.

5. Teach students that taking risks and making guesses is good. This is an effective strategy in many cases of comprehension breakdown.

6. Teach the students that comprehension can break down at one of four levels—word, sentence, paragraph, or passage. Tell them that the first step in remedying a breakdown is to identify the level where it occurs.

7. Use explaining and modeling (see Chapter 5) to teach the taxonomy of remedies for comprehension failures. Help students use it when they let you know they are having problems with comprehension.

8. Whenever students come to class with reports of comprehension problems ("I didn't understand it!"), you have a golden opportunity to teach comprehension monitoring. Don't explain the material to them. Instead, help them clarify the source of the breakdown. Help them remedy the situation by getting the information they need.

chapter 23.   MONITORING COMPREHENSION
Activities

    A. DIRECT INSTRUCTION
        1. Comprehension Strategies   P I J H A
        2. Monitoring Cards   P I
        3. W–I–K Textbook Comprehension Monitoring   I J H A
        4. Comprehension Rating   P I J
        5. Text Look-backs   I J H A
        6. Find the Errors   P I
    B. FINDING AND FIXING COMPREHENSION PROBLEMS
        1. Improving Instructions   I J H A
        2. How Confident Are You?   P I J H A
        3. Question Pairs   P I J H A
        4. Comprehension Code   I J H A
        5. What's Wrong?   P I
        6. Self-Evaluation   P I J

A. DIRECT INSTRUCTION

1. Comprehension Strategies   P I J H A

Procedure: 1. Find a passage with some unknown words.

    2. Explain that a word can be difficult for at least two reasons:

        a. You don't know the word.
        b. The word is used in a new way.

    3. Present on the board or overhead a list of possible strategies for dealing with the problem:*

        a. *Ignore* and read on—the problem may be clarified later, or it may never appear again if it's not important.
        b. *Change* the rate of reading—read more slowly.
        c. *Suspend* judgment—maybe the problem will be cleared up later.
        d. *Form* a tentative hypothesis, to be checked out as you read.
        e. *Reread.*
        f. Go to an *expert source,* such as a reference book or a teacher.

* Adapted from Collins and Smith, 1980.

    4. Model and explain the use of these comprehension-monitoring strategies using the hard text.

    5. Have the students practice the strategies with duplicated material containing word-level problems. Provide a chart with a column for each strategy.

    6. Assign independent work with textbook passages.

    7. Move on to sentence-level metacognitive practice, using steps 3–6 above. The questions students might ask themselves are: Does this sentence have meaning? Does it fit in with my prior knowledge? Does it fit with the rest of the passage?

8. Students continue to use the list of strategies until they are able to apply all of them independently when reading self-selected materials.

2. Monitoring Cards*   P I

Materials: for each student, a set of nine cards reading as follows:

1. *Click* (I understand)
2. *Clunk* (I don't understand)
3. *Read On*
4. *Reread* (the sentence)
5. *Go back* (and reread the paragraph)
6. *Look* (in the glossary)
7. *Ask* (someone)
8. *What did it say?* (to check paragraph comprehension)
9. *What do I remember?* (to check page-level comprehension)

cards 1–2: $4\frac{1}{2}$ by $2\frac{1}{2}$ inches
cards 3–7: $4\frac{1}{2}$ by $1\frac{1}{2}$ inches
cards 8–9: $8\frac{1}{2}$ by $2\frac{1}{2}$ inches

Procedure: Part I: *Developing the concept of reading*

A.   Ask what reading is. Develop the idea that although reading is pronouncing words, this may not be effective when the students are reading content-area texts, which may contain words they can pronounce but do not *know*.

B.   Develop an analogy between reading and sports, asking what strategies people use to win in various sports. After asking the same question about reading, point out that reading is also flexible and strategic: readers monitor their progress, adapting as necessary until they have won their goal of comprehension and recall.

C.   Present five questions for students to consider before they read:

1. What is reading?
2. What is my goal?
3. How difficult is the text?
4. How can I accomplish my goal?
5. How can I check on whether I accomplished my goal?

D.   To give students practice in using these questions, have them complete a reading plan sheet (Figure 23-3) when they read textbooks for the purpose of factual recall.

E.   Continue practice until students can use the questions independently.

Part II: *Using the Cards*

A.   Students read silently, responding to the text at their own pace. The cards should be used both at home and school, for preparing for tests, reading fiction and nonfiction, and so on.

B.   Students read the first sentence of text and pause to reflect whether they have understood it. If so, they raise their *Click* card; if not, the *Clunk* card.

FIGURE 23-3   Reading Plan Sheet

Questions	(Possible) Answers
1. What is reading?	Reading is thinking, understanding, remembering, and making pictures in my head.
2. Goal?	Understand and remember.
3. Text?	Hard.
4. How?	Cards. (Tell students that instruction in the use of cards to monitor comprehension will begin in the _____ lesson.)
5. Victory?	Try to say it and write it down.

Source: Babbs, 1984, p. 201. Reprinted with permission of Patricia J. Babbs and the International Reading Association.

C.   Students move on to the next sentence if they have raised the *Click* card.

D.   If they have raised the *Clunk* card, they use one or more of the five strategies on cards 3–7 to resolve the difficulty.

1.   Students decide *where* the difficulty is, with a word or with a sentence.
2.   Students select and hold up one of the five strategy cards and begin remediation. If the problem is with a *word,* they:
   a.   reread the sentence;
   b.   read on—read the next sentence;
   c.   look in the glossary if they think it will be defined there; or
   d.   ask someone.
If the problem is with a sentence, they:
   a.   reread the sentence;
   b.   go back and reread the paragraph;
   c.   read on; or
   d.   ask someone.

E.   After reading each paragraph, students look up from the page, raise the "What did it say?" card, and answer the question. If they cannot answer it, they reread the paragraph, not using the *Click* or *Clunk* cards.

F.   Students look up from each page after reading it, raise the "What do I remember?" card, and answer the question. If unable to do this, they reread the page, using the "What did it say?" card after each paragraph.

G.   If the students' reading goal is to answer prereading questions or locate specific information, they respond to cards 8 and 9 with relevant information.

Part III: *Teaching Comprehension Monitoring*

A.   Model a comprehension failure. Introduce the use of the different cards gradually.

B.   With each card, have students model the process just introduced.

C.   Students practice using the procedure silently with texts.

D.   Students fill out a reading plan sheet and use the cards independently.

* Babbs, 1984.

3.   W–I–K Textbook Comprehension Monitoring*   IJHA

Procedure: I.   *Preparation*

A.   Choose a lesson in the text that uses students' prior knowledge of the subject.

B.   Be sure this chapter or excerpt uses a clear method of development, such as problem–solution or description.

II.   *Describing the task to the students*

A.   Before the students read, distribute What-I-Know (W–I–K) sheets to them (see Figure 23-4). Explain that they are going to learn to become better readers by describing what they already know about a subject and how they learn information from the text.

B.   Instruct students to write their reading topic on their What-I-Know sheet—for example, "marsupial animals of Australia."

C.   If appropriate, use a concrete prereading activity that focuses on meaningful prior knowledge needed—for example, knowing where Australia is on the map.

FIGURE 23-4   What–I–Know Sheet

Column A What I already knew	Column B What I know now	Column C What I don't know
kangaroos	animals with a pouch	carnivores
Australia a continent	dry climate	why few predators in Australia
koala bears	spiny anteater and duck-billed platypus	
southern hemisphere		Is a predator a carnivore?
possums	special class of animals: monotremes	
	egg-laying mammals	
	kangaroo babies = joeys	
	kangaroo herd = mob	

ANSWER TO THE PURPOSE QUESTION: Marsupials are different from other animals in the following ways: They raise their young in a pouch. Most live in Australia or New Guinea. They are very small at birth, crawl from the birth canal to the mother's pouch, attach to the mother's milk gland, and develop into maturity in the pouch.

D.   Question students to activate their prior knowledge (see the activities in Chapter 7, section B).

E.   Model surveying the reading assignment. Create a teacher–student purpose that will require inferential thinking—question for example, "How are marsupial animals different from other animals?" Explain that this purpose question provides the reason for their reading.

F.   Write the purpose on the overhead or chalkboard.

G.   Students write the purpose on their W–I–K sheet.

III.   *During reading:* how to use the W–I–K sheets

A.   Explain to students that upon reading they will find both old and new information that applies to their purpose question. Information they knew before reading but did not remember until they read it in the text belongs in column A of their W–I–K sheet.

B.   In column B students write new concepts (words and sentences) that they think they understand and that they think will be useful when they answer the purpose question.

C.   In column C students write confusing concepts that may interfere with their answering the purpose question.

D.   Tell students you will fill out your own sheet and show it on the overhead or board to demonstrate.

IV.   *After reading*

A.   Students write their answer to the purpose question on their sheet.

B.   Show your completed sheet on the overhead or board.

C.   Have students look at the beginning of the section you used to complete your sheet.

D.   Describe the metacognitive strategies you used when filling out the sheet.

E.   Students compare their answers with yours.

F.   Focus on:

1.   setting the purpose for reading (What am I supposed to learn?);

2.   activating prior knowledge (What did I already know?);

3.   recognizing text structure (How did I know this was description?);

4.   knowing that one understands (What have I learned?);

5.   knowing that one didn't understand (Why did I stop here and reread?)

G.   Have students form discussion groups of three to four. Each student describes what she or he did to achieve the purpose for reading. Students compare their sheets with yours, deciding which strategies seemed most useful.

H.   End the activity by having students write a paragraph on the topic "Knowing What I Know," in which they describe their own understanding of how knowing what they do and don't know can help them become better readers.

Variations: 1.   Introduce the procedure one portion at a time.

2.   Have students model the procedure for the class.

3. For the postreading activity students write a paragraph about the content, including information about what they didn't understand but now do.

4. Keep the W–I–K sheets in a folder, to be used both as a reference for future comprehension-monitoring activities and in content-area review.

5. If you are responsible for various content areas, vary the subjects used in the procedure.

* Heller, 1986.

4. Comprehension Rating*   P I J

Procedure:

1. Develop the students' view of reading as a meaning-getting process:

    a. Using sample materials such as cloze passages or materials with nonsense words, model how readers don't need all the information to predict meaning.

    b. Model comprehension breakdowns and fix-up strategies (rereading, reading ahead, and so on).

    c. Have the students interview parents or other teachers about strategies they use when their comprehension breaks down.

2. Focus attention on silent reading for meaning: Begin with single sentences involving word-level difficulties. Have students, working in groups or individually, respond to the question "How well do you understand?" by holding up one finger to indicate "I understand," two fingers to indicate "I don't understand." Use sentences with nonsense words or sentences with real words that make no sense—for example, "The weight of the water is caused by the power of the garage."

3. Establish the criteria for understanding:

    a. Extend the two-point rating system to a three-point system: 1 = "I understand well (I have a clear, complete picture in my head and I could explain it to someone else)"; 2 = "I sort of understand (I have an incomplete picture in my head and I couldn't explain it to someone else)"; 3 = "I don't understand."

    b. Model finding the source of comprehension failure, at the word or idea level. Use a "source-of-difficulty" check system consisting of these two categories. After group practice with nonsense words and embedded errors in the text, have the students practice with a variety of materials.

    c. Have students practice the three-point rating system with appropriate materials at the sentence, paragraph, and selection levels. Response cards or finger signals can also be used.

    d. Share your ratings and group ratings in order to illustrate the reasons for different responses. (Explain, for instance, why you gave the text only a 2.) Develop the idea that understanding is a personal decision: what some people clearly understand others may not understand.

    e. Demonstrate how the purpose for reading makes a difference when readers are deciding how satisfied they need to be at any point. For example, if one were reading only for the general ideas, it would be appropriate to have only a partial understanding.

4. Develop fix-up strategies—all modeled by yourself and practiced and evaluated by the students.

     a.   word-level strategies:
     predict meaning from context
     use structural clues within words
     sound out words
     use the dictionary
     ask someone else
     b.   idea-level strategies:
     read on
     look back
     look again at visual aids and headings
     look at the punctuation
     ask yourself questions
     put information into your own words
     picture the ideas in your head
     ask an expert

Post the strategies for use as prompts.

5. Provide independent practice with a variety of materials from school and outside.

* Davey and Porter, 1982.

5. Text Look–Backs*   **I J H A (used with mildly handicapped students)**

Procedure: DAY 1

a.   Explain to students the purpose for learning the strategy—to help them comprehend and remember better.

b.   Give students a 200-to-300 word passage on two pages. Tell them to read silently, and let them know you will ask them three questions after they have finished.

c.   When students have finished tell them that as you ask each question they may look back at either or both pages to find the answer. Have them restate these directions in their own words.

d.   Ask the questions.

e.   Give students another passage, but write on the board a hint that will help them: "*Why* should you look back? You look back because you can't remember everything you read." Ask if this makes sense.

f.   Give students a similar passage with the same directions.

g.   Go over the answers, having students explain how they decided on their responses.

h.   Have students summarize the lesson in their own words.

DAY 2

a.   Review the previous class.

b.   Write hint 2 on the board: "*When* should you look back? You look back when the questions ask about what the author or article said, not about what you think.''

    c. Point out the difference between text-based questions (find answers in the text) and reader-based questions (use prior knowledge to answer). Use the first day's questions to model this.

    d. Before students read the new passage, repeat the two hints on the board.

    e. After students read the passage, they answer both text- and reader-based questions. Students explain their responses.

    f. Provide feedback. Have students summarize the class.

DAY 3

    a. Review the previous day's work. Repeat hints 1 and 2 and write hint 3: ''*Where* should you look back? Skim the whole article to find the part that might be useful.''

    b. Use the previous day's text to model skimming. Explain that skimming replaces rereading the whole article.

    c. Read look-back questions and model choosing key words or phrases from the text, rereading the sentence or paragraph in which you found them.

    d. Have students read a longer passage. Remind them to use all three hints.

    e. After they have answered the questions, have them explain how they found the answers.

    f. Provide feedback and instructions as required (see Figure 23-5).

* Reis and Leone, 1985.

FIGURE 23-5 Text Look–Back Checklist

> 1. WHY SHOULD I LOOK BACK?
>
>   I will look back to pages I have read so I can locate information I don't remember.
>
> 2. WHEN SHOULD I LOOK BACK?
>
>   I will look back when I think the questions ask about what the author or article said.
>
>   I will not look back when the questions ask me what I think.
>
> 3. WHERE SHOULD I LOOK?
>
>   I will skim the article and look for key words and phrases.
>
>   I will then reread sentences and entire paragraphs if necessary.

Source: Reis and Leone, 1985, p. 418. Reprinted with permission of Ron Reis and the International Reading Association.

6. Find the Errors*   P I

Procedure: 1.   Select a highly predictable selection of eight to ten sentences.

2.   Replace some of the predictable words with anomalous words.

3.   Tell students that they are going to practice finding errors in written material—a very useful strategy for them to use when reading. Provide relevant examples of material to apply this strategy to (movie timetables and directions for tests, for instance), and have them suggest other examples.

4.   Demonstrate finding errors in the selection, explaining the clues you used (syntax, prior knowledge).

5.   Provide supervised practice for the students. Have them share results, and be sure they explain *how* they decided where there was an error. Be sure to specify how many errors there are in a selection.

6.   Provide copies of a selection for students to work on individually. Have students share their results with the class and specify how they found the errors.

Variation: Content-area review: Use a summary from a content-area text and replace predictable and important words with errors. Have students correct the summary.

* Goodman and Burke, 1972.

B. FINDING AND FIXING COMPREHENSION PROBLEMS

1. Improving Instructions*   I J H A

Procedure: 1.   Give each student a set of incomplete or misleading instructions—for example, faulty recipes, incomplete driver's manual instructions, or unclear directions for finding a classroom.

2.   Students rate the instructions on a scale of 1 (very bad) to 5 (really good).

3.   Students list under two columns—*What I Know* and *What I Don't Know*—the salient information from the instructions.

4.   Students discuss their ratings and the information they listed under the two columns.

5.   Working in groups, students rewrite the instructions for other students of their age.

6.   Students share their rewritings orally, discussing the changes they made and the needed information their additions supplied.

7.   Students work individually on provided material.

* Fitzgerald, 1983.

2. How Confident Are You?*   P I J H A

Procedure: 1.   Provide students with a passage difficult to understand.

2.   Students read passage.

3.   Ask questions about the passage.

4.   Students write answers on a sheet and rate their confidence in their answers on a scale of 1 (not sure at all) to 5 (very sure).

5.   Answers and ratings are discussed.

6.   Demonstrate how the ratings, in relation to the answers, indicate that a reader is aware of what she or he does and does not know, an important skill in comprehension.

7.   Point out that a low rating does *not* indicate failure; it indicates only that more information is needed. Therefore, a low rating is a good response because it shows an awareness of comprehension.

8.   Reinforce comprehension awareness with real reading tasks.

* Fitzgerald, 1983.

3. Question Pairs*   P I J H A

Procedure: 1.   Tell students the purpose of the activity: to develop self-questioning strategies that will help them be aware of what they know—and what they don't know.

2.   Students divide into pairs and read the first section of a story or text.

3.   Each pair creates and writes down three questions about important information in the text.

4.   The students repeat this process for another section of the material.

5.   Pairs exchange lists and try to answer the questions without looking back at the text.

6.   Papers are returned, and pairs exchange oral feedback about the answers.

7.   Reinforce the lesson by restating the importance of asking oneself questions such as these when reading, in order to be aware of what one knows and doesn't know.

* Fitzgerald, 1983.

4. Comprehension Code*   I J H A

Procedure: 1.   Tell students that they will be using a code to evaluate their texts, indicate the state of their comprehension, and let both the teacher and the class know about the characteristics of the assigned material.

2.   Give students strips of paper to affix to the margins of assigned text pages.

3.   Develop the code for the students. For example, for a social studies text A = *agree*, B = *bored*, C = *confused*, D = *disagree*, M = *main idea;* for a science text C = *clear*, D = *difficult*, I = *important*, S = *surprising*. The code is determined by the characteristics of the text, the curriculum objectives, and/or the responses you want from the students.

4.   Students record their responses on the strips of paper as they read.

5.   Postreading discussion focuses on their response. For example, a *confused* rating for a paragraph provides the opportunity to determine what caused the difficulty and what strategies can be used to facilitate comprehension.

6.   Student responses can also serve as diagnostic data for future lessons in content and reading skills.

* Smith and Dauer, 1984.

5.   What's Wrong?   PI

Procedure: 1.   Prepare passages with inconsistent information inserted.

2.   Explain to students that their task is to figure out what's wrong in each paragraph—what information doesn't make sense—and to underline (or highlight) that section.

3.   Demonstrate this procedure with a passage.

4.   Have students work on one or two passages. Give them immediate feedback.

5.   Students work independently or in small groups.

6.   Students discuss results when finished, focusing on *why* the information was wrong.

7.   After sufficient practice, give students passages with and without inconsistent information.

Variation: Students create the passages to be used.

BIBLIOGRAPHY

Babbs, P. J. "Monitoring cards help improve comprehension," *Reading Teacher,* 38, November (1984), 200–204.

Casazza, M. "The Effects of Direct Macroprocessing Instruction on College Students' Comprehension Monitoring Strategies." Ph.D. dissertation, Loyola University of Chicago, 1988.

Collins, A. and E. Smith. *Teaching the Process of Reading Comprehension.* Technical Report no. 182, Center for the Study of Reading, University of Illinois. Urbana-Champaign, 1980.

Davey, B. and S. M. Porter. "Comprehension-rating: A procedure to assist poor comprehenders," *Journal of Reading,* 26, December (1982), 197–201.

Fitzgerald, J. "Helping readers gain self-control over reading comprehension," *Reading Teacher,* 37, December (1983), 249–53.

Goodman, Y. and C. Burke. *Reading Miscue Inventory Manual.* New York: Macmillan, 1972.

Heller, M. F. "How do you know what you know? Metacognitive modeling in the content areas," *Journal of Reading,* 29, February (1986), 415–22.

Reis, R. and P. E. Leone. "Teaching text lookbacks to mildly handicapped students," *Journal of Reading,* 28, February (1985), 416–20.

Smith, R. J. and V. L. Dauer. "A comprehension-monitoring strategy for reading content area materials," *Journal of Reading,* 28, November (1984), 144–47.

chapter 24

USING STUDY STRATEGIES

Definition: *Using reading strategies designed specifically to maximize recall*

RATIONALE

In this book, study skills are defined as those specific reading strategies that increase recall. Remember, however, that many of the processes described earlier in this book also increase recall. Active inferencing, summarizing, outlining, imaging, elaborating with prior knowledge, and so on, all increase recall of content and should also be used in study situations. Thus, study strategies can be seen as those specific strategies that go beyond the basic use of the other comprehension processes in some structured way.

General study-reading skills can be divided into strategies that are used before, during, and after reading. *Before* reading, students should preview the material, noting the organization and the topics to be covered, as well as reviewing their prior knowledge. *During* reading, students should focus on key concepts and review at periodic intervals. They may also want to underline or take notes. *After* reading, students should review and/or take notes if they haven't yet.

During all these processes, students should make maximum use of the other comprehension processes, focusing especially on the organizational pattern and on making elaborations that will help them connect the material with things they already know. For instance, during previewing students should think about what they already know about the topic, make predictions about what will be said, and note the organizational pattern. When they begin reading, they should attend to main-idea selection by deciding at the beginning of each section what they would like to find out in that section. This decision can consist of forming a question from the subheading, to be answered in subsequent reading, or it can simply be the decision to look for the key idea. Note-taking should focus on summarizing and organizing, as should periodic rehearsal. Many of our students have found that making a tape recording in which they recite the main ideas as they go along works well for periodic rehearsal. Study guides can also be used to encourage students to recite summaries or main ideas in an organized form while they are reading. After-reading review should also include all these things—elaboration, organization, and summarization in the reader's own words.

One of the most powerful study principles to

teach to students is the power of review. In a classic experiment, Spitzer (1939) found that students who reviewed immediately, a week later, and then several weeks later remembered over 60 percent more than students who did no reviewing. Students are very impressed when they see how this can work for them. Conduct a classroom experiment in which some students review and others do something else. Then give a quiz.

The implications of the importance of review are obvious. Students should be encouraged to review immediately after reading and again at intervals of about a week. You can structure these review sessions with study guides and class discussions until students are independent enough to do this themselves.

Though study skills are usually taught only in high school, we have known many teachers who have taught the basics of studying in elementary school. Teachers can model previewing when they give assignments. They can provide study guides that model note-taking and review. They can show students how to review material from the previous day's class. Other suggestions are also provided in this chapter. The point is that establishing good study habits as early as possible seems advisable.

The activities in this chapter have been divided according to whether they help students (1) read and study textbooks, (2) study for tests, or (3) take notes and underline. They should be used in real reading situations. Nothing sells a technique like success when it is needed!

INFORMAL DIAGNOSIS

Many study-skill inventories are available for assessing students' study strategies (see McWilliams & Rakes, 1979, p. 210–11 and study-skill manuals). Of course, there are two levels to assess: (1) Do the students know what to do? (2) Do they do it? The first is an awareness level, and the second is behavioral. Surveys will assess the former but not the latter. Good study strategies must be habitual. To determine whether your students regularly use study strategies you will need to observe them in study situations.

GENERAL TEACHING SUGGESTIONS

1. Try to make study strategies habitual among your students by regularly making these behaviors part of other content assignments. Students, like all of us, need constant reminders if they are to make something a habit.

2. Consider teaching study strategies in parts: first previewing, then during-reading strategies, and finally review strategies.

3. Demonstrate the efficacy of study strategies by having half the class use them and half not. When the students not using them see the others getting better scores on quizzes, they will be won over!

4. Because study skills require the use of all the other basic processes, you may find yourself teaching other processes when you meant to teach study skills. For instance, if you try to teach note-taking to a student who cannot summarize or organize, you will and should find yourself teaching those skills first.

5. Have students pair up to review material and then "test" each other.

6. Establish good study habits whenever you teach. Always preview what you are going to teach. Always focus the students' attention. Always pause and let them summarize and review. Always have them summarize and review at the end of the lesson. Always review the lesson within twenty-four hours.

chapter 24. USING STUDY STRATEGIES
Activities

A. READING AND STUDYING TEXTBOOKS
   1. Guide a Friend   I J H A
   2. Consciousness Raising   I J H A
   3. Step-by-Step SQ3R   I J H A
   4. Guided Reading   I J H A
   5. ConStruct Procedure   I J H A
   6. 3-Zone Defense   H A
   7. Textbook-Reading Pretest   I J H A
   8. Why Prequestions   P I J
   9. Guided Study   I J H A
B. INCREASING RECALL AND STUDYING FOR TESTS
   1. Review Now (RN)   I J H A
   2. Write a Fair Test   I J H A
   3. Mnemonics Help *Mnemory*   I J H A
   4. Study How?   I J H A
   5. Make Your Own Test   P I J H A
   6. Self-Questioning   I J H A
C. NOTE–TAKING AND UNDERLINING
   1. SQ5R   I J H A
   2. What's Next?   H A
   3. Underline Less to Underline More   J H A
   4. Beginning Underlining   P I
   5. Test Teams   I J H A
   6. OH RATS   J H A

A. READING AND STUDYING TEXTBOOKS

1. Guide A Friend*   I J H A

  Procedure: 1. Ask students to create study guides for material they have read. Have models of study guides available. (See Chapter 17 for a demonstration of how to make a study guide that focuses on the organizational pattern.)

                   2. Explain to students that the criterion for a good study guide is that it asks questions only about important information.

                   3. Students complete each other's guides and evaluate them on how well they helped them focus on important points.

  Variation: Divide a chapter to be read into sections and have different students work on different sections. After reading their own sections, they use other students' guides to read the remaining material.

  * Irwin 1986.

2. Consciousness Raising*   I J H A

  Procedure: 1. Make copies of a content-area text selection about which you and your students have little prior knowledge.

2.   Ask them to read the selection and take notes about the strategies they use as they read. For example, ask them to note whether they procrastinated before reading, what they did when encountering unfamiliar words, what procedures they used when the text became difficult, how many breaks they took, whether they took notes or underlined, and so forth. Tell them to do whatever they need to do to understand the new material, and explain that you will also read and take notes on your own strategies. (One way to make this more student-directed would be for the students to choose the unfamiliar material.)

3.   Set a time limit of two or three days (or whatever is convenient) for the task.

4.   After the reading is completed, ask the students the strategies they used. Write these on the board and classify them. Categories could include *prereading strategies,* such as skimming the chapter; *reading strategies,* such as rereading difficult passages and figuring out word meanings from context; *nontext activities,* such as dealing with procrastination and taking breaks; and *study/memory activities,* such as taking notes and making graphic overviews.

5.   Demonstrate the flexible strategies that you and some of the students used—for example, skimming easier material to get an overview and reading material with many unfamiliar terms more slowly, and sometimes using context to figure out word meanings and other times looking up words.

6.   Point out that you and some of the students also tended to talk to someone who knew something about the subject—that discussing the new material was a good way of monitoring comprehension. Using only the text material is probably one of the most difficult and constraining ways to learn.

7.   Emphasize the need for students to take breaks when studying new material, to give themselves time to "incubate" the new knowledge and to make the task more manageable.

8.   Compile a list of the study strategies found most useful. Have the students use this class-generated list when studying.

* Adapted from Smith, 1982.

3.   Step–By–Step SQ3R*   I J H A

Procedure: 1.   Model all steps in the SQ3R process using guided work sheets. First, have students survey an assigned text chapter and complete the first page of the SQ3R work sheet (see Figure 24-1).

2.   Then, to develop vocabulary, students identify italicized or boldface words in the text and complete page 2 of the work sheet, using context to define words.

3.   Students then relate supporting ideas and vocabulary by filling in page 3 of the work sheet.

4.   Students complete page 4 of the work sheet, creating questions for each heading that incorporate key vocabulary and answering those questions.

* Powell, 1982.

FIGURE 24-1 SQ3R Work Sheet

PAGE 1

Subject _____

Main Idea (chapter heading/title) _____

Supporting ideas (section headings):

1. _____

2. _____

PAGE 2

Special Terms: If you can, define each term in your own words, using ten
words or less.

FOUND IN SECTION NO.

1. _____   _____

2. _____   _____

PAGE 3

List supporting ideas and headings and special terms found in each section.

_____

_____

PAGE 4

Change supporting ideas and headings into *who, what, why, where,* or *how*
questions. Be sure to use all special terms found in that section when
answering the question.

1. _____

2. _____

Source: Powell, 1982, p. 263. Reprinted with permission of Glen Powell and the International Reading Association.

4. Guided Reading*   **I J H A**

Procedure: 1. Students survey an assigned section of a text chapter, reading only
chapter title, headings, graphs, charts, maps, vocabulary lists, and chapter questions.

2. Students close books and orally state everything they can remember
from the preview.

3. Record verbatim on the board all the students' information.

4.   Students then check the chapter for information not included, and this is added to the summary on the board.

5.   Discuss with the students the results of this text survey and organize the information into a topical outline on the board.

6.   Students read text silently.

Variation: Students use the survey to predict possible test questions on the material.

* Bean and Pardi, 1979.

5.   Construct Procedure*   I J H A

Procedure: 1.   Explain the purpose of the lesson. The students will use diversified multiple readings of their textbook material to create a graphic overview of the concepts, adding details with each reading. Model the remaining four steps, using a current textbook.

2.   *Survey-Read:* Read quickly, focusing on such things as introductions, headings, and subheadings. Construct a general framework for a graphic overview (a graphic representation similar to a map; see Figure 24-2).

3.   *Study-Read:* Read to understand all the material. Add details to the graphic overview. (See Figure 24-3, p. 238.)

4.   *Comprehension Check:* Reexamine portions of the text not understood earlier. Insert clarified material into the overview. (See Figure 24-4, p. 239.)

5.   *Review-Read:* Skim the selection and the overview to reinforce comprehension.

* Vaughan, 1982.

FIGURE 24-2   Top-Level Graphic Overview

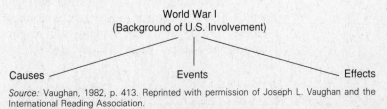

Source: Vaughan, 1982, p. 413. Reprinted with permission of Joseph L. Vaughan and the International Reading Association.

6.   3–Zone Defense*   H A

Procedure: 1.   Tell students that the purpose of the strategy they are about to learn is to help them develop study habits based on specific course needs.

2.   Ask the students to think of a course where they will have to take a test soon. Ask, "Does the instructor in that course lecture directly from the text?" If the answer is yes, they are now in Defense Zone A: they must read the text material before it is covered in class, to facilitate listening and note-taking. The

FIGURE 24-3 Second-Stage Graphic Overview

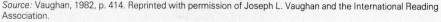

Source: Vaughan, 1982, p. 414. Reprinted with permission of Joseph L. Vaughan and the International Reading Association.

most effective way to use study time in this zone is to review class notes and coordinate them with the text. Display the 3–Zone Defense map (Figure 24-5, p. 240) on the board or overhead.

3.   If the answer is no, ask, ''Are the tests based on text material?'' If the answer to this is no, the students are in Defense Zone B: a cursory reading of the text is sufficient, because the text serves merely as background information for the students. However, *note-taking* is critical in this zone.

4.   If the answer to this question is yes, then the students land in Defense Zone C. This is a danger zone, because although the instructor does not lecture directly from the text, the students are responsible for the text material when they take the tests. Therefore, the course is really a reading comprehension course.

5.   Add to the 3–Zone Defense Map an overview of the reading strategies needed for each zone (see Figure 24-5). Define the reading terms:

a.   Pre-READ: set a purpose for reading; self-question; use visual aids; skim.

b.   READ: take notes; outline or underline text.

c.   Free-READ: read easy material on the topic being covered in class—before the lecture, before you READ, or after the lecture.

d.   Re-READ: combine what you have learned from your notes and your reading; make comparison charts, graphic overviews, or other aids to comprehension.

* Adapted from Radencich and Schumm, 1985.

FIGURE 24-4   Completed Graphic Overview

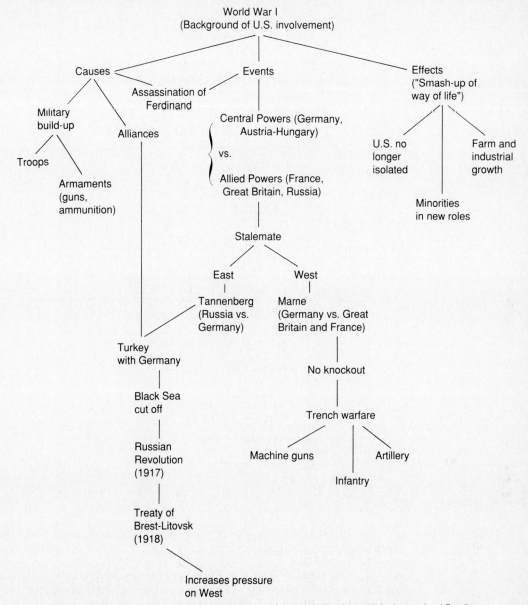

Source: Vaughan, 1982, p. 412–22. Reprinted with permission of Joseph L. Vaughan and the International Reading Association.

8. Why Prequestions*   P I J

Procedure: 1. Read text and create a *why* question for each paragraph. These questions focus on the main ideas of the paragraphs.

2. Students use these questions as they read, to help themselves focus on the main ideas.

Variation: Students create *why* prequestions for each other on new material.

* Memory, 1983.

FIGURE 24-5   3–Zone Defense Map

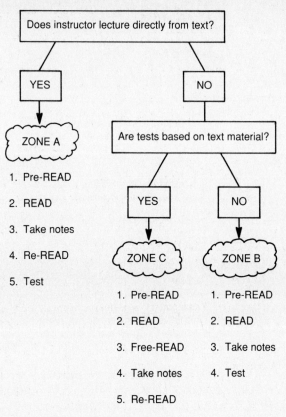

Source: Radencich and Schumm, *Reading World,* 24(3), p. 89. Reprinted with permission.

9. **Guided Study***   **I J H A**

Procedure: 1.   Explain the purpose of the lesson and model steps 2–6. Choose a student to act as your partner.

2.   *Previewing:* Preview a few pages of the text assignment and generate a skeleton outline consisting of numbers and letters corresponding to the sections and subsections.

3.   *Reading:* Read the assignment in sections, filling in the outline as you proceed.

4.   *Outlining:* For each subsection, write in a main idea *in your own words* (see A and B in Figure 24-6). If you wish, add details (see numbered items in Figure 24-6.). At the end of a major section, write a main idea for the section *in your own words* (see I in Figure 24-6). Then summarize the subsection in a key phrase and write that phrase in the left margin. (See Figure 24-6.)

5.   *Studying:* After the reading is finished, review your outline.

6.   *Retelling:* Finally, tell your partner what you learned from reading the assignment. Your partner then tells you what he or she learned.

* Taylor, 1982.

FIGURE 24-6   Sample Outline

I. Puritan cultural values that still influence our society.
   A. Puritans respected education.
      1. Most towns built schools.
      2. Harvard College was supported by taxes.
      3. Today we have public education for all.
   B. Puritans believed that work was for God and leisure was bad.
      1. They disliked games and holidays.
      2. They associated wealth with work and poverty with illness.
      3. Thus, poor people were sinful.
      4. Today, we still respect people who work and are wealthy.

Source: Irwin, 1986, p. 54.

B.   INCREASING RECALL AND STUDYING FOR TESTS

1.   Review Now (RN)*   I J H A

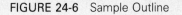

Procedure: 1.   Ask students how they would remember a new phone number if they had no paper or pencil to write it down. (repetition)

2.   Ask if repetition would work if they waited until the next day to repeat the number. (no)

3.   Discuss the reasons it wouldn't work: they wouldn't have rehearsed it enough to remember it, other information would interfere, they would have no written text to refer to.

4.   Elicit other analogies illustrating why they need to practice new knowledge immediately in order to learn it. (a basketball play, knitting stitch, etc.)

5.   To demonstrate that it is better to *review now* when learning, instead of waiting until the next day, set up an experiment. Divide the class into two groups, equal in ability. Group A will review new material the same day they learn it; group B will not review until just before the test on the assigned material.

6.   Use classroom situations, such as teacher questions and discussion, to illustrate the comparative learning of the groups.

7.   Have the two groups keep track of the amount of time they spend studying for the test on the material (see Figure 24-7).

FIGURE 24-7   Review Now Record Sheet

GROUP ____   Name _____

Directions: If you are a member of group A, review the new material the same day you learned it. Enter learning dates, review dates, review times, and test result in the columns below.

If you are a member of group B, review the new material just before the test. Fill in the columns as above.

DATE NEW MATERIAL LEARNED   DATE REVIEWED   TIME SPENT REVIEWING   TEST RESULT

8.   Compare the test results. Discuss the amount of time each group needed to spend reviewing for the test.

9.   Discuss the results of the experiment—group A remembered the material better and needed less time to review for the test—which demonstrate that *reviewing now* is the key to successful recall.

* Irwin, 1986.

2.   Write A Fair Test*   I J H A

Procedure: 1.   After reading a selection or completing a unit of study in which there are many important details, tell the students that you want to test them on the information.

2.   When students ask, "What will be on the test?" respond with "What do *you* think should be on the test?"

3.   On the board, write the material they suggest. Discuss their reasons for choosing one piece of information over another.

4.   Continue to encourage responses until you get all the important information on the board. Have students take notes on all the board information.

5.   Ask the students to work individually (or in pairs or small groups) on a test of their own about the material. Be sure to ask, "What kinds of questions would be appropriate?" Explain that the kind of information they are looking for may determine the type of question they ask. Demonstrate possible matching, true-or-false, fill-in-the-blank, and essay questions.

6.   Assign the test as a written task to be turned in. Specify the number (and type, if you choose) of questions to be included. Students must supply an answer sheet for their test.

7.   When the tests are turned in, any of several alternatives can be followed:

a.   Students can take each other's tests and then mark their partner's answers.

b.   A discussion lesson can be built around one student reading his or her test and others indicating whether they had similar questions. Other students can supply questions not included, and the class can choose the questions they think would make a fair test.

c.   You can give a test made up of the best questions turned in.

* Irwin, 1986

3.   Mnemonics Help Memory   I J H A

Procedure   1.   Write on the overhead a list of twelve items—for example, *bulb, ship, firefly, train, candle, glue, car, tape, truck, flashlight, submarine, horse.*

2.   Ask students what they would do if they had to memorize this list. Work on their suggestions on the overhead (alphabetizing, etc.)

3.   Develop the idea that organizing information is a way to remember it better. Ask the students to help you put the items into categories, and help them create the categories—for example, transportation on land, transportation on the

sea, things that give light, animals, things that stick. Label each item as you do this—L (light), TL, TS, and so on.

4. Condense the categories to transportation (*horse* can fit here), things that give light (*firefly* fits here), and things that stick.

5. Organize your three lists, count the number of items in each, and ask the students if it would be easier to remember the list this way. You will have four Lights, six Transportations, and two Stickies. Ask if there is any way they can remember the items in each list.

6. Give example of acronyms used to remember lists—HOMES for the Greak Lakes (Huron, Ontario, Michigan, Erie, and Superior), or acrostic sentences Every Good Boy Does Fine for the lines of the music scale (EGBDF).

7. Help the students develop mnemonic devices for each list. Alphabetize each list, use mnemonic sentences (Bees Can Fly Fast for *bulb, candle, flashlight, firefly*), use mnemonic words (chsstt for *car, horse, ship, submarine, train, truck*), and so on.

8. Option: Pretest students on the list before they learn mnemonic devices and posttest after, to illustrate the efficacy of the strategy.

9. Students work in small groups on lists provided, developing mnemonic devices.

10. Groups share results, get teacher feedback.

11. Have students work on relevant textbook materials. Assign each group different sections. Share results.

4. Study How?   I J H A

Procedure: 1. Ask students what techniques they use when they want to remember what they read, whether for a test or for personal use.

2. Write on the board all their suggestions.

3. Have the students help you organize the suggestions into categories. You will probably have *writing, saying it over,* and *rereading*.

4. Elaborate on these categories, eliciting the similarities and differences among them. All include going over the material again; writing and saying involve using other senses.

5. Point out that using other senses is a good way to remember information, but only writing gives you something permanent that you can use again, unless you *tape* yourself.

6. Divide students into small groups. Each group must try to think of eight to ten ways of reviewing material for a test. These may *not* include rereading the text. Groups must try to include the use of as many senses as possible in their strategies.

7. Share the results in a class discussion. Possible strategies might include the following:

    a. making a review tape of questions, silence (allowing the student to answer), and answers
    b. 3-by-5 cards of questions and answers

   c.   writing possible questions on yellow sticky pads and posting them
   d.   making a time line
   e.   making a graphic overview
   f.   reviewing with friends
   g.   writing your own test
   h.   asking yourself questions in the SQ3R format
   i.   making mnemonic devices
   j.   making a Trivial Pursuit game of the material
   k.   making a song of important information

8.   The class may want to vote on—and try out—the most useful suggestions. Students may want to experiment—some using one strategy, others another—to see which is most effective.

9.   Point out that they are adding to their repertoire of study strategies. They now have more to choose from; it's possible that more than one strategy should be used, and different strategies may be appropriate for different materials.

5. Make Your Own Test   PIJHA

Procedure: 1.   After students have completed a unit of study, ask them to hypothesize possible test questions. Go over one small section of the material (for example, the amount falling under a textbook subheading), demonstrating how to create possible test questions. Show how a subheading is itself a possible test question: "Spaniards Go to the New World" becomes "Why did the Spaniards go to the New World?"

2.   Mention that it is important to know the teacher's style, as he or she is going to create the test. The students will have to decide the type of question the teacher would most likely give. They can decide this on the basis of (a) previous tests, (b) the teacher's classroom style, (c) student reports, and/or (d) asking the teacher.

3.   Have students create questions for a section of material.

4.   Discuss the questions.

5.   Ask students to each create a test for the unit. Specify the number and type of questions required. You may have to teach them how to create matching, short-answer, multiple-choice, or essay questions.

6.   Students make an answer key for their test.

7.   Students bring tests to school and exchange, take, and mark them.

8.   Class discussion focuses on the most common test items—the ones everyone expects to find. Students who did not include these items should add them to their test.

9.   Have students turn in tests for you to see. Return the tests and have the students use them for review for the actual test.

10.   Use as many of the student test questions as you can on the actual test.

6. Self–Questioning*   IJHA

Procedure: 1.   Tell students that they are going to participate in a memory experiment. Have them all read a passage.

2.   Give a difficult quiz on the passage. Have students mark their own quizzes.

3.   Discuss the results, emphasizing that since they spent time reading the material, as they would an assignment, it is unfortunate that they did not remember the material very well. Reading so that one can remember is an important skill.

4.   To develop this skill in the students, suggest that asking themselves questions while they read will help them remember. Model the process with a passage.

5.   To demonstrate that self-questioning is effective, give the students questions to ask themselves while they read another passage. Tell them what makes good self-questions.

6.   Test the students on this passage.

7.   Compare their results on this quiz with their results on the first one. The difference should prove the effectiveness of the strategy.

8.   Give students questions to answer for assignments until they become comfortable with the strategy.

9.   Students write their own questions for assigned material, sharing them in group discussions.

10.   Students work independently.

* Irwin, 1986; see also Andre and Anderson, 1978–79.

NOTE-TAKING AND UNDERLINING

1. SQ5R*   IJHA

Procedure: 1.   Ask the students what they would do if they had to drive to Detroit right away. Refine their answers to reveal that they would want to look at a map.

2.   Ask why they would need a map. (They would need to know where their destination is, how long it would take, and so on.)

3.   Tell them that studying new material is exactly like that: they need to know where they are going so that they can get there the fastest way and won't get lost.

4.   Using a current content-area textbook, model an SQ5R sequence for the students:

S: *Survey* the material to get an idea of what it contains.

Q: As you read, turn each heading or subheading into a *question*. This will give you a purpose for your reading. For note-taking, draw a vertical line one third of the distance from the left edge of a sheet of paper. *Write the question in this left-hand column.*

R: *Read,* answering the question you have created.

R: *Restate* the answer to the question in your own words. Draw a vertical line one third of the distance from the right edge of your paper, and *write this answer in the right-hand column.* This will give you material to review.

R: *Restate* any question that your reading indicates was inappropriate, and answer the restated question. For example, the heading "The War in New England" might have caused you to ask "Why was there a war in New England?" Upon reading, you might have found that the passage *described* the war and did not mention the causes, so you would have to rephrase your question.

R: *Recite* the answers to your questions. Using another sense helps you strengthen your memory.

R: *Review* your notes regularly to get a bird's-eye view of where you've been—the various ideas and their relationships to one another. This quick review will improve your memory.

5.   Demonstrate how to use the notes for review: cover the right-hand column of your paper with your hand and ask yourself the questions in the left-hand column. Answer the questions orally, and check your answers.

6.   Work on each of the steps in the sequence individually, supervising student practice and assigning independent work on relevant material.

7.   Have students turn in written work for each of the steps so that you can monitor their progress.

8.   Regularly discuss the effectiveness of the strategy, eliciting student comments about any changes they made because of the content they were reading.

* Pauk, 1984 Adapted from Robinson, 1970.

2.   What's Next?   H A

Procedure: 1.   Ask students which strategies they have found useful for taking lecture notes, and what difficulties they have encountered.

2.   Discuss one of the major problems of note-taking—people speak 125 to 150 words per minute, but can write only about 25 words a minute. Tell the students that if they can pick up the clues that lecturers give about the organization of their lectures, they will have an important skill that will help them organize their lecture notes better.

3.   Review some of the most common lecture structures:

    a.   description or narration
    b.   time sequence
    c.   cause and effect
    d.   a definition with attributes
    e.   a list
    f.   comparing and contrasting

Ask which disciplines they could be found in. (They can be found in all disciplines.)

4. Tell students that lecturers' opening sentences often give clues about the format of the lecture. Give examples of opening sentences and ask students to identify the structure. Then ask "What were the words that gave you the *clue* about the organization?" Here are some sample opening sentences, with the clue words underlined:

What do we <u>mean</u> when we talk about gravity? (definition)

Let's <u>trace</u> the events that led to the southern states' decision to secede from the Union. (time order)

Today's topic is: <u>how</u> does photosynthesis occur? (cause and effect)

As we look at the Industrial Revolution and its effect on family life, <u>four</u> basic truths emerge. (list)

It is important in our study of this period to <u>distinguish</u> totalitarianism from dictatorship (compare and contrast)

Before we go any further, let's <u>review</u> the <u>events</u> in the novel so far. (narration, time order)

The <u>characteristics</u> of arthropods <u>are</u>: . . . (list)

If you had lived in Europe in 1900, <u>what would</u> your life <u>have been like</u>? (description)

5. Emphasize that knowing the organization alerts you to what is coming next. Demonstrate different note-taking techniques that you might use for each pattern. For example:

compare and contrast—two columns

time order—dates in left-hand column

cause and effect—label C and E and use an arrow to connect them

6. You might want to give a short lecture, using clues, and have students note the clues.

7. For homework, have students make a list of the clues their lecturers use, with example of the sentences in which they appeared.

8. Share clues in class.

3. Underline Less To Underline More*   J H A

Procedure: 1. Ask how many students like to underline their textbooks as a study aid. Ask how many take written notes.

2. Ask *why* underlining is more popular. (takes less time)

3. Ask what advantages they can see in underlining (reading the text more actively, thinking while they are reading, having smaller chunks of material highlighted for test review)

4. To find out if underlining really works, give students two content-area passages with the main-idea sentences underlined. Use material new to the students. After they have read the passages, have them write down what they remember of them without looking back.

5. Discuss the responses, focusing on *why* the students tended to remember the underlined sentence—the underlining attracted their attention to certain material.

6. Distribute two more passages, this time with trivial sentences underlined. Repeat the sequence used with the first two passages.

7. Ask if the material remembered this second time was different from that from the previous time. Discuss whether it would be the kind of material they would want to remember for a test. Point out that if the underlined material is not important, not only will they have wasted their time underlining the wrong items, but it is those trivial items that they will be studying.

8. Students read two passages almost completely underlined. Repeat the procedure.

9. Discuss which type of underlining produces material that is easiest to review (underlining the main-idea sentences). Other advantages of this approach are as follows:

   a. It takes less time.

   b. Less time on underlining means more time to review.

   c. The reader can review more often, getting more chances to rehearse the material and remember it.

Therefore, *underlining less is really underlining more.*

10. Ask when they think that underlining might *not* work (math-problem solving, etc.). Material not suitable for underlining may require a different study strategy, such as reworking the problem.

11. Using text material having explicit main-idea sentences, have students underline one sentence in each of several passages.

12. Discuss responses, giving feedback.

13. Students work independently on a content-area text, underlining one sentence per paragraph.

Variations: 1. If underlining is not feasible for your students, you can demonstrate how to write down main-idea sentences.

2. Demonstrate how you would underline a text differently for an essay than for a multiple-choice test. Have students duplicate the procedures with text material.

* Adapted from McAndrew, 1983.

4. Beginning Underlining   P I

Procedure: 1. Explain to students that they are going to learn a skill that they will need in school to help them study—underlining.

2. On an overhead, show a long sentence, such as ''John and Mary, the happy-go-lucky Smith twins who live across the street, just won $1000.''

3. Model selecting the main idea of the sentence (John and Mary won $1000), and underline it in red.

4. Practice selecting the main idea from sentences, eliciting help from the students. Use relevant content-area material.

5. Have students work on sentences of their own, using felt pens.

6. Discuss sentences and give feedback.

7. Students work independently on sentences from content-area texts.

8. Move on to content-area paragraphs containing explicit main-idea sentences. Demonstrate selecting the sentences and rereading them for review.

9. Students work on a relevant content-area assignment, writing down sentences to be underlined if underlining is not feasible.

10. Discuss sentences chosen. Hypothesize possible test questions that these sentences would answer.

11. Practice this procedure, steps 8–10, with your content-area reading assignments.

5. Test Teams*   IJHA

Procedure: 1. Explain the purpose of note-taking—to write text material in your own words as a rehearsal for remembering for a test.

2. Demonstrate the skill by reading a relevant text paragraph, formulating a possible test question based on its main idea, and writing down the note in your own words—the answer to the question.

3. Supervise students as they practice this skill with relevant content-area paragraphs.

4. Discuss the possible test questions formed, and the answers (notes) created.

5. Divide students into small groups. Assign a section of text for all to read and take notes on.

6. When all are finished, give them time to study their notes by asking each other questions, reciting, and so on.

7. The next day, have a Test Team Time. Groups ask each other test questions they have created. Groups may use only their own notes as the sources for answers. Points are awarded for each correct answer. The textbook is the authority in case of disputes. *Note:* Be careful to discourage picky detail questions. The questions must be those you would legitimately ask about the material.

8. Use this procedure throughout the year to develop students' note-taking skills.

* Schilling, 1984.

6. Oh Rats*   JHA

Procedure: 1. Explain to students that they will learn a note-taking method useful for remembering what has been read and for reviewing for tests.

2. As you explain each step, give the reasons students should use it. Model each step, teaching each one as a separate lesson and allowing the students to

practice it separately, before putting them all together. This method is excellent for some subjects but not for *all* subjects. Be sure your students know this.

3.   Step O: OVERVIEW

a.   *what* you do

(1)   Look at the chapter, article, or story to be read.
(2)   Read the title.
(3)   Read all the headings.
(4)   Look at the illustrations.
(5)   Read the captions.
(6)   Read the introduction, if there is one.
(7)   Read the summary, if there is one.
(8)   Read the questions at the end of the chapter.

b.   *Why* you do it: This warm-up before studying is similar to the warm-up you use before sports. It's the opportunity to get the right mind-set. You will have to know what kind of reading you have to do, how difficult it is, and how interesting it will be to you.

4.   Step H: HEADINGS

a.   *what* you do

(1)   Set aside a notebook or part of a three-ring binder to be used only for the notes for this course.
(2)   On the top of the page write the chapter title and page number.
(3)   Fold the notebook page in half lengthwise.
(4)   On the left side of the fold, write down the first heading in the chapter.
(5)   *Think* about the information this section will contain. Ask yourself these questions: Who? What? Where? Why? How?

b.   *Why* you do it: You want to know what you will be reading. Authors usually choose the main idea of a section as the heading. If you write the heading, you will know the main idea. By asking yourself questions, you will focus on reading for a specific purpose, which will help you understand and remember what you read.

5.   Step R: READ

a.   *what* you do

(1)   Read the section and answer your questions.
(2)   As you are reading, think about the heading. Try to:
(a)   remember the details that support the heading;
(b)   remember the details that answer your questions;
(c)   decide which information is relevant, essential, and specific to the heading.

b.   *Why* you do it: Because you are now reading for a purpose, established by the heading and your questions, you are thinking about what you are reading.

6.   Step A: ANSWER

a.   *what* you do

(1)   In the right-hand column of your folded note page, list the essential and relevant information from the section.

(2)   Do not include irrelevant, nonessential details.

(3)   Answer the questions from step H.

(4)   Include major points, the specific emphasis, specific dates, facts, and numbers in your answers.

(5)   Write on only one side of the page.

(6)   Continue with steps H, R, and A until the assignment is completed.

b.   *Why* you do it: Taking notes will force you to think about what you are reading. You will need to organize and select the information that you think is relevant and essential to remember. Writing notes also reinforces your thinking and helps you to comprehend and remember.

7.   Step TS: TEST–STUDY

a.   *what* you do

(1)   Reread your notes, making any corrections, inserting any additions, and omitting any incorrect or inappropriate questions from the heading column. Remember that headings are the main ideas and your notes are the supporting details.

(2)   Fold your page in half so that you are looking only at the headings.

(3)   Ask yourself the heading questions.

(4)   *Say* the answers without looking at the other half of the paper.

(5)   Check your answers or study them by reading the answer column.

(6)   If you have forgotten the information, read your notes.

(7)   Saying the information aloud helps you to remember it.

b.   *Why* you do it: Editing and then rereading your notes lets you interact with the information again, forcing you to select the information you think is important for the course. The folded-page strategy allows you to test yourself, to see what you have retained and what you need to study.

* Adapted from Berrent, 1984.

BIBLIOGRAPHY

ANDRE, M. AND ANDERSON, T. "The development and evaluation of a self-questioning study technique." *Reading Research Quarterly,* 14 (1978–79), 605–23.

BALAJTHY, E. "Using student-constructed questions to encourage active reading," *Journal of Reading,* 27, February (1984), 408–11.

BEAN, T. W. AND R. PARDI. "A field test of a guided reading strategy," *Journal of Reading,* 23, November (1979), 144–47.

BERRENT, J. L. "OH RATS: A note-taking technique," *Journal of Reading,* 27, March (1984), 548–50.

CUNNINGHAM, P. M. AND J. W. CUNNINGHAM. "Improving listening in content area subjects," *NASSP Bulletin,* 60, December (1976), 26–31.

IRWIN, J. W. *Teaching Reading Comprehension Processes.* Englewood Cliffs, N.J.: Prentice-Hall, 1986.

MCANDREW, D. A. "Underlining and notetaking: Some suggestions from research," *Journal of Reading,* 27, November (1983), 103–8.

MANZO, A. V. "Guided Reading Procedure," *Journal of Reading,* 18, January (1975), 287–91.

McWILLIAMS, L. AND T. A. RAKES. *Content Inventories: English, Social Studies, and Science.* Dubuque, IO: Kendall/Hunt 1979.

MEMORY, D. M. "Main idea prequestions as adjunct aids with good and low-average middle grade readers," *Journal of Reading Behavior,* 15, Spring (1983), 37–48.

NICHOLS, J. N. "The content reading–writing connection," *Journal of Reading,* 29, December (1985), 265–67.

PAUK, W. *How to Study in College.* Boston: Houghton Mifflin, 1984.

POWELL, G. "SQ3R for secondary handicapped students," *Journal of Reading,* 26, December (1982), 262–63.

RADENCICH, M. C. AND J. S. SCHUMM. "Script'n Scribe: Parallel and flexible study/writing strategies for college students," *Reading World,* 24, March (1985), 88–96.

ROBINSON, F. R. *Effective Study.* New York: Harper & Row, Pub., 1970.

SCHILLING, F. C. "Teaching study skills in the intermediate grades: We can do more," *Journal of Reading,* 27, April (1984), 620–23.

SMITH, S. L. "Learning strategies of mature college readers," *Journal of Reading,* 26, October (1982), 5–12.

SPITZER, H. F. "Studies in retention," *Journal of Educational Psychology,* 30, (1939), 641–56.

TAYLOR, B. M. "A summarizing strategy to improve middle grade students' reading and writing skills," *Reading Teacher,* 36, November (1982), 202–5.

VAUGHAN, J. L., JR. "Use the ConStruct procedure to foster active reading and learning," *Journal of Reading,* 25, February (1982), 412–22.

ADJUSTING TO PURPOSE AND TASK DEMANDS

Definition: *Adjusting one's use of the comprehension processes according to the demands of the purpose and text involved*

RATIONALE

No two comprehension acts are exactly alike. For instance, good readers adjust their strategies according to their purpose. (A table of purposes and appropriate strategies can be found in chapter 2 of this text.) For example, if one were reading *National Geographic* for fun, one would probably read each article straight through, pausing only to enjoy the pictures. If one were reading it for a research paper, one would pause and take notes on the parts that applied to the paper. If one were reading it for a test, one would use all the study strategies described in Chapter 24.

Good readers also read different genres and different content areas differently. Table 25-1 provides a chart of some of the different materials students may have to read in different content areas. If you are in doubt about strategies for reading any of these, you may wish to consult a content-area reading book. A bibliography of useful references is included at the end

of this chapter. Other activities designed to help students read specific content-area materials are included in section A of this chapter.

Finally, good readers also adapt their strategies to the demands of the text. For instance, if the relationships between sentences are unclear, the reader will want to emphasize inference while reading; if the material is very descriptive, the reader might choose to use more imaging than he or she would with less descriptive material. Two strategies not discussed earlier in this book are using flexible reading rates and

TABLE 25-1 Content-Area Reading Materials

Science	Social Studies	Math	English
lab directions	maps	word	poetry
charts, tables	charts	problems	drama
definitions	time lines	formulas	grammatical
diagrams	narrative	symbols	rules

reading visual aids. The activities in section B of this chapter deal with these skills. Activity B.4 contains a chart of commonly used reading rates.

INFORMAL DIAGNOSIS

You will get a lot of information just by asking students how they plan to approach different tasks. You may also want to observe them while they are reading, or ask them after the fact. Activity A.1 describes a method for assessing students' ability to read and use the textbook.

GENERAL CONSIDERATIONS FOR TEACHING

1. Always discuss the purpose for reading and help the students to look at the demands of the particular text. Make sure students have decided on a reading method that reflects these two things.

2. Never assume that students know how to adjust their comprehension strategies to the reading task.

3. Provide students with a variety of tasks and texts so they can learn to be flexible.

4. Not everyone will approach every task and text in the same way. Be prepared for individual differences.

chapter 25. ADJUSTING TO PURPOSE AND TASK DEMANDS
Activities

A. SPECIFIC CONTENT–AREA DEMANDS

1. Inventory of Textbook–Specific Study Skills*   I J H A

Procedure: 1. Prepare an inventory of textbook-specific study skills for your current text (see Figure 25-1). Ask three types of questions, to elicit:

  a. students' use of aids for locating information;
  b. students' use of typographical aids;
  c. students' use of pictographic aids.

2. The questions on the use of pictographic aids should focus on both reading the aids accurately—"How many women were in the armed forces in 1987?"—and interpreting the aids—"What changes have you noticed in the number of women in the armed services in the past five years? What reasons might there be for these changes?" Be sure to focus on the types of questions that you, as instructor, will typically ask during class discussions and tests.

3. Tell the students that you are going to have them fill out a survey that will indicate how efficiently they read their textbooks. Explain to them that the first three questions are blank; they will answer questions you ask orally and write the answers there (see Figure 25-1).

4. The procedure for these three oral questions is simple:

  a. Ask the question.
  b. Stop the students five to eight seconds later.
  c. Have the students record the *page number on which they are looking at that moment.*

For example, ask "On what page does Chapter _____ begin?" After five to eight seconds say "Stop! On your answer sheet record the number of the page you are looking at *now*."

FIGURE 25-1   Inventory of Study Skills for a Typical History Text

1. _____
2. _____
3. _____
4. What is the subject of Chapter 12? _____
5. What are the main points of Chapter 9? _____
6. What is the main topic of Part Three? _____
7. Why is the word *enlightenment* on p. 324 in italics? ____
   _____
8. Look at the map on p. 389. What does the key to the map tell you about the wars of Louis XIV? _____
9. Look at the graph on p. 524. How many ships did the British Navy have in 1870? _____
10. Look at the illustration on p. 634. Why did the authors include this in the textbook? _____
11. Look at the graph on p. 574. What does it tell you about the relative naval strength of the two countries? What reasons might cause this difference? _____
12. What does the cartoon on p. 390 mean? _____

    5.   Other oral questions can focus on use of the index, glossary, and other aids mentioned in step 1 above.

    6.   Items 4–6 of the inventory require the student to write the answers to given questions.

    7.   The remaining questions focus on maps, graphs, tables, charts, diagrams, pictures, appendixes, and other supplementary materials.

    8.   You may use the results of the inventory in several ways—as a guide to what should be taught, with groups possibly needing instruction, or as an instrument to discuss in class as a means to develop efficient textbook reading skills.

* Carvell, 1980.

2.   Ten Good Questions to Ask About a Novel*   I J H A

Procedure: Use the following questions in any manner you wish!

    1.   What would this story be like if the main character were of the opposite sex?

    2.   Why is the story set where it is? [*Note:* The question does *not* ask what the setting is.]

    3.   If you were to film this story, which characters would you eliminate if you couldn't use them all?

    4.   Would you film this story in black and white or in color?

    5.   How is the main character different from you?

    6.   Why would this story (or why wouldn't it) make a good TV series?

    7.   What's one thing in this story that's happened to you?

8. Reread the first paragraph of Chapter 1. What's in it that makes you read on?

9. If you had to design a new cover for this book, what would it look like?

10. What does the title tell you about the book? Does it tell the truth?

* Peck, 1980. Reprinted with permission.

3. Secret Assignment   P I

Procedure: 1. Choose a concept in a content area that you wish to reinforce, such as adjectives.

2. Write a series of clear, step-by-step directions for students to follow to create a picture (see Figure 25-2). Be sure that each listed step contains only one direction.

3. Include directions that will reinforce the skill you have selected.

4. Next to each direction place a box or line for students to check off as they complete the step.

5. Try out the secret assignment on yourself or a friend to get some idea of the time required to provide you with a model to use when evaluating students' completion of the task.

FIGURE 25-2   Secret Assignment (Language Arts)

> YOU HAVE ON YOUR DESK IN FRONT OF YOU:
>   WHITE PAPER
>   FELT PENS OR CRAYONS
>   BROWN PAPER
>
> *READ ALL DIRECTIONS BEFORE BEGINNING WORK.*
>
> 1. On the brown paper draw a rabbit. _____
> 2. Cut the rabbit out. _____
> 3. Paste the rabbit on the bottom right-hand side of the white paper. _____
> 4. Draw 4 flowers along the bottom of the white paper. _____
> 5. Write above the rabbit an adjective that describes rabbits. _____
> 6. Write above each flower an adjective that describes it. DO NOT RE-PEAT ADJECTIVES. _____
> 7. Draw the sun in the top right-hand corner of the paper. _____
> 8. Under the sun write an adjective describing it. _____
> 9. Write your name on the top left-hand side of the white paper. _____
> 10. Under your name write two adjectives describing you. _____
> 11. Put your paper scraps in the waste basket. _____
> 12. Sit with your right hand on your left ear so that the teacher knows that you are finished.

6.   Explain rules to the students:

    a.   No talking.

    b.   No asking questions.

    c.   Read all the directions first.

    d.   When you are finished, I will come to your desk to see if the assignment is completed according to the directions.

7.   Once the activity is finished, post all the secret assignments along with a direction sheet. This is a good way to show that there are different ways of doing the same assignment.

4. Textbook Treasure Hunt* I J

Procedure: 1.   Explain the purpose of the activity—to preview the content-area textbook.

2.   Students complete Textbook Treasure Hunt, working in pairs or small groups (see Figure 25-3).

3.   Class discussion focuses on the items the students discovered while completing the Treasure Hunt—textual aids such as chapter previews, bold type, italics, the index, the preface, and so forth.

* Adapted from Bryant, 1984.

5. Science Reading Kits* P I J

Procedure: 1.   Prepare a list of concepts for students to research. Explain to students that their task will be to research a topic that interests them, and to prepare a Science Reading Kit containing activities for teaching that topic to other students. Topics that have been used successfully include solar heating, baboons, and computers.

2.   Model the steps that students can use in preparing a kit, focusing on many kinds of materials at many different reading levels. Activities might include the following:

    magazine articles and books to read

    TV videos

    crosswords

    blueprints, plans for building models

    vocabulary

    task cards

    filmstrip and tapes (student-made or premade)

    slides

    spelling words

    an evaluation instrument

FIGURE 25-3 Textbook Treasure Hunt*

There are many hidden treasures in your history book. After you have completed the path below, you will have discovered some interesting facts. Write your answers, the page numbers, and the source (map, picture, graph, index, or whatever, if you found the information in a source other than the narrative) on a clean sheet of notebook paper.

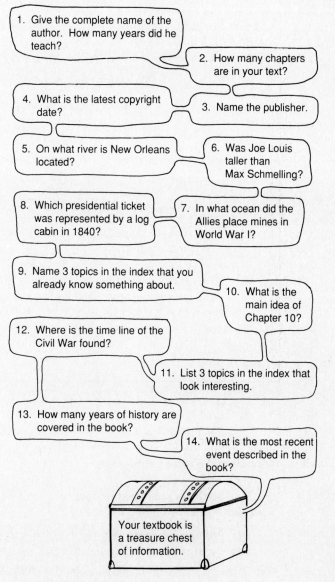

1. Give the complete name of the author. How many years did he teach?

2. How many chapters are in your text?

4. What is the latest copyright date?

3. Name the publisher.

5. On what river is New Orleans located?

6. Was Joe Louis taller than Max Schmelling?

8. Which presidential ticket was represented by a log cabin in 1840?

7. In what ocean did the Allies place mines in World War I?

9. Name 3 topics in the index that you already know something about.

10. What is the main idea of Chapter 10?

12. Where is the time line of the Civil War found?

11. List 3 topics in the index that look interesting.

13. How many years of history are covered in the book?

14. What is the most recent event described in the book?

Your textbook is a treasure chest of information.

* Adapted from Bryant, 1984.

3. Have a model kit for students to consult for format and ideas (see Figure 25-4).

4. You might want to set a deadline for students to demonstrate their kits. This would be a good activity to share with parents.

* Cochran, 1979.

FIGURE 25-4   Science Reading Kit: Solar Heating

(A partial list of a student's kit contents)

Consumer's Guide to Solar Heating and Cooling (fictional publication)

All About Solar Energy (fictional publication)

Spelling words: condenser, distiller, photosynthesis

Spelling activities: Make a crossword puzzle using 10 of the words.

Write the definitions of all the words.

Create a code and write the words with it.

Write a sentence that includes each word.

Task cards: Build a solar grill. (directions in *Consumer's Guide*)

Build a solar water distiller. (")

Write a report about solar furnaces.

Burn a piece of paper using a magnifying glass, and write up the process.

Test: [The test included true-or-false, fill-in-the-blank, and evaluation questions involving inferential thinking, such as "What do you think will be the future of solar energy in the United States? Why do you think so?"]

A bibliography

Source: Cochran, 1979, pp. 12–13. Reproduced with permission from *Science and Children,* March, 1985. Copyright 1985 by the National Science Teachers Association, 1742 Connecticut Avenue, NW, Washington, D.C. 20009

6.   On My Own: Independent Social Studies Reports*   I J

Procedure: 1.   Students choose any topic that can be researched in the school library. Set a time limit for finding a suitable topic.

2.   Provide students with activity lists (see Figure 25-5). Students must select two assignments from each section of the list. The assignments must be applicable to their report topic. You may want to demonstrate your thinking as you choose two general assignments from each list.

3.   Students work with you and the librarian in finding books at the appropriate reading level to use in completing their assignments.

4.   Students write answers, stating the specific assignment and summarizing their answers in at least half a page. You may want to alter requirements for various students and/or assignments. A bibliography of sources is required.

5.   Students publish and/or share their research in class.

* Kratzner and Mannies, 1979.

FIGURE 25-5   Activity List

A. GETTING THE FACTS
1. Find at least 10 interesting and important words related to your topic. Define them.
2. List 10 events and when they occurred, in time order.
3. List 10 people and tell why they were important.
4. List 10 events and where they occurred. Show the locations on a map.
5. Describe how 5 objects work.
6. Describe 3 theories given.
7. List 10 general principles given.
8. List 5 values mentioned.
9. Choose an event and give 5 reasons why it happened.
10. Describe how someone does something.

B. TRANSLATING THE FACTS
1. Describe some person, place, object, or event.
2. Make a picture, graph, or map from a written description.
3. Write a description from a picture, map, or graph.
4. Summarize 3 major ideas.
5. Explain something in such a way that a third grader could understand it.
6. Draw a poster of something described.
7. Draw a cartoon or comic strip about something described.
8. Write a radio or TV script.
9. Write a commercial for something described.
10. Write a news release for an event described.

C. FINDING RELATIONSHIPS
1. Predict 5 trends based on information.
2. Guess what would have happened if things had not happened as they did.
3. Identify 3 different ways a group of people, places, or things could be regrouped.
4. Outline 10 different pieces of information.
5. Identify 5 main ideas in a chapter you read.
6. Make a chart comparing 2 related sets of information.
7. Write a one-page essay combining information from at least 3 sources.
8. Compare and contrast two people, places, or objects.
9. Give 5 causes of some event.
10. Give 3 reasons someone might have done what he or she did.

D. APPLYING THE FACTS
1. Choose some real problem not yet solved and gather information on it.
2. Write a two-page theme on the problem. Include (a) a paragraph explaining what the problem is, why it is important, and the meanings of some key words; (b) the more interesting and important findings of your research; (c) your own reactions, conclusions and recommendations; and (d) a bibliography.

E. TAKING THINGS APART (ANALYZING)
1. Identify 5 unstated assumptions in your readings.
2. Identify when the author is using opinion rather than fact.
3. Identify 3 propaganda techniques.
4. List common characteristics of persons, places, or objects.
5. Tell why two people are likely to disagree on some aspect.
6. Explain why some cartoon is funny.
7. Suggest 5 additional facts the author could have included to make the reading more interesting.

FIGURE 25-5   continued

> 8. Identify some mistake in reasoning.
> 9. Write a general statement, give an example of that statement, and draw a conclusion from it.
> 10. Guess about someone's motive for something he or she did.
>
> F. PUTTING THINGS TOGETHER (SYNTHESIZING)
>   1. Suggest a novel use for some common object, relating it to the topic.
>   2. Suggest something that needs to be invented.
>   3. Make a 3-dimensional object.
>   4. Suggest a way to find the answer to some unsolved problem.
>   5. Write as many different titles as you can for a story.
>   6. Do something truly different that has not been suggested here or by anyone else you know.
>   7. Invent a cartoon character as a symbol for something related to the topic.
>   8. List as many words as you can think of related to the topic.
>   9. Make up a poem about a person, idea, or object.
>   10. Write a short play about some mythical event.
>
> G. WHAT'S SO GOOD ABOUT IT? (EVALUATION)
>   1. List at least 5 strengths and 5 weaknesses of an event, object, or person.
>   2. Identify at least 3 actions taken by someone and explain why you approve of them.
>   3. Identify some action and explain why you disapprove of it.
>   4. Pretend you are a manufacturer of some object related to your topic and list 5 ways to make it better.
>   5. Choose some object and identify ways it has been improved.
>   6. Describe your feelings about some value judgment related to your topic.
>   7. Describe the strangest part of your topic.
>   8. Explain why one description of some person, event, or object is better than another.
>   9. Tell which of your sources was most useful and why.
>   10. Predict how the teacher will evaluate you on this project and why.

Source: Kratzner and Mannies, 1979, pp. 503–4. Reprinted with permission of Roland R. Kratzner and the International Reading Association.

7. PGR: Problem–Guided Reading for Math–Related Courses*   IJHA

Procedure: 1. Demonstrate that comprehension of new material in a math-related course can be made easier by:

A. reading the problems before reading the text

B. determining what is needed to learn to do the problems

C. reading to get that information

(PGR works best if the problems can be solved by reading a section at a time—if, for example, some can be answered by reading section 1, some by reading sections 1 and 2, some by reading sections 1, 2, and 3, and so on.)

2. Students can use the following seven-step procedure:

a) Classify homework problems. Look through an assigned chapter, group similar problems, and label them according to where in the chapter they are discussed. Make an overview of the chapter.

b) Begin with the easier problems.

c) Start solving the problems that you can do without consulting the text, using what you remember from the lecture.

d) Consult your sources. Read the sections of the text that are applicable to the problem. Stop reading when you feel you can work more of the problem, and return to working on it. Read carefully, with purpose and concentration.

e) Go on to the next problem and repeat the process.

f) Review your reading. Read through the text assignment, completing any parts not read while doing the problem.

g) Keep solving problems.

* Adapted from Johnson, 1984.

8. Packet P.E.*   I J H A

Procedure: 1. Prepare packets that guide students through physical education lessons (see Figure 25-6).

2. Use these packets to add variety to your content presentations.

3. Use the packet lessons to give individual instruction while other students are following packet instructions.

Variation: Use packets for other content-area subjects.

* Maring and Ritson, 1980.

FIGURE 25-6   Sample Physical Education Packet Lesson

All of the following skills are to be worked on with a partner (choose a different partner for each class session). Each person progresses at his or her own pace. You may work one skill from each of the following 3 sections. Before you begin, though, make sure you understand the proper warm-ups from your instructor's demonstration in the first session. Develop a new flexibility exercise of your own and fit it into your warm-up pattern.

Section One: Rolls. For help, consult *The Tumbler's Manual* (LaPorte and Renner, 1938) on the pages indicated.
    1.   forward roll—p. 10
    2.   backward roll—p. 18
    etc.

Section Two: Balances
    10.   tripod—p. 26
    etc.

Section Three: Partner Stunts
    13.   hand-balance pull-over—pp. 32–33

Source: Maring and Ritson, 1980, p. 29. Reprinted with permission of Gerald H. Maring and the International Reading Association.

B. VISUAL AIDS AND FLEXIBLE READING RATES

1. Visual Aid Search   PIJHA

Procedure: 1.   Demonstrate to students the importance of using visual aids by having them read a long description of an object such as a nutcracker and try to figure out what it looks like, and then showing them a picture. A prose selection and a graph could also illustrate the point.

2.   Using a relevant textbook chapter, model how to get information from visual aids. Fill in a Visual Aid Search chart with relevant information (see Figure 25-7).

3.   Students practice using visual aids by filling in the Visual Aid Search chart. Students share results and get teacher feedback.

4.   Students work independently on text material, using the Visual Aid Search chart before, while or after reading chapters.

2. Visual Aid Test (VAT)   PIJHA

Procedure: 1.   Demonstrate to students how to develop an overview of the contents of a textbook chapter by using only the visual aids in the chapter. Outline or map the overview on the board or projector.

2.   Based on the overview, hypothesize possible test questions that could be asked.

3.   Model answering the questions.

4.   Have students make a visual-aid overview of a relevant text chapter. Share results. Provide feedback.

5.   Students create and answer visual-aid test questions, discussing results.

6.   Students work independently on new material using the VAT strategy. Regularly reinforce the skill by assigning VAT tasks for content-area material.

FIGURE 25-7   Visual Aid Search Chart for a Social Studies Chapter

Visual aid _____ Page _____

Next to each category below, list information in note form that you can learn by observing the picture, graph, or chart. You may not be able to fill in all the categories for every visual aid. Also list questions you would like to answer about the subject.

CLOTHING _____
GEOGRAPHY, ENVIRONMENT _____
TRANSPORTATION _____
ART AND ARCHITECTURE _____
INVENTIONS, ARTIFACTS _____
ECONOMICS, MONEY, COMMERCE _____
RELIGION _____
WAY OF LIFE, CUSTOMS _____
DIVISION OF LABOR _____

3. Picture Search   **P I J H A**

Procedure: 1. Demonstrate to students the types of information you can learn from an illustration, using an illustration from a textbook section they have not yet read. Point out how much information you learned this way before you even began to read the chapter.

2. Use a chart (see Figure 25-8) to list the information you find and to guide your self-questioning.

3. Provide students with charts and work with them on another illustration.

4. Have students use a Picture Search chart for a current textbook assignment. Share results.

5. Reinforce the skill by assigning a Picture Search for textbook assignment preview.

4. What For?   **I J H A**

Procedure: 1. Bring to class a wide variety of reading materials, such as phone books, driver's manuals, insurance forms, magazines, cookbooks, instructions for appliances, bills, travel folders, warranties, novels, newspapers, and tax forms.

2. Ask students if people always drive at the same speed. Discuss reasons for driving at different speeds.

3. Ask if people always drive in the same manner. Discuss reasons for driving in different manners (very carefully in a city, and so forth).

4. Repeat these questions, this time on the subject of reading. Develop the idea that the purpose for reading, the type of material, and our own ability and

FIGURE 25-8   Picture Search Chart

Name _____

Subject of Illustration _____ Page _____

Directions: Next to each category below, list information in note form that you can learn about the category by observing the picture. You may not be able to fill in all the categories.

CLOTHING

_____

TRANSPORTATION

_____

(Other categories might include education, religion, way of life and customs, geography and environment, weather, division of labor, economics (money and commerce), art and architecture, and inventions and artifacts in use at the time.)

familiarity with the subject will determine how we read. Use the materials you brought in to illustrate this point and to initiate a discussion on various reading rates.

	Speed	Purpose
Scanning	very fast	to search material for one item, such as number in a phone book or the amount of flour in a recipe
Skimming	fast	to get a general idea of what the material is, such as previewing a chapter or looking at a travel folder
Recreational Reading	moderate	to enjoy oneself
First Reading	moderate	to get a fairly good idea of the specific ideas in the material—for example, reading an assignment
Studying	slow	to find material you will need for tests and to remember that material
Critical Reading	slow	to examine material to form your own opinions—for instance, reading a travel folder because you may want to go to the place described
Analytical Reading	word for word	to study difficult material that requires careful attention to almost every detail, such as a warranty or a contract for buying a car

5. Students complete a work sheet on hypothetical reading situations, deciding the type of reading speed required (see Figure 25-9). Discuss answers in class.

FIGURE 25-9   What Speed?

Good readers don't always read at the same rate. You should choose your reading speed to fit the *type* of material you have to read and your *purpose* for reading that material.

Here are some different reading situations. Indicate the best reading style and speed to use for each.

	Purpose	Reading Style	Speed
1.	Reading an editorial to decide which way to vote on a particular issue.	_____	_____
2.	Reading an insurance policy for your car.	_____	_____
3.	Reading an article about a TV star.	_____	_____
4.	Reviewing class notes for a test.	_____	_____
5.	Looking over a magazine to decide what to read.	_____	_____
6.	Reading a recipe to see how many eggs are needed.	_____	_____
7.	Reading a science textbook for instructions for an assigned lab procedure.	_____	_____
8.	Reading a short story to get a general idea of the plot.	_____	_____

[*Note:* You may want to include the preceding chart of reading speeds and purposes on this worksheet.]

6. Have students choose (or pass out) different types of reading material. Students create four or five hypothetical reading situations for that material that would demand different reading speeds. They develop questions related to these situations and attach the questions to the material.

7. The next day students exchange materials, answer reading questions, and discuss answers.

8. Reinforce the strategy by regularly setting or asking the purpose for reading and the speed required for an assignment.

5. Graphic Information Lesson (GIL)* I J

Procedure:

1. Students read a text containing graphic aids.

2. Lead a discussion focusing on two questions:

   a. What information is found in the graphic aids?
   b. How does this information relate to the content in the text?

3. Students' contributions may focus on literal information. If so, model using inferences and making connections between the text and the graphics. Encourage students to make similar efforts.

4. Help students decide if the information in the graphic aids was:

   a. redundant
   b. complementary to the text
   c. supplementary to the text

5. You may also want to discuss the purpose of the captions or titles of the aids.

6. Pseudographics (invented by you) form the second stage of the lesson. Present some examples of graphic information that, although not included in the text the students read, are related to the text. Make some of these graphics appropriate and consistent with the text; make others inconsistent (see Figure 25-10). The important consideration in creating these is that they be credible. List page numbers if the information is found in the text.

7. Students, working individually or in groups, decide whether each of the pseudographics is believable, based on their reading of the text and their prior knowledge.

8. Students share and discuss their decisions.

9. The final stage of a GIL allows students to work independently with graphic aids and a text. They may:

   a. create additional pseudographics
   b. decide on the most important graphic in the text—and defend that decision
   c. develop the connection between two graphic aids, such as a picture and a map
   d. suggest additional useful graphics aids for the text

* Adapted from Reinking, 1986.

FIGURE 25-10   Examples of Teacher's Pseudographics

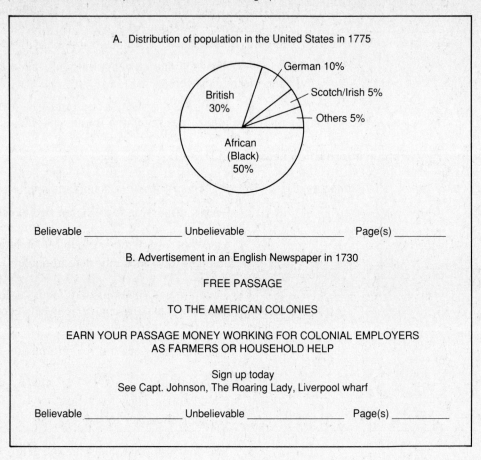

A. Distribution of population in the United States in 1775

German 10%

British 30%

Scotch/Irish 5%

Others 5%

African (Black) 50%

Believable _____ Unbelievable _____ Page(s) _____

B. Advertisement in an English Newspaper in 1730

FREE PASSAGE

TO THE AMERICAN COLONIES

EARN YOUR PASSAGE MONEY WORKING FOR COLONIAL EMPLOYERS
AS FARMERS OR HOUSEHOLD HELP

Sign up today
See Capt. Johnson, The Roaring Lady, Liverpool wharf

Believable _____ Unbelievable _____ Page(s) _____

BIBLIOGRAPHY

BRYANT, J. A. R. "Use a treasure hunt with a new content area book," *Journal of Reading,* 27, March (1984), 546–48.

CARVELL, R. J. "Constructing your own textbook-specific study skills inventory," *Reading World,* 20, March (1980), 239–45.

COCHRAN, CHERYL. "Science Reading Kits," *Science and Children,* 17, no. 3, November/December (1979), 12–13.

ELLIS, E. "Computers, technology, and learning disabilities." Paper given at The Learning Disabled Student in Higher Education, conference, Rutgers University, New Brunswick, N.J., July 24, 1986.

HAFNER, L. E. *Developmental Reading in Middle and Secondary Schools: Foundations, Strategies, and Skills for Teaching.* New York: Macmillan, 1977.

JOHNSON, L. L. "Problem-guided reading for college math-related courses," *Journal of Reading,* 27, April (1984), 602–8.

KRATZNER, R. R. AND N. MANNIES. "Building responsibility and reading skills in the social studies classroom," *Journal of Reading,* 22, March (1979), 501–5.

MARING, G. H. AND R. RITSON. "Reading improvement in the gymnasium," *Journal of Reading,* 24, October (1980), 27–31.

PECK, R. "10 Good Questions to Ask about a Novel." In *The Avon Apple.* New York: Avon Books, 19.

REINKING, D. "Integrating graphic aids into content area instruction: The graphic information lesson," *Journal of Reading,* 30, November (1986), 146–52.

OTHER CONTENT-AREA TEXTBOOKS

CHEEK, E. H. AND M. C. CHEEK. *Reading Instruction through Content Teaching.* Columbus, Ohio: Chas. E. Merrill, 1983.

ESTES, T. H. AND J. L. VAUGHAN. *Reading and Learning in the Content Classroom,* 2nd ed. Boston: Allyn & Bacon, 1985.

SHEPHERD, D. L. *Comprehensive High School Reading Methods,* 3rd ed. Columbus, Ohio: Chas. E. Merrill, 1982.

VACCA, T. H. AND J. L. VACCA. *Content Area Reading,* 2nd ed. Boston: Little, Brown, 1986.

PUTTING STRATEGIES TOGETHER

There are many excellent reading comprehension activities that cannot be separated by strategy. You may have noticed that some of the activities earmarked for specific strategies earlier in this book actually included some reference to others as well. This is as it should be. When students are actively comprehending, all of the processes discussed in this book should be working together. They all assist each other, and in some ways the attempt to divide activities by strategy is just an illusion. No matter what process you are teaching, the others play a part.

The activities provided in this chapter could not be classified under one specific strategy. For instance, section C includes activities that teach students to ask and answer questions about their reading. These questions may require many of the processes discussed earlier. Section A contains general directed-reading

activities, and section B includes lessons that encourage students to use the same processes when listening. Finally, the three activities in section D also cover multiple strategies.

Moreover, there is one very effective comprehension activity that is not specifically included anywhere in this text. It is the one that arises incidentally from purposeful reading situations. Students reading for fun might become confused, and an opportunity for teaching comprehension monitoring might then present itself. Students who do poorly on a test might suddenly request instant study-skill advice. It is not necessary for all of your comprehension instruction to be planned ahead of time. *The core of your instruction must be meaningful reading tasks.* The planned lessons then complement and enhance real reading needs rather than create artificial reading needs of their own.

chapter 26.   PUTTING STRATEGIES TOGETHER
Activities

    A. DIRECTED READING
       1. I Know I Can   P I J H A
       2. Listen-Read-Discuss   I J H A
    B. DIRECTED LISTENING
       1. Guided Listening   I J H A
       2. Directed Listening Activity (DLA)   I J H A
    C. INVOLVING STUDENTS IN QUESTIONING
       1. InQuest (Investigative Questioning) I J H A
       2. Request   I J H A
       3. Question Only   I J H A
       4. Question–Answer Relationships (QAR) I J H A
    D. USING MULTIPLE STRATEGIES
       1. Chapter-Review Scenario   I J H A
       2. K–W–L Plus   I J H A
       3. Self-Selected Reading for Success P I J H

A.   DIRECTED READING ACTIVITIES

1.   I Know I Can*   P I J H A

Procedure: 1.   Ask if any student remembers the children's story of "The Little Engine That Could." After discussing the plot, ask for the moral or meaning of the story. Discuss the idea of self-fulfilling prophecies: people who think they *can* do something often do succeed, and people who say they can't do something very often cannot. Ask for reasons for this, and elicit from students both examples from their lives and examples of famous people who succeeded or failed because of their attitudes.

      2.   Suggest that the students can themselves use this strategy by forming an image of themselves as competent readers before they begin reading. Demonstrate that approaching reading material with the idea that "I can read this—it *is* going to make sense" can help readers read more actively and facilitate comprehension.

      3.   Elicit from students the strategies they have learned to help them comprehend new material—previewing, asking questions, and so forth. List these on the board. Emphasize that knowing many strategies for reading means they can be flexible when they read, choosing a different strategy if the one they are using doesn't work.

      4.   Discuss with the students the fact that knowing these strategies will help them to attain their goal in reading—the comprehension of their reading material and the acquisition of new knowledge.

      5.   Have the students read some new material using this strategy.

      6.   Discuss the results, focusing on their feelings and how they may have influenced their approach.

      7.   Regularly encourage students to take the "I Know I Can" approach when reading.

* Adapted from Smith, 1982.

2. Listen–Read–Discuss* **I J H A**

Procedure: 1.   Choose a well-written, well-organized section of text.

2.   Present this section in some sort of "favored format" (usually a lecture) for half the class period.

3.   Have the class read the section of text. You may want to give the students various purposes for reading—for example, to compare their understanding of the lecture with their understanding of the text, or to find words, facts, or ideas that are difficult to them or about which they are unsure.

4.   Lead a class discussion focusing on clarifying the basic meanings and reducing uncertainties.

5.   Follow this with a more critical approach towards the material, raising uncertainties.

6.   Discussion questions such as the following (Smith, 1975) can provoke meaningful discussion and encourage positive attitudes towards the lesson:

    a.   What did you understand best from what you heard and read?
    b.   What did you understand least from what you heard and read?
    c.   What questions or thoughts does this raise in your mind about reading, learning, or related issues?

7.   Express any of your own thoughts or questions about the material, thus modeling comprehension monitoring and critical thinking.

Variations: 1.   Tell the class that your lecture will omit a few important details. The students read the text to find these details.

2.   Tell the students that the lecture will cover all the details of the lesson but that they will need to read the text to find what questions the details answer, or what basic concept holds them together.

3.   Tell the class that a quiz will follow the discussion. This strategy is recommended particularly for students who have difficulty staying alert unless the class activity is grade-related.

4.   To reinforce skills in lecture note-taking have the class take notes and then answer quiz questions using only those notes.

5.   Turn the process around occasionally. Students read first, for fifteen minutes, and then you lecture. Discussion follows the lecture. This procedure improves listening and the skill of learning from an effective lecture.

6.   Ask the students which parts of the text seem to be "inconsiderate" of the reader (poorly written or organized and difficult to comprehend). Show them where they may have had problems understanding because of text deficiencies. This strategy will show students how to monitor their comprehension when reading, and how to ask for teacher assistance.

7.   Give a definitive purpose for reading and discussion that will require critical or creative expression or application. Write this purpose on the chalkboard as a reminder for the students to read analytically.

8.   During the discussion, ask the students (and yourself) what they did differently when they got good grades rather than poor grades. Reinforce the

study techniques that they suggest. Use the teaching behaviors that they indicate facilitate comprehension, thus giving the students a chance to influence classroom procedure.

* Manzo and Casale, 1985.

B. DIRECTED LISTENING

1. Guided Listening*   I J H A

Procedure: 1.   Select some material for the students to hear—a lecture, record, or tape not exceeding ten minutes. The total time for the process is about fifty minutes.

2.   Tell students to try to remember *everything* they hear.

3.   Lecture, read, or play the recorded or taped selection. If you lecture, record yourself.

4.   Remind the students that they were supposed to try to remember everything. Write on the board everything they remember, making no corrections and asking no questions.

5.   Read everything listed on the board, directing the students to look for incorrect or missing information.

6.   Play the tape, record, lecture, or reading again so that students can correct the wrong information and obtain the missing information.

7.   Add to and amend the information on the board where needed.

8.   Ask the students which ideas on the board seem to be the main ideas— the most important ideas, the material they think they should try to remember for a long time. Mark these items.

9.   Since the students have now mastered the literal level of the material, raise any inferential questions that you feel are vital for complete comprehension.

10.   Erase the board and test students' short-term memory with a test that does not depend on reading or writing skills—for example, an oral true–false or multiple-choice test.

11.   Do not grade the tests; students can exchange papers or mark their own. Students record their scores and chart their growth in short- and long-term listening retention by keeping two separate graphs in their notebooks (see Figure 26-1).

12.   Test long-term memory with a similar test containing different items several weeks later.

* Cunningham and Cunningham, 1976; Manzo, 1975.

2. Directed Listening Activity (DLA)*   I J H A

Procedure: 1.   Readiness Stage

a.   Establish motivation for the lesson. Let's use the high cost of beef in hamburgers as an example.

FIGURE 26-1   Guided Listening Procedure (GLP) Graph

	GLP 1	GLP 2	GLP 3	GLP 4	GLP 5
1					
2					
3					
4					

(y-axis: Number of questions correct)

Source: Cunningham and Cunningham, 1976, p. 30. Reprinted with permission.

b.   Introduce any new or difficult concepts or words—complete and incomplete proteins, grams, and so on.

c.   Set the purpose for listening—to find out which protein foods are complete, which incomplete.

2.   Listening–Reciting Stage

a.   Have students listen for the information designated in the purpose set in step 1c.

b.   Ask both literal and inferential questions about the purpose.

c.   Have students comment on the lesson and discuss it.

d.   If you discern any errors or gaps in the students' understanding, have the students relisten to certain parts of the lesson.

3.   Follow-Up Stage: Provide opportunities for students to engage in activities, such as reading, writing, art, and small-group discussion, building on the concepts of the lesson. For example:

Keep a one-week record of foods you eat that contain protein.

Estimate the cost in dollars and grain of your own protein intake.

Variations: 1.   Tape the lesson and the directions for the DLA for students who need additional listening time.

2.   Videotape the DLA.

3.   Have older students create a DLA for younger students.

4.   Assign DLAs as alternatives to term papers.

* Cunningham and Cunningham, 1976.

C.   INVOLVING STUDENTS IN QUESTIONING

1.   InQuest (Investigative Questioning)*   I J H A

Procedure: Part I: How to ask good questions

A.   Obtain a videotape of a local or national TV interview. If videotapes are not available, tape a radio news interview or arrange your class time to coincide with such an interview.

B.   Choose an interesting short segment of the interview that provides examples of both good and bad questions.

C.   Before viewing or listening to the interview, ask the students to think about what kinds of questions are used in an interview and why they are asked.

D.   After the interview, ask the students what kinds of questions were better, and why.

E.   After this discussion, role-play a famous person, living or dead, and ask each student to think up a good question to ask this person at the time of an important event in his or her life. Ask them also to think of what type of response they anticipate.

F.   After the conference, evaluate the questions and answers. Here are some ideas to elicit about questions:

1.   Questions that get longer responses are the most desirable.
2.   Questions that receive a yes or no answer can be followed by "Why?" to get a longer response.
3.   Interview questions usually elicit information, reflections, evaluations, or predictions.
4.   Good interviews contain a variety of questions.

Part II: InQuest Strategy

A.   Choose a story that has interesting characters and an interesting plot. Find in it a high point of action.

B.   Suggest that students think of questions they might like to ask a particular character as the story develops.

C.   Read the story only up to the critical incident.

D.   Role-play a news conference in which the story character is to be interviewed, and choose a volunteer to play the character. Have other students play the role of investigative reporters. The character answers questions revealing the story as seen by him or her. The teacher may want to play the character role the first few times this procedure is practiced.

E.   Evaluate the interview. Have students briefly evaluate the questions and answers. Reinforce the good questions.

Variations: 1.   Use the procedure with basal readers as a break from the teacher-questioning approach.

2.   Use the procedure with books read aloud to students.

3.   Use the procedure with biographical material that can be integrated with content-area subjects.

* Shoop, 1986.

2. Request*   I J H A

Procedure: 1.   Prepare a selection suitable for the students' reading level. Decide how much material will be read at a time. Identify the appropriate points in the selection where you can elicit predictions.

2.   Tell the students that they will be asking you questions after they read a certain amount of text. You will answer the questions, and in return ask questions of them about the material.

3.   Students read and ask you questions. Answer their questions, and refine and develop them by asking questions of the students. You will be modeling good questioning behavior. For example, if you are asked "When did the American Revolution begin?" answer, and in return ask "What causes led up to the American Revolution?"

4.   After an adequate amount of material has been read, ask the students to predict the outcome of the selection. Students provide reasons for their predictions, pointing to places in the text for support.

5.   Students silently read the rest of the selection to find out if their predictions were adequate.

6.   Discuss the reading, focusing on the accuracy of the students' predictions.

* Manzo, 1979.

3. Question Only*   I J H A

Procedure: 1.   Tell students the topic of study.

2.   Tell them they must learn all they can about the topic by questioning you. Explain that you will answer all their questions fully, but without elaboration.

3.   After the questioning is finished, give a test on all the material about the topic that you think is important.

4.   The class discusses which questions ought to have been asked. The questions will fall into categories of study needed for the discipline. For example, history will necessitate cause–effect questions in the areas of society, religion, the military, and economics.

5.   A retest can be given after the class discussion to determine the amount of improvement.

* Manzo, 1980.

5. Question–Answer Relationships (QAR)*   P I J H A

Procedure: 1.   Explain to students that when they are answering questions about texts, there are two basic places they can look to get information:
   a.   In the Book
   b.   In My Head

2.   Illustrate this by having all students read a sample text. Ask questions about the text and have students show you where they got their answers.

3.   Once students have mastered the two categories, expand each. The In the Book category includes two types of situations:
   a.   Right There: The answer is explicitly stated in the text in one sentence.
   b.   Putting It Together: The answer is in the text, but to find it the reader must put together information from different parts of the text.

Draw a figure on the board or overhead to clarify these subcategories for the students.

4. Demonstrate the use of both of these subcategories by having the students read sample texts and answer questions about them.

5. For upper elementary and middle school students, you may want to expand the In the Book category to show the specific strategies needed to find the Right There questions:
  a. looking in a single sentence
  b. looking in two sentences connected by a pronoun
  The Putting It Together subcategory can focus on the text structure—for example, cause–effect, compare–contrast, list–example, or explanation. Once again, drawing a figure will help clarify this subcategory for students.

6. The In My Head category also has two subcategories:

  a. Author and Me: Students must consult the text *and* use prior knowledge to answer the question. "What do you think Ricardo might have done if the bus was late?" is an example of a question requiring this strategy.
  b. On My Own: Students can answer the question by using prior knowledge. They don't have to have read or understood the story. Students could use this strategy for a question such as "What do you do when you are happy about something, as Jenny was in the story?"

7. Reinforce these strategies during instruction by having students identify the types of questions you are asking. For example, you will ask mainly On My Own questions before the reading and Think and Search and Author and Me questions after the reading. Have students also identify the types of questions the book uses.

8. In addition, knowledge of the QAR can help you diagnose your own questioning strategies. For example, if you find that the Right There subcategory tend to dominate your questions you may be focusing too much on literal and detail questions.

9. Reinforce the skill by having students create different types of questions about their reading, identifying each type.

10. A poster indicating the types of QAR helps remind students to use the skill.

* Adapted from Raphael, T., *Reading Teacher*, 39, pp. 516–522. Printed with permission of Taffy Raphael and the International Reading Association.

D. USING MULTIPLE SKILLS

1. Chapter–Review Scenario*   IJHA

Procedure: 1. Ask students if they know which industries rely on their age group for part of their sales: "For which industry are you important consumers?" Encourage discussion.

2. Develop the characteristics of a good consumer (is familiar with the merchandise, comparison-shops, knows what to look for).

3.   Say "One of the industries you are important consumers for is the textbook industry. What do you think you should look for in textbooks?" Develop the idea that organization, readability, text aids such as questions and examples, and graphic aids are the characteristics they should look for.

4.   Demonstrate, using the Chapter-Review Scenario with a current text chapter (see Figure 26-2).

5.   Provide supervised practice for the students by using this format with their next chapter assignment.

6.   Discuss in class the paragraphs or purchasing reports the students develop from the scenario.

7.   Assign scenarios when appropriate throughout the year.

Variation: Have the students summarize their recommendations for a series of chapters and send these recommendations to the textbook editor.

* Nichols, 1985.

FIGURE 26-2   Chapter–Review Scenario for a Fictional Text

Textbook publishers frequently hire teachers to review their texts before they publish them. As student-consumers, you also should review your texts. Pretend that you have been hired by the school board to review Chapter 24, "The Arthropods," in our text *Biology Today.* Your recommendations are important and will decide whether the publisher makes or loses millions of dollars. Therefore, be careful what you say. Write one paragraph for each of the following tasks, using the questions as guidelines.

TASK 1:   Review the *organization* of the chapter. Is it organized in a logical, easy-to-follow sequence? Are the headings, subheadings, and marginal aids helpful?

TASK 2:   Read the *questions* and *other activities* suggested at the end of the chapter. Are these appropriate? Are they easy to understand?

TASK 3:   Is the chapter content *readable?* Are the new vocabulary words clearly explained? Are enough practical examples given to illustrate each new term?

TASK 4:   Review the *chapter pictures* and *graphs* as to quality and quantity. Do they clearly illustrate the chapter's ideas? Are there enough of them?

TASK 5:   Write a paragraph summarizing the *strengths* and *weaknesses* of the chapter. What recommendations would you make for improving the chapter?

Write each paragraph not only as an answer to the question but as a report to the editor of the textbook.

ALTERNATIVE: Pretend you are part of a Student Search Committee that has to advise the principal whether to adopt or reject this text. Tasks 1–4 stay the same. Task 5 will be an argument for purchasing or not purchasing this text. Write this argument out and be prepared to defend it orally in class.

Adapted from Nichols, 1985.

2. K–W–L Plus*   IJHA

Procedure: There are three sections to this procedure: activities for monitoring comprehension, mapping activities, and summarizing activities. The first section involves presenting the K–W–L process.

I.   COMPREHENSION MONITORING

A.   Step *K—What is known* (prereading activities)

1.   Have students brainstorm ideas about the assigned topic in order to activate prior knowledge.

2.   Students save unanswered questions about specific points.

3.   Students write on work sheets what they feel they already know about the topic (see Figure 26-3).

B.   Model categorizing the known information. Have students categorize the information they have generated. Have them anticipate what other categories of information they may find about the topic.

C.   Students complete the Anticipated Categories section on the work sheet.

D.   Step *W—What you want to know:* Encourage students to generate questions they want answered in their reading. These questions go in column W on their sheets.

E.   Divide the text into manageable sections. Eventually, after students become familiar with the technique, they will do this independently. For the first lessons, one or two paragraphs may be all they can handle before you interrupt the reading and look for answers to the questions in column W.

FIGURE 26-3   A ninth grade disabled reader's K-W-L worksheet on killer whales

K (Know)	W (Want to know)	L (Learned)
They live in oceans. They are vicious. They eat each other. They are mammals.	Why do they attack people? How fast can they swim? What kind of fish do they eat? What is their description? How long do they live? How do they breathe?	D — They are the biggest member of the dolphin family. D — They weigh 10,000 pounds and get 30 feet long. F — They eat squids, seals, and other dolphins. A — They have good vision underwater. F — They are carnivorous (meat eaters). A — They are the second smartest animal on earth. D — They breathe through blow holes. A — They do not attack unless they are hungry. D — Warm blooded A — They have echo-location (sonar). L — They are found in the oceans.
Description Food Location		

Source: Carr and Ogle, 1987, p. 628. Reprinted with permission of Eileen Carr and the International Reading Association.

Final category designations developed for column L, information Learned about killer whales:
A = abilities, D = description, F = food, L = location.

F.   Students continue to add questions to column W as they work on the material.

G.   Step *L—What has been learned:* Students put new information in column L of the work sheet. This column also provides an instrument for later review.

H.   Postreading: Students discuss what they have learned and which questions have been answered. Students should be encouraged to seek answers to unanswered questions in additional materials.

II.   MAPPING

A.   Students create maps of the material (Figure 26-4) by first categorizing the information in column L by asking themselves "What does this statement describe?" and by categorizing the questions in column W.

B.   Students use the title of the article as the center of a map.

C.   The categories which have been developed under K, W, and L now become the major concepts of the map, with relevant details listed under each.

D.   Students can use the map to create test questions and to study for exams. Be sure to encourage students to ask key questions about main ideas as well as detail questions.

III.   SUMMARIZING

A.   Students can use the map as an outline for a summary. First, they number the categories of the map in the sequence they would prefer for a summary.

B.   The title of the map is the title of the summary.

C.   Each category becomes the topic for a paragraph. The supporting details in the categories are used to explain the topic sentence and expand the paragraph.

* Source: Carr and Ogle, 1987, p. 628. Reprinted with permission of Eileen Carr and the International Reading Association.

FIGURE 26-4   The ninth grader's concept map

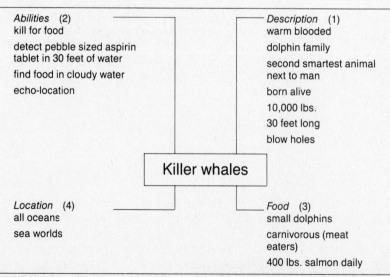

(1) through (4) indicate the order of categories the student chose later for writing a summary.
* Carr and Ogle, 1987.

3. Self-Selected Reading for Success*   P I J H

Procedure: 1. Tell your basal reading groups one or two weeks before you begin this strategy that there will be a change in the group reading lessons. Model the strategy.

2. Students will preselect a library book. To determine the difficulty level of the new book, use this method:

Unknown Words Per Page	*Difficulty Level*
0–1	too easy
2–4	good for growth
5 or more	too hard

3. Because vocabularies will vary in these self-selected books, students can read during the time you formerly spent on word and concept development.

4. While the group reads silently, meet with one student at a time. During these meetings, held slightly apart from the group, you can choose from several activities: oral reading, questions about the story, predictions about the story, discussion of new words, and so on.

5. Twice-weekly three-to-five minute meetings should be possible with each child in a twelve-student group.

6. You can close group meetings by sharing highlights from any of the individual meetings.

7. At the conclusion of each book, encourage the children by asking higher-level questions, such as "What do you think will happen next?" "Suppose the main character had been _____. What would have happened then?"

8. Keep a record of the books read. Note the developing vocabulary skills. Have students keep their own records. Share these records with parents and administrators to show continuing skill development.

9. Alternate this activity, either weekly or daily, with use of the basals.

10. A supply of quality paperback books is needed for this reading approach to be successful.

11. To demonstrate the developing positive attitudes towards reading, you may want to include "On My Own" comments from students about self-selected reading in communications to parents. The students may want to illustrate these comments in a short newsletter.

* Smith, 1986.

BIBLIOGRAPHY

CARR, E. AND D. OGLE. "K–W–L Plus: A strategy for comprehension and summarization," *Journal of Reading,* 30, April (1987), 626–31.

CUNNINGHAM, P. M. AND J. W. CUNNINGHAM. "Improving listening in content area subjects," *NASSP Bulletin,* 60, December (1976), 26–31.

MANZO, A. V. "Three 'universal' strategies in content area reading and languaging," *Journal of Reading,* 24, November (1980), 146–49.

MANZO, A. V. "The ReQuest procedure." In *Reading Comprehension at Four Linguistic Levels,* ed. Clifford Pennock. Newark, Del.: International Reading Association, 1979, pp. 57–61.

MANZO, A. V. AND U. P. CASALE. "Listen-read-discuss: A

content reading heuristic," *Journal of Reading,* 28, May (1985), 732–34.

NICHOLS, J. N. "The content reading–writing connection," *Journal of Reading,* 29, December (1985), 265–67.

OGLE, D. M. "K–W–L: A teaching model that develops active reading of expository text," *Reading Teacher,* 29, February (1986), 564–70.

RAPHAEL, T. E. "Question–answering strategies for children," *Reading Teacher,* 38, November (1982), 186–90.

RAPHAEL, T. E. "Teaching Question–Answer Relation-ships, revisited," *Reading Teacher,* 39, February (1986), 516–22.

SHOOP, M. "InQuest: A listening and reading comprehension strategy," *Reading Teacher,* 39, March (1986), 670–75.

SMITH, F. *Comprehension and Learning.* New York: Holt, Rinehart & Winston, 1975.

SMITH, L. B. "One method for conducting individualized reading," *Reading Teacher,* 40, November (1986), 242–44.

SMITH, S. L. "Learning strategies of mature college learners," *Journal of Reading,* 26, October (1982), 5–12.

appendix A

COMMON ROOTS AND AFFIXES

Root, Affix	Meaning	Example	Root, Affix	Meaning	Example
a	no, not	atypical	ab	away	absent
ad	to, toward	adjacent	anti	against	antisocial
ambi	both	ambivalent	ante	before	antecedent
audi	hear	audible	auto	self	automatic
bene	good, well	benefit	biblio	book	bibliography
bi	two	bicycle	bio	life	biology
chrono	time	chronic	cide	kill	suicide
circum	around	circumference	cogni	know	recognize
con, com, col	with, together	community	con, contra	against	contradict
de	down, away	depose	deo	god	deity
dict	say	diction	dis	not, opposite	discontent
duct	lead	conduct			
ex	out of	export			
-fy	to make, cause	magnify	fact	to make	manufacture
gen, generis	race, birth	generate	geo	earth	geology
graph	write	autograph			
hemi	half	hemisphere	homo	same	homogenous
intor	between	intermediary	in, im, il	not	impossible
intra	among	intramurals	-ist	one who is associated with	monotheist
magni	large	magnificent	mal	bad	malicious
mis	incorrect	mistake	mono	one	monocle
multi	many	multiply	man(u)	hand	manual
mini	small	minimum	maxi	large	maximum

non	not	nonsense	neo	new	neolocal
ology	study of	geology	omni	all	omnipotent
ped	foot	pedestrian	per	through	permeate
phobia	fear of	claustro-	phon	sound	telephone
poly	many	polygon	pre	before	prefix
pro	forth, for	propose	post	after	postnatal
rex, reg	king	regal	re	again	renew
script, scrib	write	manuscript	specto	look	retrospect
sub	under	submarine			
tele	far	television	trans	across	transport
terra	earth	terrestrial	theo	god	atheist
urb	city	urban	uni	one	unified

DIRECTIONS FOR GAMES

CONCENTRATION

1. Cards are shuffled and placed face down in rows before players. Player A turns over two cards.

2. If the cards match (for example, a vocabulary word and its definition or synonym), A keeps the pair and has another turn.

3. If the cards do not match, A turns them face down again in the same position and B attempts to find a matching pair.

4. All players need to concentrate to remember the positions of the cards.

5. Play continues until all cards are matched.

6. The player with the most pairs wins.

FISH

1. The whole deck is dealt to the players. It doesn't matter if some players have an extra card.

2. Players pick up their cards and fan them out.

3. Players with pairs of matching cards stack them face down next to themselves.

4. Play begins with player A, on the dealer's left, asking any other player, B, for a card that matches one A reads from his or her hand. If B holds the card, B must give it to A. If A gets a matching card, she or he has another turn. If not, the turn passes to B.

5. The player who is asked for a card but does not have it always has the next turn to "go fish." A player can keep on asking for cards as long as she or he gets the one asked for.

6. The player with the greatest number of pairs wins.

ODD PERSON OUT

1. The entire deck is dealt out to the players, who fan out their hands.

2. If players have pairs of cards, they lay them face down on the table in front of them.

3. When all players have discarded all pairs they hold, play begins. Play always moves in turn to the left.

4. The dealer, A, draws one card, seeing only its back and not knowing what it is, from the hand of B on his or her left.

5. If A can use the card to make a pair, he or she places the pair face down. A does not get another turn.

6. If A cannot use the card, she or he must keep it in hand.

7. B now draws from C, on the left.

8. Play continues in this manner around the table.

9. Finally, all cards but one are paired. The holder of that card is the *odd person out*.

RUMMY

1. Each player is dealt five cards. The players sort the cards in their hands into whatever order the game goal indicates.

2. The rest of the deck is placed face down in the middle of the table. This is the *draw pile*.

3. The top card is turned up and placed next to the *draw pile*. This is the *discard pile*.

4. The first player begins and draws the top card from the draw pile or the discard pile, and discards a card onto the discard pile.

5. Only the top card in the discard pile may be picked up by a player. All cards under it are dead and cannot be used.

6. The next player draws a card from either pile and discards a card of his or her own.

7. The first person to have all cards match calls "Rummy" and puts down his or her hand.

8. The person who gets rummy receives ten points, and the deck is redealt. Fifty points wins the game.

Variation: Students create a deck of rummy cards.

INDEX